IN COMMON THINGS

Commerce, Culture, and Ecology in
British Romantic Literature

In Common Things

Commerce, Culture, and Ecology in British Romantic Literature

MATTHEW ROWNEY

UNIVERSITY OF TORONTO PRESS
Toronto Buffalo London

© University of Toronto Press 2022
Toronto Buffalo London
utorontopress.com

ISBN 978-1-4875-4348-8 (cloth)   ISBN 978-1-4875-4349-5 (EPUB)
                                  ISBN 978-1-4875-4347-1 (PDF)

Library and Archives Canada Cataloguing in Publication

Title: In common things : commerce, culture, and ecology in British Romantic literature / Matthew Rowney.
Names: Rowney, Matthew, author.
Description: Includes bibliographical references and index.
Identifiers: Canadiana (print) 20210265337 | Canadiana (ebook) 20210265469 | ISBN 9781487543488 (cloth) | ISBN 9781487543495 (EPUB) | ISBN 9781487543471 (PDF)
Subjects: LCSH: English literature – 19th century – History and criticism. | LCSH: English literature – 18th century – History and criticism. | LCSH: Ecology in literature. | LCSH: Commerce in literature. | LCSH: Culture in literature.
Classification: LCC PR468.E34 R69 2022 | DDC 820.9/36–dc23

This book has been published with the assistance of the College of Liberal Arts and Sciences at the University of North Carolina, Charlotte.

We wish to acknowledge the land on which the University of Toronto Press operates. This land is the traditional territory of the Wendat, the Anishnaabeg, the Haudenosaunee, the Métis, and the Mississaugas of the Credit First Nation.

University of Toronto Press acknowledges the financial support of the Government of Canada, the Canada Council for the Arts, and the Ontario Arts Council, an agency of the Government of Ontario, for its publishing activities.

In memory of my father
Michael John Rowney
(1937–2011)

Contents

Acknowledgments ix

Introduction 3

1 "The Bones of the World": Mary Wollstonecraft's Social Geology 21

2 Broken Arbour: Deforestation and the Cultural History of Trees in "The Ruined Cottage" 45

3 "Strange Look'd it There!": The Paradox of the Palm in the Poetry of Felicia Hemans 75

4 Preserver and Destroyer: Salt in *The History of Mary Prince* 101

5 "Lin'd with Moss": John Clare's Rhizomatic Poetics 123

Conclusion: Plastic Rime 149

Notes 165

Works Cited 193

Index 211

Acknowledgments

Though this book would eventually take the shape of my own wanderings, it could not have done so without the many people who, with patience and generosity, have pointed out places on the map and led me through numerous landscapes of language, of history, and of the mind. The debt is endless, both in what can be traced and in all those unremembered acts that have unconsciously guided my steps along the way. Foremost among those to whom I owe this debt is Alan Vardy, whose mentorship and friendship over the years has been crucial to this project all along. I would also like to recognize the mentorship of Alexander Schlutz, who has been a great source of intellectual and personal encouragement. A special thanks to Joshua Wilner, Joseph Wittreich, and Nancy Yousef for their invaluable expertise and example.

I have been lucky to have a number of readers who have read and commented on chapter drafts in ways that have contributed materially to the book's current form. I am most grateful to Anne-Lise François, Jonathan Mulrooney, Alan Bewell, Julia S. Carlson, Kristina Huang, Chris Washington, Kate Singer, Alan Rauch, Kirk Melnikoff, Beth Gargano, Clayton Tarr, David Sassian, Seth Reno, Bonnie Shisko, Thomas Manganaro, Carol Summers, Joseph Bowling, Christopher Bischoff, Robert Volpicelli, and Mimi Winick. For his invaluable feedback that helped shape the introduction and conclusion to this book, I am indebted to Sean Barry. Katey Castellano and the other anonymous manuscript readers deserve more thanks than I can provide; their patience and insight have helped me to make this a better book. I thank Mark Thompson, my editor at University of Toronto Press, for expertly shepherding this project through its various stages.

A number of my colleagues at the University of North Carolina at Charlotte have made the work of this book possible through conversations, professional advice, help in obtaining funding, recommended readings, and in many other ways. Kirk Melnikoff and Lara Vetter have been an inexhaustible source of support, information, and encouragement - my warmest thanks to you both. For many hours of conversation and camaraderie, I thank Juan Meneses, Allison Hutchcraft, Phil Kaffen, David Boyd, and Bibi Reisdorf, as well as Alan Rauch and Clayton Tarr, also mentioned above. I thank Katie Hogan, Paula Connolly, Janaka Lewis, Jennifer Munroe, Chris Davis, Rebecca Roeder and Jeffrey Gillman for their interest and support. I thank my chairs, Mark West and Paula Eckard, for all they have done on my behalf.

I also thank the following friends (some of whom are mentioned above) who have supported the completion of this book in ways beyond what they could know. I thank Kristina Huang, Michael Krynski, Yair Solan, Kultej Dhariwal, Erin Garrow, Leila Walker, Andrew Dicus, Kaitlin Mondello, Daniel Allegrucci, Meira Levinson, Julie Fuller, David Sassian, and Joseph Bowling.

The College of Liberal Arts and Sciences at UNC Charlotte has generously supported this project both through grants and through a reassignment of duties that allowed me to concentrate on completing the manuscript. I am grateful to Dean Nancy Guitterez for making all of this possible.

An earlier version of chapter two, titled "Broken Arbour: *The Ruined Cottage* and Deforestation," was published in *European Romantic Review*, vol. 26, no. 6, November 2015. A conference paper version of chapter four, titled "Preserver and Destroyer: Salt in *The History of Mary Prince*," was published in *European Romantic Review*, vol. 29, no. 3, June 2018. I am grateful to the editors of this journal for the dissemination of this work.

Finally, I must thank the family and loved ones who have been an important part of the process of this book's composition. My late father, Michael J. Rowney, to whom this book is dedicated, was a life-long lover of literature, and though the novel was his favored genre, he carried something of the poet about him. I thank my mother, Kathleen Keller, for her continuous support, willingness to listen, and understanding. To my siblings, Caroline, Joe, and Andrew, thank you for your encouragement. To Seirin, my partner, I cannot express the fullness of my gratitude for sharing with me not only in this project but in everything, the good, the bad, and the indifferent; thank you for deciding that the good is worth the rest.

IN COMMON THINGS

Commerce, Culture, and Ecology in
British Romantic Literature

Introduction

A small thing may give an analogy of great things, and show the tracks of knowledge.

– Lucretius[1]

The history of the last 250 years in the West has been one guided by the assumption that the ultimate end of human endeavour is the ownership of property. That assumption has proven woefully inadequate to the realities of our relation to the world. By valuing natural substance not primarily as something to be owned but as a part of what we are, as that which inhabits our motion and thought, Romantic literature describes another way of being, one that puts us in touch with something largely lost; it connects us to neglected and forgotten histories, it reminds us of their strangely familiar forms.

Like Lucretius, this book is interested in things for what they show about the "tracks," or *vestigia*, of knowledge. The traces or remains studied here are both literary and material, each inflecting the other. *In Common Things* describes a relationship between people and things, sometimes one of intimate union, and sometimes one of historical violence (*vestigia* are often the remains of violence[2]), but always one that is mutually defining. The "In" of the title offers a lexical bridge that describes this mutual inflection.

To talk about the "common" means to talk about the history of the shared use of land and resources. The ancient custom of "the commons" in England was rapidly disappearing during the Romantic period, as enclosure laws and industrial methods of agriculture transformed landscapes and cultural practices, dramatically overturning the traditional rights and values of the labouring poor.[3] The historical context of commonly held property has become important to various strands of utopic political and theoretical discourse,[4] but my focus here is slightly different. I define the "common" as that shared[5] across the human and non-human, something Stacey Alaimo calls "transcorporeality," or "the movement across human corporeality and non-human nature" (3).[6] Because British romantic literature focuses on non-human agency at the historical moment when the introduction of industrial methods of production and the spread of capitalist methods of exchange would forever alter the human relation to the natural world, it is a particularly productive location for this reconsideration of the common. This is not a retreat from the political questions raised by "the commons" but, rather, an entry more deeply into the historical life of things that lie at their heart. Rather than thinking about the utopic possibilities of a "commons," I am instead interested in the historically observable interactions between humans and common things.

I define "things" in terms of five substances – stone, wood, palm oil, salt, and moss – that were critical to cultural life in the Romantic period. "Thing" is a term, like "common" that has received a large amount of critical attention.[7] My use of it here is confined to natural substances and how they inhabit cultural, economic, and ecological history in ways that challenge traditional divisions of social and natural, subject and object. Romantic authors demonstrate that our relationship with natural things is constitutive of our relationship with the environment and with each other, as much as this is often understood the other way around. The long evolution of life on this planet over billions of years has been guided by the relation between organisms and natural substances. Humans as a species have been shaped by overwhelmingly uncountable evolutionary interactions, the vast majority of which are pre-linguistic, prehistoric, and pre-hominid. Romantic literature, with its deep investment in the natural object, provides a structure for understanding the centrality of this intimate and epochal unfolding within our everyday and commonplace experience.

The dynamic interplay of the "common" and the "thing" is exemplified by Wordsworth's arrival in Grasmere, as described early in *The Prelude* (1805):

> I spare to speak, my friend, of what ensued –
> The admiration and the love, the life
> In common things, the endless store of things
> Rare, or at least so seeming, every day
> Found all about me in one neighbourhood.   (1.116–20)

The hesitation to communicate expressed in the first line is repeated and enhanced by the pauses created by the aside and the dash; the voiceless plosives also momentarily block the airstream, contributing to the overall effect. These lines appear within a larger narration of a meandering journey, and the formal stops of the first line reinforce the sense of an arrival, dramatically framing the sense of overflowing abundance in which the human and common things become momentarily blurred. This explains the hesitation to speak, as if human language might intrude upon the grounds of communion.[8] The words "communicate," "common," and "communion" all indicate something shared (*commūnis*), whether it be knowledge, material, or experience. These lines describe a fabric woven from the communal. Poetic language unfolds a sense of the texture (*texere*) of this fabric in ways other forms of knowledge cannot.

When we use the word "thing" today, we are more likely to think of an inanimate, made object than a tree or a flower, and this is symptomatic of our contemporary way of life. Things, for Wordsworth, are not made, or even given, but "found," and this is a crucial distinction, for it implies seeking, even if somewhat passively (the action comes late, in the passive voice). We are also more likely to use the word as indicating a limitation – this specific thing and not that one. This is again distinct from the "endless store of things" found here, expansively transforming the countable thing into uncountable substance. The following enjambment, "endless store of things/Rare" appears to skirt the limits of sense, until one recognizes the unique form that individual natural objects present upon close observation. The "every day" chimes with the "one neighbourhood," a unified rhythm of space and time, of "every" in "one." The uniqueness of the natural object and the wholeness of the scene call to each other, not as metonym but as metaphor.

The preposition "in" is central to the poetic sentence not only in its positioning but because it forms the bridge between the speaker's poetic vocation and these "common things" (itself nested within another relationship, the "I" and the "neighbourhood" that open and close the sentence). The multiple meanings of the preposition (the *OED* lists dozens) allow for the implication of participation, rather than merely describing an inherent quality ("shared with" rather than "inside"). The centrality and openness of this "in" provides multiple possibilities of connection. According to Andrew Burkett, "For Wordsworth, each happenstance detail of nature is ... connected to myriad other uncertain events, processes, beings, things, and phenomena both synchronically and diachronically" (19). My attempt in this book is to draw together seemingly disparate processes, beings, and things, both in terms of the Romantic period and our current moment, to reinvoke a lost heritage of cultural relations with common substances. Though we have long occupied our energies with things, it is time we pay attention to the way the energies of things occupy us.

This book seeks to contribute to an already vibrant conversation about the relationship between literature and the biosphere and to advance it in a direction that is, at once, both old and new. Romantic authors' interest in the "common thing" takes on a new importance in our own era, not only because they witnessed a fundamental shift in the relation between people and their environment but because we continue to live within the implications of that shift in ways that both exceed and include issues like climate change, species extinction, and environmental injustice. The networks, pathways, and structures formed by British empire and the spread of industrial capitalism provided the framework for globalization and for an unprecedented human-induced change to the biosphere. By attending to the movements and qualities of substances and the ways they are culturally inscribed during this period, this book offers an alternative history of a shift at the root of what has become an existential crisis. And by treating these substances, not merely as passive materials or resource but as agents in themselves, I seek to contribute to a rethinking of our cultural and ecological presence, one that is both desperately necessary and that offers new possibilities for understanding our shared corporeality.

Because of the necessarily transdisciplinary[9] nature this book takes, drawing on literary history, popular culture, several scientific disciplines, commercial and commodity history, the history of race, and the history of empire, it at times departs from some general tendencies of literary criticism. Readers will at times find scientific studies where literary criticism might be expected, or a history of commodity production where discussion of literary theory might be more typical. This does not mean these generic expectations are entirely neglected but that they are not always strictly followed. Reading Romantic literature through the lens of the common natural object opens routes for interpretation that are historical in nature but that also question what the proper subject of history should be. This book contributes to a notion of literary history that foregrounds the non-human as central to our vision of literature, place, and time. This refocusing addresses both the urgency of our current ecological moment and the history of the neglect of the centrality of the non-human, especially in the West, in the stories that we tell about ourselves.

Becoming With

Though the need to address the relationship between literature and the natural world has long been recognized,[10] and the role that specific natural objects have played in human history has long been of interest to political scientists, historians, sociologists, and anthropologists, the relevance of the material history of these objects to literature and its criticism has not received the same attention.[11] Several critically significant ventures have been made, however, to broaden the scope for the investigation of the natural object and how it might contribute to such a study. Arjun Appadurai, in *The Social Life of Things*, points out that "even though from a *theoretical* point of view human actors encode things with significance, from a *methodological* point of view it is the things-in-motion that illuminate their human and social context" (5). *In Common Things* is in many ways a study of "things-in motion" as they cross-pollinate and "become with"[12] through history and literature. Bill Brown, summarizing some new approaches to materialism, sees the focus "not about things themselves but about the subject-object relation in particular temporal and spatial contexts" (7). This book is also about a relationship between people and things, studied across economic, cultural, and ecological lines within the literary and historical contexts of the Romantic period.

Yet rather than focus on discrete subject and object relations, I am more interested in how these categories blur because they all too often create assumptions that identity and power somehow congeal into these forms. Indeed, the subject/object dialectic is often more obscuring than clarifying, more concerned with human encoding than with "things-in-motion." To capture this motion we need to consider the way subjects and objects can and do change place. As Bruno Latour, in "The Berlin Key," explains: "Consider things, and you will have humans. Consider humans and you are by that very act interested in things. Bring your attention to bear on hard things, and see them become gentle, soft or human. Turn your attention to humans, and see them become electric circuits, automatic gears or softwares" (20). Even here, however, we are describing a process that is human-centred and evaluative, and while it is, of course, impossible for us not to see things from a human perspective, we might do so while recognizing that other agents are at work, even within that supposedly independent unit we label "human." We "become with" these other agents, both through evolutionary and cultural history and in our everyday interactions. Understanding our immersion in these processes and flows disrupts the Enlightenment notion of an independent subject and interrogates the historical organization of knowledge around this subject in the West.

Because our very being is the product of a long process of evolution, humanity has been shaped by an inconceivable number of interactions and intimacies with the physical world. This becoming part of has implications for constructions of the "human," a seemingly self-evident but actually slippery concept. It is elusive, in part, because of the type of participation just described. The material world informs our biological structure, not merely in terms of the latent qualities of things, their fluidity, plasticity, or hardness, but in the active processes in which they partake, the way they sustain themselves, how they grow or change, how they interact with other things in their environment. These things are not something outside of us that we become aware of; they are constitutive of our being through our evolutionary history. Any construction of a "subject," (human or otherwise) in this view, cannot be as a sequestered unit, but exists as a shared assemblage of uncountable interactions over huge stretches of time. This assumed centrality of a subject has been full of other assumptions, beginning with those about what the "human" is in the first place. As we continually increase our knowledge of how much the non-human plays a role in the human (in the microbes in our gut, in the viral matter in our DNA, and in countless other ways), and as it becomes increasingly obvious how much we are undermining the life systems that support us, traditional ideas about the place and purpose of humanity are increasingly being reexamined.

This book examines the work of five Romantic period authors: Mary Wollstonecraft, William Wordsworth, Felicia Hemans, Mary Prince, and John Clare, in terms, respectively, of five natural substances: stone, wood, palm oil, salt, and moss. Each of these substances is important commercially, culturally, and ecologically in ways that exceed virtually any other natural artefact from this period. This transdisciplinary intimacy gives a better historical understanding of the role of these substances than any one discipline can do alone. This intimacy corresponds, I argue, with the kind of intimate relations established with these substances in the literature studied here. The array of authors dealt with, Black and white, both in and out of the canon, male and female, English and non-English, middling and poor, represent different and important stakeholders within British empire and its legacy. There is a need within Romanticist studies for a broadening of the kinds of texts and authors it studies, and I seek to contribute to this broadening by offering a more inclusive study of literary material history than most attempts have provided. "Becoming with" refers not only to how our modern subjectivities are informed by natural substances but also to the recognition that our history has been forged by diverse groups of people, despite the tendency in the West to elide this fact and privilege a white male European perspective.

Things not only inform our being biologically, they provide the means for the construction of modernity. We choose stone for our most ceremonial and symbolic structures, but it is also that from which the ore was mined to produce the currency necessary for the expansion of capitalist markets. Wood was not only indispensable in all aspects of daily life, it also was necessary to the expansion of industry and for the ships with which Britain would build its empire. Palm oil, found today in thousands of products, both lubricated Britain's early industrial machine and provided an essential ingredient in soap, appealing to changing attitudes towards the body. Huge amounts of salt were crucial to the movement of people and goods around the world at this time, due to salt's key role as a preservative. Moss had a host of domestic uses in the history of the four nations, became an internationally traded commodity, and, as peat moss, was an important fuel with geopolitical significance. Though other substances were also important during this period, these substances are powerfully dynamic in their significance across literary, social, and economic practices, and considering them together lends added significance to each. Similarly, by combining an understanding of the intrinsic qualities of these substances, how people interacted with them, and how authors inscribed them into literature, each of these areas is productively broadened, producing an approach that finds otherwise unlooked-for attachments and exchanges at the heart of Romantic cultural production.

The hardness of stone, the pliant strength of wood, the fluidity of palm oil, the crystalline nature of salt, and the vegetable qualities of moss, each speak to elemental forms of experience that describe a way of being in and understanding the world. These qualities are representative of the basic features of materiality. Cultural practices flow from these forms, as do the observations and structures of the sciences. They are, respectively, the foundational, indispensable, often hidden, preserving, yet humble fabric of our existence. A fundamental shift took place in Europe in how these substances were valued and used, from a system in which "personal property … had very little importance" to one in which "the acquisition of personal property became the chief concern of individuals and an important focus of the law" (Lamb 135). This shift would obfuscate the role these substances play at the root of both our experience and our knowledge and define their value primarily in terms of capital: as mineral resource, as building material, in industrial applications, as preservative, and as fuel, respectively.

Literary language does not imprint its form on the world as much as narrate the form it has taken in its coalescence with the world. We think through things as they *thing* through us. The strata of stone, the grain of wood, the veins of a palm leaf, the lattice parameters of a salt crystal, or the rhizome[13] of moss ("objects where no brotherhood exists/To common minds"), are all traceable lines that make possible other lines, lines of thought, lines of text, lines of being ("that interminable building reared/By observation of affinities").[14] The qualities and characteristics of physical substances are apparent in every form of cultural expression, and Romantic literature, with its investment in the natural object, is a primary site for demonstrating this presence and participation.

Belonging To

The transformation of the relation between people and things leading up to and including the Romantic period was codified in law and political practice, perhaps most notably in the great social contracts of the late eighteenth century. Ownership would become the basis for a new political subjectivity and cultural standard of value. As Hardt and Negri explain, "In the dominant line of European political thought from Locke to Hegel, the absolute rights of people to appropriate things becomes the basis and substantive end of the legally defined free individual" (13). Freedom, as this legacy would have it, is the freedom to own things. This notion of freedom depends on the creation of a "legally defined free individual" that fundamentally changes the way social value is created, expressing a "fantasy that private life is the real in contrast to collective life" (Berlant 283). Yet in the Romantic literature examined here, it is largely the freely available thing, and not private property, that provides the basis for thinking about how human agency is shared with a collective that includes the natural world.

If a new "republicanism" was forming based on the assumed rights of property, then we can read a good deal of Romantic literature, through its investment in common things, as resisting this foundation and suggesting the possibility of alternate constructions of the subject and of society. On one level, this would appear to position the Romantics as hopelessly nostalgic for a lost object, out of touch with the developments of their era, in which the natural thing was rapidly disappearing into the commodity. But if we consider the long participation of the natural object in human life and culture, then the Romantics' achievement becomes more clearly provocative, not at all "romantic" in the pejorative sense but rooted in a material and cultural history informed by the productions of the natural world. This is all the more relevant today as we face the existential threat of a variety of ecological crises that will inevitably reshape human society as we know it.[15]

A sense of belonging doesn't come from the things that belong to us but from a sense that we belong to things. Put another way, we cannot experience what Wordsworth calls "the life/In common things" if we are not able to invest ourselves in these things. This is not a surrendering of agency but a recognition that constructions of human agency in the West have inadequately addressed the role of the natural world: it is a rethinking of agency as something that is always shared. As Jeffrey Jerome Cohen asserts, "Humans themselves emerge through 'material agencies' that leave their traces in lives as well as stories" (36). Wordsworth finds home, another word for his poetic calling, in this shared agency, where the unique natural thing can represent the world itself (one possible meaning of the "one neighbourhood"). Similarly, John Clare understands shared agency in terms of the origins of his poetic career, as evidenced in the last stanza of "My Early Home was This":[16]

> The old house stooped just like a cave
> Thatched o'er with mosses green
> Winter around the walls would rave
> But all was calm within
> The trees they were as green agen
> Where bees the flowers would kiss
> But flowers and trees seemed sweeter then.
> – My early home was this –   (17–24)[17]

In the village and environs of Helpston, where Clare lived most of his life, moss was a constant companion, an often familiar and comforting presence for the poet. In "My Early Home was This," moss partakes in an activity that would normally be considered something only humans do: thatching a roof. It is not merely a poetic device Clare employs here but a stated faith in the agency of moss to provide this service, as if it existed at least in part just for this purpose. Moss offers shelter, helping keep the cottage cool in summer and warm in winter, providing the distinctive space for the poet's growth. This type of intertwining of substance with human life and cultural production is the thread running through this book. Moss, for example, can offer a soothing relief to the eyes, something simply pleasant to gaze upon, but it also can have commercial importance, such as its common use in the packaging of flowers during the Romantic period (amounting to millions of bundles per year in metropolitan London alone[18]), or in its role, in the form of peat moss, as a fuel, both warming individual homes and driving a wide variety of industries, notably providing the grounds for the Dutch Golden Age and its colonial expansion.[19] A bed of moss can provide a comfortable spot to rest, but it is also important ecologically because of the large amount of carbon it stores and the wide variety of microscopic creatures that make moss beds their home. Like literature itself, moss can evince endurance across vast stretches of time, and its ecology and growth demonstrate productive parallels with literary form and structure. Though simple substances such as this garner little attention today, they are integral not only to the history of the human species and its culture but to their future. The moss-thatched home is the image of human dwelling on the earth.

For all the pleasantry of Clare's description, there is a mild sadness that emerges, particularly in the penultimate line, one that appears nostalgic at first, but on closer inspection reveals a breaking down of distinctions between time and place, where and when that explodes the safe-seeming distance of nostalgic longing. The title of the poem, also the refrain at the end of each of its three stanzas, evokes a sense of being, a "this"-ness, or at-handedness of the past, of its enduring life within the present. The poem appears to be set in both the past and present at once, not merely in the sense that in this place little has changed but that the text of the poem replaces a broken link between the past and the present. "This" is, finally, the poem itself, not a time or a place but a series of images, mostly of things that provide a map or field guide to the poet's sense of belonging. In this way, the poem extends well beyond its localized setting, and its depiction of loss and imagined recovery can be read in terms of various global phenomenon in Clare's time and our own, from the effects of enclosure on the labouring classes across England and the dispossession that affected millions as Britain colonized the world, or in terms of contemporary climate refugees and others displaced by violence in the struggle for control of "natural resources," often the very substances that Romantic poetry evokes as constitutive of poetic identity.

What the Romantic texts studied here expose, I argue, is not simply a reaction against this shift (urbanization, colonization, environmental degradation) nor an ideology for it but a way of both recording its effects and reminding us of the long interface between the human and the non-human. Rather than view the natural object as something standing in opposition to human culture, this study understands these formations as a kind of amalgam, that is, what Latour (echoing Wordsworth's "one neighbourhood"), refers to as "the public life of a single collective" (31). And as Michel Serres argues in *The Natural Contract*, we have allowed our views of social relations to occlude the material world to our detriment and must begin rethinking the basis of our relation to the world and to each other. Rather than assuming natural things exist merely for human use and manipulation, we need to recognize the myriad ways our identities are formed through a belonging to these things, both historically and biologically. *In Common Things* argues that substances provide a key link to our past and that understanding our connections with them is necessary to the possibility of our future.

Global Intimacies

Stone, wood, moss, oil, and salt provide necessary ground for examining the relationship between literary expression, environment, and economy during the Romantic period, and for understanding the origins of our current global challenges. These substances were a ubiquitous part of daily life and shaped a way of living, a way of thinking, and a way of acting in the world from pre-history to the present. As Clare writes of his local natural objects, "Things seem the same in such retreats/As when the world began." Yet, as Clare knew well, this landscape and its objects were undergoing rapid transformation, causing environmental degradation and restricting traditional practices of the peasantry. Enclosure and related laws passed in the latter half of the eighteenth century made various activities illegal that had been practiced for centuries, such as gleaning, the use of the commons for a variety of purposes (e.g., grazing, subsistence farming, dwelling, sport, leisure), and the use of traditional footpaths that now passed through enclosed land. As Clare writes, "Inclosure came and trampled on the grave/Of labour's rights and left the poor a slave."

Clare describes how the legislation that limited the access of the labouring class to the natural world and its objects would leave an indelible mark on the structure of English rural life. Substance, the humble companion of everyday life, was increasingly the subject of international trade and geopolitical conflict, transforming the lives of those far from Britain's shores. The application of narrowly defined notions of culture and property were extended to the places Britain colonized. The transformation of colonized spaces in many ways parallels the deforestation, drainage, and enclosure of land in Britain in the seventeenth, eighteenth, and early nineteenth centuries, a harbinger of the conversion of landscapes around the world into monoculture plantation zones. It was not only land that was enclosed. In England, "A massive prison construction program accompanied the enclosure of agricultural production" (Linebaugh 1).[20] This program, which went hand in hand with the increased criminalization of formerly customary rights of the poor, must also be considered in light of the rise of workhouses and the increasing institutionalization of the underclasses (Wordsworth's "The Old Cumberland Beggar" dramatizes precisely this process). The transformation of land and its relation to the treatment of people was also visible, if in drastically different form, in the plantation zones. The transatlantic slave trade was bound up in all forms of Atlantic trade; the history of capitalism is also the history of this commodification of human beings. The colonial plantation system produced natural products for consumption in Europe and North America, forming the grooves on which later commerce and empire were to run.[21] The close attention Romantic authors paid to the natural object must be read in the context of these global processes then unfolding.

The trans-corporeal sense of "becoming with" and "belonging to" described above take on another valence in this global context. The historical relationship with substance looks more fragile and fraught, compounded with unremitted suffering and industrialized modes of being. Wordsworth's "endless store of things" found in "one neighborhood" read differently when considered in terms of the unprecedented movement of people and things around the globe over the eighteenth century.[22] The hesitation to describe his coming into possession of a home clashes with the violence of colonial dispossession, suggesting a geo-historical reason to give pause over "what ensued," in this case the simultaneous exploitation of human beings and of the natural world that has resulted in ocean and air pollution, environmental racism, species extinction, global inequality, climate change, and climate refugee-ism. The complexity of our relations to things today has its roots in the global movements of the Romantic period; the literature of this period acquires a different weight when considered in terms of the multiple forms of speech that are in danger of lapsing (or have already lapsed) into silence due to the forces unleashed by instrumentalist forms of production and consumption. This trans-corporeality runs through our historical, cultural, and biological being.

The reality of this exploitation should not efface the extent to which an interdependence developed between Britain and its colonies.[23] This interdependence is central to this book's argument, as the diversity of authors studied demonstrates the increasing inextricability of text from the textures of relations dictated by global capital. In *The Intimacies of Four Continents*, Lisa Lowe points out that "we actually know little about" these global interrelations "despite separate scholarship about single societies, peoples or regions" (1), in part because Western disciplinarity has historically tended to focus on the specific and discrete subject or nation rather than the interconnections between things and people. This book traces the movement of substances through Romantic literature and culture to reveal how they represent and portray the material intimacies of a globalizing world. Notions of closeness and distance, home and abroad, become intrinsically involved in how the things studied here imbue everyday life. The trans-corporeal movement of substance across human/non-human boundaries is also a movement across continents, movement that requires treatment across disciplines to begin to address.[24]

The march towards globalization depended on the circulation of material goods. Even substances seemingly valueless were put to work in the pursuit of capital. The Romantic period saw an exponential increase in commodity exchange and the infrastructure which supported it and has thus been often associated with the outset of globalization. What Evan Gottleib explains about the role of "sociohistorical convergences" during the Romantic period might be read as located within substances, "that suggest themselves as catalysts or facilitators of the spatiotemporal transformations that characterize global processes" (6). These substances catalysed and facilitated global transformations and were at the same time the subject of these transformations. As Alan Bewell has shown, "[d]uring the eighteenth century, the ground on which natures had stood since time immemorial began to move. The effects of this mobilization ... are central to understanding the history of colonialism and what natures are today" (27). Substances provide, therefore, a double affordance, both as the commodities that have shaped our modern world and as the natural objects that underwent an unprecedented transformation in which we can read both our colonial and environmental history. This is apparent in Wordsworth's "The Ruined Cottage" in which wood is both what Robert uses to carve "uncouth figures," a sign of his alienated labour, and the material forming the ship which would carry him "to a distant land." The historical transformation in the use of this substance in the context of deforestation is reflected in Robert's desperation as he enlists to fight in one of Britain's colonial conflicts and in the death of his family members in his absence. Wood, so relied on for its strength and versatility, becomes intimately involved in the process of a mourning that words cannot express.

The Romantic generation were among the first to experience the flood of commodities (and what Marx called their "fetishism") into everyday life and culture that heralded the phenomenon we now refer to as globalization. Globalization presents the illusion of a newly common world, one quite distinct from what the authors studied here would recognize. This metamorphosis has its roots in the shift in value from land (fixed and held provisionally from the crown) to capital (portable, held personally, and protected by a new system of laws). Romantic authors were particularly attuned to the importance of natural objects in their work and anxious about what the development of a commodifying culture would produce. There is a paradox in their championing of the natural object, as the "nature" they knew, and the way of life intertwined with it, was disappearing and being steadily replaced by a host of products, goods, and commodities, accompanied by an insatiable desire for possession. In some cases, the shift was just underway, as in Wollstonecraft's Scandinavian letters (1796), where the author praises the advance of industry but critiques it once it disrupts the harmony of the landscapes through which she travels. The stone she poetically depicts as evoking the wild and timeless throughout her travels, the Scandinavian gneiss, would soon be shipped to Germany and Denmark to pave city streets. In some cases, the cultural shift had already taken place, and the natural objects they depicted had largely become defined in commercial terms. The formerly enslaved Mary Prince narrates this shift in her *History* (1831), where salt, an essential substance for the preservation of food that made transcontinental travel possible, becomes an invasive and corrosive substance for those who produced it. Standing in the salt ponds day after day caused the salt to "eat down in some in some cases to the very bone" (72). Prince demonstrates the monstrosity of being eaten by a substance she is producing that will be shipped abroad to be eaten by others. Prince's narrative, like the other texts I examine here, foregrounds the paradoxical qualities of the Romantic-era depiction of substance. These Romantic texts reveal how the simultaneous exploitation of human beings and the environment lay at the root of the unequally shared social and ecological woes of our current "globalized" world.

In following substances where they lead, whether through their historical use and exchange, or in their metrical nooks and autobiographical crannies, I offer a type of "history from below," where substance performs a role elided by normative ways of conceiving history as human centred and enshrined by text. *In Common Things* draws on ecocritical, new materialist, postcolonial, and new historicist scholarship to highlight the continuing importance of the Romantic era to our own. This importance often remains, like many of the ingredients of contemporary commodities, and the labour which goes into them, hidden from view. This is apparent today in the palm oil industry, which has its roots in the British import of palm oil from West Africa during the Romantic period. The palm appears more often in the poetry of Felicia Hemans than any other major Romantic poet, providing an ideal textual location for a discussion of its historical role during the period. Just as palm oil is hidden away in so many of our current products and foods, so it maintains an important, though unacknowledged, cultural presence in Hemans's England in its use as an industrial lubricant and in soap. Hemans exclaims of a palm tree in an English garden, "Strange look'd it there!" and this sense of strangeness identifies the alienation the tree has undergone, which is also the alienation of the individual from the natural world that is a central element of capitalist modernity. Current social and environmental upheavals in Indonesia and Malaysia, where the vast majority of the world's palm oil is produced, demonstrate the undeniably destructive nature of globalized forms of consumption.[25] As foreign products became assimilated into the everyday lives of British subjects, they remained entangled in systems of exploitation and their social outcomes that informed, and continue to inform, the conditions of their consumption.

In Common Things

In Common Things's first chapter, "'The Bones of the World': Mary Wollstonecraft's Social Geology," addresses the stark rock formations that crop up throughout her Scandinavian travels in the 1790s in *Letters Written During a Short Residence in Sweden, Norway and Denmark* (1796). Before Wordsworth's Simplon Pass or Shelley's *Mont Blanc* became representative of Romantic attitudes towards rock formations, Mary Wollstonecraft's *Short Residence* took them as a central preoccupation, both evoking their foundational presence and their imminent destructive power. In this chapter, I consider the formation of this stone (geologically known as "gneiss") over thousands of years in a process known as "compositional layering" and consider this in terms of Wollstonecraft's own compositional strategies. This stone is important in architecture, as it also helps form the affective structure of Wollstonecraft's text. Stone is the source of the ore that produced the currency necessary for the expansion of capitalism during this period and is the source of Wollstonecraft's aesthetic contemplation as she pursues a mission to retrieve stolen silver. In this chapter I argue that her troubled landscapes disrupt Enlightenment notions of progress and picturesque forms of viewing she otherwise engages in. The "vast shadows of the rocks" hang over the narrative of Wollstonecraft's journey, interrogating Enlightenment notions of human telos and anthropocentric historiography.

If stone provides the ore necessary for the expansion of capitalist markets, then wood provides both the fuel and the means of transportation in creating and maintaining those markets. In chapter two, "Broken Arbour: 'The Ruined Cottage' and Deforestation," I consider how the increased use of wood, as both material for ship building and fuel for industry, drove the destruction of Britain's forests. This destruction, I argue, has unexplored consequences for poetic depiction of landscape during the period. The desolate plain in Wordsworth's "The Ruined Cottage" (c. 1797) provides a site from which to consider this broad environmental disruption. This chapter attends to both the forces that motivated deforestation and the cultural associations with elm and oak, trees important within Wordsworth's poetry and English culture more broadly. It also considers deforestation and literary responses to it in the places Britain colonized. It traces the relationship, increasingly visible in our own time, between the destruction of the natural world and human tragedy. An attention to the cultural responses to deforestation challenges the model historically offered through the English pastoral of a "natural" landscape.

It was not only wood but its products that were integrally important to British industry and empire. Palm oil, of which the world consumes over sixty million tons annually today, was first imported in significant amounts into Britain during the Romantic period. Chapter three, "'Strange Look'd it There!': The Paradox of the Palm in the Poetry of Felicia Hemans," examines Hemans's employment of palms in her poetry of the 1820s and early 1830s in terms of the exponential increase of palm oil importation from West Africa during this time, the beginning of the modern global dependence on this substance. The palm tree and its oil, I claim, are directly involved in European ways of seeing the colonial other and in the slavery and exploited labour on which Europe depended for its growing wealth. Attending to the use of the palm as an image in Hemans's poetry provides insight into the increasing necessity of palm oil to Britain, both as a lubricant for the gears of Britain's industrial machine and in the production of soap to meet new standards of cleanliness. The palm works in Hemans's poetry as both an exoticized other and as an emblem of interiority, and I connect this figuration with the applications of palm oil in Britain at the time she is writing. The chapter closes with a consideration of the compelling relationship between the palm's literary and commercial past, the ubiquity of palm oil in contemporary products, and the social and environmental costs of palm oil production today.

Chapter four deals with a substance humans cannot survive without. In this chapter, "Preserver and Destroyer: Salt in *The History of Mary Prince*," I attend to the ubiquitous presence of salt in the *History* (1831) and investigate the literal and metaphorical uses of a substance that has ineluctably shaped the geology and culture of the planet. Salt has been used as currency, has provided the word "salary" (from the Latin *sal*), has played an important role in religion and ritual, and has been essential to any type of travel. In the first published account of enslavement by a woman, Prince records ten years working in the salt ponds of Turks Island. Prince's long and daily exposure to salt, to the point where it invades the bodies of those working in the salt ponds, documents an intense investment of psychic energy into this substance that parallels the attention commodities would command in Western societies. Prince employs an imagery of both physical and metaphorical swelling that is connected, through conditions such as edema, to salt retention and the epidemic of hypertension among members of the African diaspora. Salt in its invasive whiteness further provides a method for reading the vexed issue of the editorial intervention in this text, and the broader invasive presence of European empire around the globe.

The last chapter treats a substance that is globally more widespread than any other treated here, yet strongly identified as a dominant feature of a specific landscape, illustrating the integration of the domestic and the global that was ongoing during this period. Chapter five, "'Lin'd with Moss': John Clare's Rhizomatic Poetics," investigates the imbrication of moss and the poetic structures of Clare's poetry. Just as moss is ubiquitous in Clare's fenny hometown of Helpston, it everywhere lines his poems. This chapter takes up the presence of moss in the middle-period (c. 1822–37) poetry of John Clare. I argue that the qualities of this plant, such as its rhizomatic root system, its fecundity, and its reproductive strategies, all illuminate Clare's poetic form. The various uses of moss, from the insulation of homes and the providing of cushioning, to its commodity history as peat moss, to its contemporary importance as a palaeo-ecological archive are also considered. I examine Clare's unique fen aesthetic in comparison to an aesthetic history that largely denigrated such landscapes, and his identification with these landscapes is considered in terms of other groups, such as escaped slaves in the American South, who established independent communities in swampy areas. Clare uniquely demonstrates the radical potential of thinking through poetics alongside the substances of everyday life.

What this book develops, through a historical treatment of substance, is a sense of the common thing as both a ground for human subjectivity and a contested site, one that offers both the possibility of social transformation and one that becomes ever more a site of violence as the competition for resources becomes more fierce. And, of course, it is the global poor that experience the brunt of this violence, whether it be more directly, through state-mediated channels (as is evident in the long history of institutional racism against members of the African diaspora) or indirectly, through the ecological catastrophe brought about by capitalist practices of production and consumption.

Though some have found in the Romantic attention to the natural object an avoidance of social and political conflict,[26] this book demonstrates how these objects and their valuations were at the very roots of these conflicts. An attention to "common things" offers a new way of seeing Romantic texts and their relevance to our current moment. Understanding the interplay of substance and society during the expansion of British empire allows for a more inclusive Romanticism by decentring human agency and the traditional canon in the construction of this historical era. As Henri Lefebvre argues, "it is in the most familiar things that the unknown - not the mysterious - is at its richest" (132), and it is through the literature of the Romantic period we come closer to these things, their construction of our present, and the unknown future our relations with them will inevitably determine.

Chapter One

"The Bones of the World": Mary Wollstonecraft's Social Geology

It, the stone, does not talk, it speaks …

– Paul Celan qtd. in Nagele (1987, 152)

Substances have a story to tell – they do not talk, but they speak. Wollstonecraft's *Letters* (1796) recognize this in returning again and again to the stone that shapes her journey through Scandinavia. Stone forms the subject of her first sustained observation, the "huge dark rocks that looked like the rude materials of creation forming the barrier of unwrought space" (7) and the last, as she approaches anticlimax at the cliffs of Dover, that are "so insignificant … after those I had seen in Sweden and Norway" (130). Stone is her constant companion whether underfoot, along the coasts, or soaring above her in massive bulwarks and towering cliffs. It speaks of the time and waiting, trauma and metamorphosis that the *Letters* unfold, as they form under huge invisible pressures, like layers of metamorphic rock.[1]

The *Letters* have long been recognized as a foundational text of British Romanticism and for the history of women's life-writing.[2] Their innovative multi-genre structure, intervention into aesthetic, philosophical, and political discourses, and contribution to the advancement of women's rights have long been matter for critical discussion. Less recognized is how they offer a method for re-envisioning the role of the material in the formation of culture and of the subject. Though Elizabeth Bohls describes Wollstonecraft's "concern with the material conditions of everyday life" (152), there has not been a study of the *Letters* that takes these material conditions as its central concern.[3] Since substances are part of the common experience of humanity, they enable a recognition of what is intrinsically shared and thus a position from which to critique socially produced inequities. A study of the qualities of stone reveal it to be not only a physical necessity to human endeavour but also a moral, aesthetic, and cultural one. The *Letters* both continue what Jeffrey Jerome Cohen calls "the long tradition of mining the philosophical from the lithic" (4) and discover a new territory for the construction of female subjectivity. Though caught in the web of human activity and shaped by that activity, it must also be recognized that stone has influenced the form of human culture and shaped constructions of the human. Wollstonecraft's multifaceted meditations on the stone of Scandinavia offer an opportunity to excavate the agency of substance in the history of human dwelling on the earth and thus to look beyond anthropocentric constructions of the subject. When considered together, the formal qualities of stone and text reveal an intimacy otherwise obscured from view.

By excavating the history of the material that appears in the *Letters*, a story emerges through a series of correspondences, not unlike the epistolary form that gives the text its shape. The most common rock type of Norway and Sweden is gneiss,[4] a metamorphic rock formed under intense conditions of heat and pressure. These conditions stretch the rock like plastic, producing foliations, and gneiss is often characterized by dark and lighter coloured bands (Marshak 193). Rather than an impenetrable monolith, these foliations present the rock as many-layered and complex. The most common process of the formation of these bands in the rock is known as "compositional layering" (Marshak 195), and this process bears comparison to the compositional organization and genre compilation of Wollstonecraft's *Letters*. In this sense, each letter represents a band in a larger formation, marking the diverse and turbulent forces which formed it, each containing the concept of the larger whole. The intense pressures under which this rock forms are comparable to the intense pressures Wollstonecraft was under as she undertook this journey (in the summer of 1795) and as she revised her letters for publication (in 1796) upon her return to England. She was a woman travelling alone with a one-year-old child, something highly unusual for the time period. She was on a delicate mission to recover the value of stolen property that required her to travel through several foreign countries and meet with various officials, as well as the family of the assumed thief. She had recently recovered from an attempt at suicide on finding her lover Gilbert Imlay, the letters' ostensible addressee, unfaithful, and had now to find the means to become financially independent of him. She was openly sympathetic with the French Revolution at a time when to be so was to risk violence, arrest, and trial for treason in England. She faced certain social banishment in England, rejected by her lover and left with their illegitimate child. Her steadfastness amidst these pressures is a triumph, as was the nearly universal critical reception of her *Letters* on publication.[5] She becomes like the stone in its perseverance, not in the sense of being unfeeling, like Imlay ("Know you of what materials some hearts are made?" [124] she asks him), but precisely through embracing and working through the turbulent pressures that surrounded her.

The bands of gneiss are also sometimes formed by a chemical process known as "metamorphic differentiation,"[6] and we might also read the *Letters* as a metamorphic process in which varying tendencies become distinct and solidified, recrystalized by the action of a kind of affective chemistry. The multilayered rock presents a narrative, something noted by early geologists. James Hutton, describing granite, a parent rock of gneiss, writes, "They have not only separately the forms of certain typographic characters, but collectively give the regular lineal appearance of types set in writing" (44).[7] The layers of stone that Wollstonecraft investigates parallels the epistolary layers of her text, foliation deriving from the Latin *folium*, or leaf (referring only to the plant at first [*OED* 1], and centuries later applied to both rock and text [*OED* 4,6] as industry and technology expanded). Wollstonecraft's *Letters* mediate these definitions, as she contemplates "having turned over a new page in the history of my own heart" (61). The formation of these foliations is full of turbulent subterranean forces that burst onto the surface unexpectedly, just as Wollstonecraft's aesthetic appreciation of the landscape is repeatedly interrupted by unexpected intrusions. For the narrator of the *Letters*, the bare stone of Scandinavia is both a raw material and a skin, a blank page and a sensitive surface that floods her consciousness and gives her pause, that draws her thoughts towards sublime expanses of time[8] and human possibility and also leaves her alone in the crisis of a barren and confining present. Like the disarticulated word in a dictionary, the stone is a raw material heavy with its own potential; its silence sinks into Wollstonecraft's narrative and informs the intricate structures she creates.

Understanding the foundational presence of stone in both human culture and in the *Letters*[9] frees the material from its limitation to mere "natural" resource or aesthetic object and makes possible a construction of the intersubjective that includes the natural world. Michel Serres has argued for the need to recognize the natural world as a legal subject, to "add to the exclusively social contract a natural contract of symbiosis and reciprocity" (38). To affirm the integral role of these substances in the formation of our notions of self, is to contribute towards a more symbiotic construction of human identity and purpose. As Nancy Yousef observes, subjectivity in the *Letters* is "shaped by vulnerability and acknowledged dependence on others" (537);[10] Wollstonecraft offers an opportunity to expand our definition of "others" and our dependence on them in her development of the presence of stone.

In this chapter, I read Wollstonecraft's "bones of the world" as more than a metaphor, as this substance has provided the material frame upon which human culture has taken shape. These bones augur both potential and ruin, and therefore speak directly to contemporary ecocrisis and its ramifications for human cultural production. The growth of capitalist markets and their associated industrial forms of production during the Romantic period have accelerated to the point that the future of human dwelling on the planet has been endangered. Wollstonecraft consistently critiques a growing devotion to commerce throughout the *Letters* but feels that her voice is lost in the tumultuous rush to profit. Late in the *Letters* she writes, "Cassandra was not the only prophetess whose warning voice has been disregarded" (128). Though Wollstonecraft's warning applies to commerce, it is Cassandra-like in its relevance to contemporary ecological crisis. How stone provides a nexus for the relationship between the economic, the ecological, and the literary will be the subject of this chapter.

Flows of Commerce and Iron-Sinewed Rocks

The silence of the stone, that "made itself be felt" (7), is bound up with the silence that motivates the narrative. The reader is never told what drives Wollstonecraft from place to place in the *Letters*, but we know she was on a mission to recover lost silver for her erstwhile lover, the American adventurer Gilbert Imlay. Wollstonecraft's contemplation of the bare and rugged stone as resource of the sublime is mirrored in the vast extraction, from the sixteenth to the eighteenth centuries, of precious metals from the mines of New Spain, at a height during Wollstonecraft's travels: "Mining and minting held near historic highs through the wars of the 1790s and early 1800s" (Tutino 174). It is difficult to underestimate the importance of silver to global trade before paper money; it provided the means of exchange for the rapid expansion of international markets. It "went round the world and made the world go round" (Frank 131), flowing from the mines of New Spain then into the coffers of Chinese emperors before returning, via the opium trade, to Britain's shores.[11] The silver stolen from Imlay that Wollstonecraft seeks harbours within itself a multilayered historical theft, as it was likely looted from imprisoned French aristocrats (Nyström 21), who before this had quite possibly obtained it from the looting of the mines of New Spain with the aid of enslaved and conscripted labour (Klein and Vinson 18–24). Wollstonecraft's wandering and its hidden motivations expresses that of the substance she seeks to recover the value of.

The various things that remain silent, or to use Mary Favret's words, "[w]hat is unvoiced or barely voiced in her writing" ("Wollstonecraft's Antigone"), include the initial response with which the *Letters* were met: Imlay's insensibility to their appeal. Wollstonecraft's words, revised and edited for publication, resound amidst this silence, as if from the surface of the barren Scandinavian stone. And while stone can appear as sterile and inhospitable, as a fundamental limit to human endeavour, it is in fact the prerequisite underlying all forms of human relations. Stone does not resist or block the word, but reflects, and even amplifies it, even when there is no one to hear, as Wollstonecraft demonstrates. As Cohen puts it, "Relations do not create things like rocks and mountains; things like rocks and mountains are what enable relations to flourish" (3). And, of course, the significance of Wollstonecraft's reconfiguration of her letters extends beyond Imlay, or any need for a patriarchal interlocutor, to enable a myriad of potential relations that necessarily include the non-human.

The area where Wollstonecraft lands in Sweden is Hallandia County, an area where gneiss was mined for centuries: "It has ... been discovered in churches from the 12th and 13th centuries and has thus been used for building purposes for several hundred years" (Schouenborg et al. 45).[12] Hallandia County would become a centre for industrial gneiss production from the 1850s, mostly for export to Germany and Denmark (also on Wollstonecraft's itinerary) for use as paving stones and as structural elements (35). Thus, this stone is not merely something that invites aesthetic and philosophical contemplation; it is a structural element in the architecture and infrastructure of nineteenth-century Europe, a commodity as well as a representative of a supposedly wild and untouched natural environment. In the first Letter, when Wollstonecraft observes, "Rocks were piled on rocks ... Come no further, they emphatically said, turning their dark sides to the waves to augment the idle roar" (9), she not only invites a consideration of the accumulative nature of capitalism (the imagery of "Rocks ... piled on rocks" is one she returns to several times), she depicts a "wild" landscape in terms of its function to harbour and protect, to make habitation and contemplation possible, even to provide the structure of that very habitation and contemplation. It is not that the rocks *seem* to say something, they "emphatically" (9) say it ("it does not talk, it speaks" in Celan's words), and in so doing shape human experience.

Wollstonecraft's evocation of and attitudes towards these rocks are complicated and at times contradictory, suggesting the uncertain ontological place of the natural object within an increasingly secularized and commodified society. That is, she captures the confusion in how something like stone can be considered both a natural object and a commodity at the same time. This uncertainty was also reflected in subject formation: as Martha Woodmansee and Mark Osteen write, "capitalist practices of representation construct various, and often conflicting, versions of subjectivity" (16). Wollstonecraft's epithets "bare," "blind," "naked," and "shivering," describe the rocks in an abject state of a purely instrumental nature, while the "immense," "grand," "fantastic," "iron sinewed" rocks exude power and sublimity. The way a lake is described as "embosomed," the body "sheltered," and that a "bulwark" or "barrier" is formed by the rocks suggests their protective and comforting power, while how they "menaced" the clouds, threatened to sink the careless boat, or left the individual "bastilled by nature" communicates a sense of confinement and impending destruction. These contradictory significations are reflected in Wollstonecraft's own attack on the blind pursuit of material wealth as she travels through the landscape as an agent of commerce.

In another figure of contrasts, Wollstonecraft combines the ecological qualities of stone with the social customs of Sweden: "the politeness of the north seems to partake of the coldness of the climate, and the rigidity of its iron sinewed rocks" (8). There is a further commentary hidden within what Wollstonecraft sees as a stiff politeness, and that is the importance of iron to the eighteenth-century Swedish economy and to the development of British industry: "Bar iron was by far the most important item in Sweden's 18th century exports," and "more than half usually went to Great Britain and Ireland" (Hildebrand 3). According to Carl-Johan Gadd, "by 1750 ... Sweden was by far the greatest exporter of iron in Europe" (120), and Britain at this time was Sweden's largest importer of iron, largely in support of the war effort (used in muskets, shot, cannon, and cannonballs). Wollstonecraft's "iron sinewed rocks" take on a different valence here and raise the question as to how many technological advances in human history were motivated by war as opposed to the "Enlightened" progress of industry. In addition, Swedish iron came to be essential[13] to a host of traditional and developing industry in Britain, used in everything from horseshoes to anchors, plows to presses.[14] It was particularly prized for its quality over other sources of imported iron (Hildebrand 24). Britain's maritime and industrial expansion was unthinkable without huge supplies of the substance, a fact of which Wollstonecraft seems well aware, as she goes out of her way to visit an iron mine while travelling through Scandinavia.

At several times in the narrative Wollstonecraft references mining as the type of activity that signals Enlightenment progress towards a more absolute command of the material world. Besides providing the source of the raw material and precious metals necessary to expand economic growth, mining was significant in a number of other ways in the Romantic period. It was directly involved in the progress of geology and other associated disciplines. It also occupied a cultural space that included mythic associations with the underworld, which bled into the description of aesthetic experiences of these spaces. Many important European Romantics, such as Goethe and Novalis, were trained as mining engineers, and this training inevitably inflected their work.[15] The Swedish mystic Swedenborg first became famous throughout Europe for a work that detailed iron and copper smelting, written during his thirty-year stint as an assessor for the Swedish Board of Mines. While this connection between mining and mysticism might seem strange, according to Lars Bergquist, "From Swedenborg's perspective, philosophy and mining were complementary realms" (114). This is not surprising given the longer history of analogizing the interior of the earth with the human mind. Advances in geology made it possible to develop these analogies further. For example, the division of the earth into crust, mantle, and core (occurring roughly around the same time that Freud was theorizing the tripartite nature of the psyche[16]) had to initially rely on theoretical grounds, as the mantle and core could not be directly observed: "study of the solid Earth necessarily relies on indirect approaches and on rare samples of deeper material brought to the surface through geologic processes" (White 493). If the "solid Earth" is replaced with the unconscious, and "geologic" with psychoanalytic, then the same holds true. The unconscious must also be approached indirectly, and the process of analysis must be relied on to bring deeper material to the surface, thus Freud's famous depiction of the analyst as an archeologist, or Jung's psychologizing of the classical *anima mundi*.[17]

Wollstonecraft's focus on the stone of Scandinavia, and her descriptions of the iron and silver being brought up from the mines of Sweden and Norway might thus be reconsidered in terms of the psychologizing of the earth. In this sense, ore is related to the latent content that psychoanalysis seeks to exploit.[18] This relation is helpful in considering a passage in Letter VIII, where Wollstonecraft describes how her "very soul diffused itself in the scene" (50). A few lines later, she details a relationship between stone, liquid, and body wherein other diffusions take place: "By chance I found a fine rivulet filtered through the rocks, and confined in a bason for the cattle. It tasted to me like a chalybeat; at any rate it was pure … I therefore determined to turn my morning walks towards it, and seek for health from the nymph of the fountain; partaking of the beverage offered to the tenants of the shade" (51). A chalybeat is "water containing iron, often from a spring, and taken for medicinal purposes" (*Letters* 180). Iron is diffused into the water through the stone, which in turn is diffused into the body through a kind of pastoral ritual. If the stone can represent the manifest content of the dream, and its ore the latent content, then the taking of the water appears something like the process of analysis, in which the repeated ritual represents an ingestion of the latent content back into the psyche, and thus a working through towards a health granted "from the nymph of the fountain."

Wollstonecraft's text may thus be compared to the stone and its products, itself something "filtered through the rocks" and offering a health-producing regimen. Yet, just as aesthetic recompense through interaction with the natural world is never very far in Wollstonecraft from the disruption of human industry, so early industrial geology was intrinsically tied to appreciation of the landscape. In describing the importance of amateur fieldwork in the development of geology, Richard Hamblyn points to "an economic coupling of industrial mineralogy with the leisure economy of movement between an itinerary of prospects" (qtd. in Heringman 142). Wollstonecraft's publication of a travel narrative depicting movement through an itinerary of prospects dominated by rock formations while on a mission to recover lost silver also retraces this economic coupling of geology with the aesthetic appreciation of picturesque landscapes.

Yet this coupling is, for Wollstonecraft, a vexed one. Though she consistently champions the improved ability of humanity to exploit the resources of the earth, she also laments the results of this exploitation. In Letter VI she describes Lauvrig as "a clean, pleasant town, with a considerable iron-work, which gives life to it" (36). In Letter VII, Wollstonecraft blames "the want of mechanical and chemical knowledge" for the lack of productivity of Norwegian mines. Yet, in Letter XIII, now writing from Moss, Norway, she strikes a different note: "I had not time to see the iron works … and I was not very anxious to see them, after having viewed those at Lauvrig" (77). What she was not anxious to see we can only guess, as she omits a description of the mines at Lauvrig, though it is apparent there was a gap between her assessment of the productivity of the mine and the visceral experience of witnessing it in operation. We know from various other passages in the *Letters* that, for Wollstonecraft, human intervention in the landscape often ruined the aesthetic recompense that landscape afforded. In Letter XV she "did not like to see a number of saw-mills crowded together close to the cataracts; they destroyed the harmony of the prospect" (133), and in Letter XVII, describing the building of a canal, she "could not help regretting that such a noble scene had not been left in its solitary sublimity" (143). Just how progress is to be attained without disturbing the landscape or the enlightened traveller appears to be something of a conundrum. Yet rather than shying away from this dilemma, the *Letters* foreground it, presenting a paradox at the heart of their formation, one also at the heart of a nascent capitalist system of value.

Environmental Trauma

The massive forces at work in the formation of stone bear a resemblance to the forces Wollstonecraft channels in the production of her narrative. In Letter XVII she describes rocks which "probably had been torn asunder by some dreadful convulsion of nature" (96), which is mimicked by the engineering project going on at the site, in which workmen were "blowing up the rocks," though this activity pales in comparison to nature's handiwork and is, in comparison, "the insignificant sport of children" (96). In 1788 John Whitehurst similarly draws a picture of the form of rocks in Derbyshire in terms of a spectacular violence. He describes the rocks as "broken, dislocated, and thrown into every possible direction, and their interior parts are no less rude and romantic; for they universally abound with subterraneous caverns; and, in short, with every possible mark of violence" (63). These marks of violence frozen into place in the landscape resemble the violence which turns figures into stone or freezes them into place in Ovid's *Metamorphoses*, and help to read Wollstonecraft's own characterization towards the end of Letter I of feeling (in Whitehurst's words) "broken, dislocated, and thrown into every possible direction": "How frequently has melancholy and even mysanthropy taken possession of me, when the world has disgusted me, when friends have been unkind. I have then considered myself as a particle broken off from the grand mass of mankind" (12). The deep time in which rock cycles operate would appear to make any comparison to human experience absurd, but Wollstonecraft, in her constant return to the stone, creates a scaled likeness through which to think her own fragility and will to permanence.

Human intervention into the landscape is often characterized as a type of "depredation." Letter XIII begins with a theatrical framing: "my eyes were charmed with the view of an extensive undulated valley, stretching out under the shelter of a noble ampitheatre of pine-covered mountains." Amidst this picturesque description Wollstonecraft inserts the following passage: "The view, immediately on the left, as we drove down the mountain, was almost spoilt by the depredations committed on the rocks to make alum. I do not know the process. – I only saw that the rocks looked red after they had been burnt; and regretted that the operation should leave a quantity of rubbish, to introduce an image of human industry in the shape of destruction" (118–19). Alum[19] is a substance that had a wide variety of applications in Wollstonecraft's day. It was produced through a six-part industrial process, involving various chemical transformations. The process has been called "a marvel of empirical industrial chemistry" (Rayner and Hemingway, qtd. in Balston, Appendix I), because there was no knowledge of the chemical interactions at the time, and the production was developed purely by a trial-and-error process. This is the reason for the large amounts of urine used in the production of alum to provide the necessary ammonia. This aligns the scene with the passage on herring, discussed below, and with the irruptive smell, in Letter XXIV, of the glue factory at Altona.

However, the need to immediately and flatly deny knowledge of the process here, followed by the pause and the "I only saw," are suggestive that the author might know more than she lets on. At the very least, she knew that alum, along with soap, were products Imlay and his business associates were importing into France. She teases him in a letter of 22 September 1794: "Well, you will say this is trifling – shall I talk about alum or soap?" (*Collected Letters* 263). Alum production was a major industry in England from the Reformation to the Victorian period, and urine was regularly collected from London and other major cities and shipped in casks to meet the necessary supply. The "rubbish" and "destruction" left behind by the chemical process would have been visible in Wollstonecraft's day in North Yorkshire, where the cliffs were eaten into, the forests cut down for the required charcoal, and the land left bare and stained. Having spent her formative years in Yorkshire,[20] it is highly unlikely that Wollstonecraft was not aware of the industry before meeting Imlay.

The way in which the site of alum manufacture is like a sore on the body of the landscape is similar to the way the functions of the body interrupted the progress of the mind for Wollstonecraft. According to Emily Sunstein: "Mary's reaction to her body's functions, even as late as … her thirties, was one of shame and revulsion" (25). There are several passages in the *Letters*, however, that demonstrate Wollstonecraft as moving away from these attitudes and expressing a greater sense of comfort and intimacy with her body. The landscape description brings attitudes towards the body into contact with fears regarding the uncontrolled growth of industry, placing both within the context of a natural world both resilient and fragile. The close relationship Wollstonecraft often draws between the body and the landscape presents a foil to the relationship between alum production and the functions of the body. The way alum manufacture produces a sore or scar upon the landscape suggests the essential ecological relationship between the body and its environment, and the resulting ramifications of violent depredation. Wollstonecraft reports a scarring that is a prelude to a much more violent and ongoing historical dismemberment.

Wollstonecraft's identification with the rocks of Scandinavia forms a stark contrast to the imagery of cultivation that often appears oddly alienating. Mark Canuel notices "a certain uneasiness that Wollstonecraft has with the conventional discourse of cultivation that crops up intermittently throughout [the *Letters*]" (140). This uneasiness may in part lie with the way a language of cultivation characterized much of the historical description of feminine traits. As she makes clear in the *Vindication of the Rights of Woman*, a language of cultivation is used to naturalize a socially created form of slavery. Yet rather than merely denounce this language, Wollstonecraft turns it on its head, substituting a language of enlightened growth for one of luxuriant decay (George 209). In the *Letters*, Wollstonecraft further complicates the use of the language of cultivation, inserting it into picturesque description and economic observation in such a way as to raise questions about how notions of value arise from forms of social organization, and how these forms both influence and are influenced by the material objects of nature. Rather than departing from her earlier philosophical tenets, the *Letters* present, as Yousef explains, "an instantiation and elaboration of preoccupations central to that work" (538). That much of the space Wollstonecraft describes is uncultivated land, paradoxical "fields of rocks," is particularly appropriate to her approach towards the language of cultivation and its social ramifications.

Agriculture is frequently a subject of discussion in the *Letters*, and it frequently enters into descriptions of landscape. In Letter V it does so in a way that not only disrupts the picturesque description of which it is a part but causes visceral disgust.

> I was particularly impressed by the beauty of the situation. The road was on the declivity of a rocky mountain, slightly covered with a mossy herbage and vagrant firs. At the bottom, a river, struggling amongst the recesses of stone, was hastening forward to the ocean and its grey rocks, of which we had a prospect on the left, whilst on the right it stole peacefully forward into the meadows, losing itself in a thickly wooded rising ground. As we drew near, the loveliest banks of wild flowers variegated the prospect, and promised to exhale odours to add to the sweetness of the

air, the purity of which you could almost see, alas! not smell, for the putrifying herrings, which they use as manure, after the oil has been extracted, spread over the patches of earth, claimed by cultivation, destroyed every other.

It was intolerable, and entered with us into the inn, which was in other respects a charming retreat. (40)

The sentimental language of picturesque description rises artfully to a climax only to meet a shocking rebuff at the moment the greatest aesthetic pleasure is expected.[21] The odour of the herring irrupts into the landscape, making further aesthetic recompense unthinkable. It invades the elaborate and artful practice of picturesque viewing and the class assumptions underlying this aesthetic. The passage further asks where the source of aesthetic pleasure is to be located. As Bohls has argued, Wollstonecraft critiques Burkean and Kantian modes of disinterested contemplation by destroying the distance between perceiver and a statically framed scene, undercutting the primacy of the visual (151). The centrality of the body here and throughout the *Letters*, suggests an alternate aesthetic that is "anchored in and arising from" the body's needs and desires (165). The atmosphere these herring create reappears within and nearly hovers over the narrative that runs through the *Letters* (as it follows the travellers into the otherwise "charming retreat") and is reminiscent of the colonizing force of capital that suffuses all objects of discourse. These herring bones, also "bones of the world," and their use in cultivation resonates in later Romantic period work, where bones are described in relation to cultivation and industry.

The *Letters* provide an early example of the environmental effects of industrial capitalism, effects which would become increasingly dire, as John Clare's "The Lament of Swordy Well" attests:

And me, they turned me inside out
For sand and grit and stones
And turned my old green hills about
And picked my very bones   (61–4)

The bones of the earth also evoke the "skin and bone" of the impoverished, to which William Cobbett would repeatedly call attention in his *Rural Rides*: "what a hellish system it must be, to make those who raise it skin and bone and nakedness" (375).[22] The rural poor and the landscape come to resemble one another in various ways, their bodies shaped by the power structures of an increasingly industrial and urban society. This is also illustrated by Wordsworth's description of the discharged soldier: "you might almost think/That his bones wounded him" (44–5). And Mary Prince indicates the invasive nature of the commodity when she writes of the effects of working in the salt ponds on Turks Island, where the salt would "eat down in some cases to the very bone" (72). The rawness and sharp contrasts of the landscapes described in the *Letters* raise implications for the ways in which capital's irruptive force complicates aesthetic formations of the natural world and the forms of subjectivity upon which these are based.[23]

The herring has further historical importance to the growth of British economic and naval power, which also hangs in the air, an important context to Wollstonecraft's experience and her work. Roger L'Estrange, writing in the seventeenth century, comments on the role of the herring in British colonial endeavour: "the only common nursery of seamen is this [herring] fishery, where every buss brings up (it may be) six, eight, or ten new men every year, so that our fishery is just as necessary to our navigation as to our safety and well being" (qtd. in *The Treasuries of the Deep* 168). What is often described as the origin of the modern British Navy, Cromwell's Navigation Act of 1651 is prompted by issues related to herring fishing. According to Arthur Michael Samuel, the Act was "one of the foundation stones upon which the commercial prosperity" of England was built (113) and was conspicuous in that it "arose from disputes based upon the visits of foreign vessels in search for herrings" (114–15). Succinctly describing the importance of the fish in the expansion of empire, the French naturalist Bernard Germain de Lacépède writes, at around the same time Wollstonecraft is composing her *Letters*: "Le hareng est une de ces production naturelles dont l'emploi decide de la destinee des empires" ("The herring is one of the natural products that decides the destiny of empires"), and Georges Cuvier writes, "The greatest statesmen, the most intelligent political economists, have looked on the herring fishery as the most important of maritime expeditions" (qtd. in "Herring and the Herring Fisheries" 378). The herring provided an important source of food, especially for the labouring classes, and was exported in great quantities in the late eighteenth century to feed slaves on British plantations in the West Indies (Samuel 134, 142).

The interruption of picturesque description takes on new significance when considering the herring's place in history. Though the roots of the word are not entirely certain, one possible source is the Old High German, "heri" or "army, host" (*OED*). The sudden presence of the herring not only evokes the irruptive violence of empire but a critique of that empire, a return of the repressed upon the underlying foundations of a dominant aesthetic. Because the herring can cheaply feed large numbers and provides a training ground for a growing seagoing nation, it proves, as Lacépède notes, an essential tool of empire. Its presence here, used up and squeezed out, its bones spread across the earth, acts as a sign pointing back to the significance of its historical context.

It is further important to note here that the Swedish herring industry was at its height at the time of Wollstonecraft's arrival in Scandinavia. Over 30,000 metric tons of herring were exported each year in the 1790s, as well as approximately 70,000 tons of herring oil, obtained by an industrial process that involved boiling the fish and skimming the fat from the liquid. Statistics for one province on the west coast of Sweden, through which Wollstonecraft passed on her travels, provides an example of the extent of the industry. According to Axel Vilhelm Ljungman, "in 1787 there were in Bohuslan 338 salting houses and 429 oil-refineries, with a total of 1,812 boilers, using 40,986 barrels of herring per day ... These figures increased considerably during the following years" (235–6). The processing of herring required vast amount of wood, not only for the barrels, but for housing, boats, and the firewood needed to fuel the vast number of boilers. It is little wonder, then, that the land was as barren as Wollstonecraft found it. According to Gadd, "The sixteenth and seventeenth centuries had already seen extensive land clearance, especially in the southern woodlands and in western Sweden, and the process continued into the eighteenth century" (143). Western Sweden was the area through which Wollstonecraft travelled extensively. Another industry that required large amounts of wood was the iron industry, which produced Sweden's primary export, as discussed above. The resulting effect of vast land clearances had distinct ecological implications. According to Per Eliasson and Sven Nilsson, "In the end of the eighteenth century, the rural Swedish economy saw signs of an ecological crisis caused by overuse of scarce land resources" (661). It seems highly likely, then, that when Wollstonecraft describes a landscape "waiting to be clothed," it is one that in former times enjoyed more plentiful vegetation.

It is not only in Wollstonecraft's overt warnings as to the evils caused by excess involvement in trade that foreshadow later environmental thought; it is also the way she depicts industry encroaching on the scenes through which she passes, and the way this industry interrupts the viewer and disenchants the scene. The relevance of these descriptions to increasing environmental, and therefore cultural, destruction is perhaps nowhere more apparent than in Letter XI, where the view of the coast as they sail along it brings about this meditation:

> I anticipated the future improvement of the world, and observed how much man had still to do, to obtain of the earth all it could yield. I even earned my speculations so far as to advance a million or two of years to the moment when the earth would perhaps be so perfectly cultivated, and so completely peopled, as to render it necessary to inhabit every spot; yes; these bleak shores. Imagination went still farther, and pictured the state of man when the earth could no longer support him. Where was he to fly to from universal famine? Do not smile: I really became distressed for these fellow creatures, yet unborn. The images fastened on me, and the world appeared a vast prison. (68)

The logic of Enlightenment improvement here meets one type of logical end, ironically comparable to the future we continue to contribute towards (as greenhouse gas emissions continue to rise), in which "the earth could no longer support" humanity. And Wollstonecraft was right in the sense that progress in industry and technology, which she everywhere praises in the *Letters*, is absolutely essential to the grossest excesses of environmental destruction from her time to our own (though the last fifty years have done exponentially more harm than any other period in human history). "Improvement" would indeed wreak a path of unprecedented destruction, and Benjamin's metaphor becomes literalized in the wake of contemporary climate change: "This storm is what we call progress" (258).

The fact that much ecological disaster is not immediately visible does not of course mean it is not occurring. The references in the *Letters* to rocks just below the surface of the water that can wreck unwary boats or rocks not visible when sailing at night are both ways of conceiving this. Rocks threaten the boat on which she sails on numerous occasions. In Letter VI we learn of the necessity "to steer clear of the rocks that lurk below the water, close to the shore" (35). In Letter X "our pilot avoided the blind rocks with great dexterity" (66). In Letter XI "we were continually obliged to tack about, to avoid the rocks, which, scarcely reaching the surface of the water, could only be discovered by the breaking of the waves over them" (68). In Letter XVI "There was … great reason to fear that we had lost our way, and were straying amidst a labyrinth of rocks" (90). On more than one occasion the rock formations are both picturesque and dangerous, a combination pertinent to our present situation, when many of the products that contribute to environmental degradation are marketed directly to the global consumer's sense of enjoyment and convenience. What lurks below the placid surface, the "normalcy" of contemporary life, is the immanence of shipwreck.

Text and Stone

The word "gneiss" is thought to derive from the old German "gneisto," or "to spark." This likely refers to the reflective minerals layered within the stone but could also refer to the action of a tool, as gneiss is of sufficient hardness to spark when hit with metal. Thus we can think of the spark as both what the material contains and what it produces when worked upon. In the *Letters* the spark is the Promethean animating principle (93), that "goes out" (51) when life ends, touching on the debates around vitalism that would so engross Wollstonecraft's daughter Mary. The spark of the stone is reflected in the sparkling eyes Wollstonecraft describes several times in the *Letters*, most notably in Letter V: "I wondered from whence the fire was stolen which sparkled in their fine blue eyes" (31). The spark is also the animating principle of the text, the eye/I through which the reader experiences the world of the *Letters*, which Wollstonecraft comments on in the "Advertisement":

> In writing these desultory letters, I found I could not avoid being continually the first person – 'the little hero of each tale.' I tried to correct this fault, if it be one, for they were designed for publication; but in proportion as I arranged my thoughts, my letter, I found, became stiff and affected: I, therefore, determined to let my remarks and reflections flow unrestrained, as I perceived that I could not give a just description of what I saw, but by relating the effect different objects had produced on my mind and feelings, whilst the impression was still fresh. (3)

There is a struggle here between the narrative "I" and the object the narrative purports to be about. This struggle is apparent is in the number of relative and dependent clauses in this passage, the use of colons to artificially prolong the sentence, and the multiplication of "I"s. This passage resembles Whitehurst's depiction of the "romantic" Derbyshire rock formations quoted above, with its implied scattering of a previously unified form. Wollstonecraft's contrast of "stiff" and "unrestrained" here recalls her description of feeling alternately hemmed in and constrained by the stone (and Scandinavian manners), and free when roaming alone in the rocky picturesque countryside. The "impression" the "different objects produced" corresponds with the impression of ink upon the page, or that made upon rock in the process of its formation. As text aspires to the seeming permanence of stone, its form attempts to capture impressions the way stone captures the fossilized impressions of life.

Text as stone would become a prominent metaphor in Wordsworth's *Prelude*, where his "little yellow canvas-covered book" (V.483) is "but a block/Hewn from a mighty quarry" (487–8). Stone would also figure prominently in the composition of *Lyrical Ballads*, which began as a way to make enough money "to defray the expense" of a tour, according to Wordsworth, "to visit Linton and the Valley of Stones near it" (qtd. in Langan 76). The Valley of Stones was visited by Robert Southey in the following year (1799), which he describes in a letter to his close friend John May as "the very bones & skeleton of the earth, rock reclining upon rock, stone piled upon stone, a huge & terrific mass" (*Collected Letters* 429). Southey's description is too close to Wollstonecraft to be accidental, and it raises the possibility that Southey, and perhaps even Wordsworth and Coleridge, had Wollstonecraft's narrative in mind when drawn to the unusual rock formations of the Valley of Stones. Coleridge would later describe the visit to the Valley of Stones as prompting the composition of *The Rime of the Ancient Mariner* (Barker 138). And though Southey echoes Wollstonecraft, it is also true that Wollstonecraft was mining a more ancient source. Barthalomaeus Anglicus, writing in the thirteenth century, claims that Saint Ambrose (in the fourth century) refers to stones as "the bones of the earth" (16.75). While I find no evidence of Wollstonecraft reading Anglicus, it is possible she came across the epithet indirectly. The idea, like what it describes, is suitably ancient.

That Wollstonecraft describes the letters as "desultory" is telling, not only because this recalls the chaotic scattering of Whitehurst's rocks but because Wollstonecraft uses this word again in the *Letters* to describe habits of reading. In Letter III she writes, "Desultory reading is commonly merely a pastime. But we must have an object to refer our reflections to, or they will seldom go below the surface" (20). The letters may appear haphazard, not following any uniform structure or genre, but that doesn't mean we should read them as not having a design upon us. Rather than recording impressions, as readers we "refer our reflections" to an object. Taking stone as an object necessarily involves going below the surface and putting tools to work upon the veins found there. Wollstonecraft's narrator consistently poses as a reader throughout the *Letters*, referring her reflections again and again to the omnipresent stone. Her movements across territories and landscapes reflect the reader's movement through the text, and text reflects stone in the way it offers a "resistance that the establishment of a place offers to the erosion of time" (Certeau 39). Stone offers a resistance upon which Wollstonecraft both reads and writes.

This paradox inheres in the very material necessary to the production of Wollstonecraft's text: the paper, ink, glue, and other materials required to produce a book. The leaf-like bands of gneiss and the leaves of the pages of her text both represent substances that have undergone metamorphosis. In Letter V she writes, "Approaching the frontiers, consequently the sea, nature resumed an aspect ruder and ruder, or rather seemed the bones of the world waiting to be clothed with every thing necessary to give life and beauty. Still it was sublime" (28). This unclothed stone, both a site of vulnerability and of strength, suggests the blank page Wollstonecraft inscribes. They may be "the bones of the world," but the metaphor of clothing brings them to life. At the end of Letter IV she describes the "varying lineaments" of "the soul, as well as the heart" (24), in Letter VII she refers to the body as a "vestment" and "habit" (49), and in *Mary* she imagines a "spirit unclothed." And literal clothes again and again come up in the *Letters* in terms of the relation between moral and aesthetic value. These relationships between naked and clothed landscape, unclothed spirit and body as clothing, are relevant to how Wollstonecraft dresses the page.

The very paper on which Wollstonecraft writes, and on which her letters will be printed, is made from disused cloth, as it would be another fifty years until wood was introduced into the paper-making industry. The repeated discussion of particular clothes and fashions throughout the letters is relevant here in terms of the rags these clothes would eventually provide for paper-making factories. The process of producing text thus involved not only authors, editors, and printers but also "rag and bone" men, human sweat, and animal parts.[24] The "bones of the world" infuse Wollstonecraft's text in more ways than one. The demand for rags was so great[25] that Britain had to import huge amounts, and some of these rags came from Sweden and Norway, so that many of the clothes discussed in the *Letters* likely became paper for the printing of a variety of texts. But Britain also got its rags from other sources, including dead sailors' uniforms, the linen of executed criminals, and the used-up osnaburgs of enslaved labourers.[26] Just as the bodies of these figures haunted the blank whiteness of the page (Burgess 372), so are Wollstonecraft's landscapes haunted by historical forces that overwhelm their description.

The process by which paper was made was undergoing a significant transformation during the latter half of the eighteenth century. For centuries the rags used for paper manufacture, after being sorted according to quality, were beaten with hammers in the early stages of the process to break down the cloth into its composite fibres. A machine known as the Hollander (so named due to its development by the Dutch) was quickly replacing the hammer. According to Alfred Shorter, "During the second half of the eighteenth century the engine replaced the older stamping method of beating the materials, and by 1800 there were very few English paper mills where the hammer and mortars were still in use" (40). The second half of the eighteenth century also saw increasing conflict between paper-mill owners and workers, which in the 1790s caused vast stoppages of work and in 1796 (the year the *Letters* were published) brought about a largely ineffective Act of Parliament to prevent workers in the paper industry from organizing (Shorter 96–7). Paper production as transformed by industrialization, and thereby a site of social conflict, reveals something of the many-layered nature of commodity form.

Materials present in the *Letters* also are important in the manufacture of the paper on which they are written. In the glue factory Wollstonecraft describes in Letter XXIV would likely have been found both glue and gelatin, essential ingredients in the process of paper production (glue was used in the rollers of presses, as well as in binding, and gelatin provided a more efficient writing surface and protected paper from deterioration). Alum, which appears in another passage in the *Letters* discussed above, was often mixed with gelatin, as it helped the gelatin bond to the paper more readily (Balston, Appendix 1). Alum was also an ingredient in James Watt's recipe for ink for his letter-copying press (Rhodes and Streeter 30), a popular device owned by a host of prominent individuals, including Thomas Wedgwood, Joseph Priestley, and William Godwin. Wollstonecraft may have made copies of her letters, though without the benefit of Watt's device. What is interesting, however, is the prevalence of the inclusion of sugar in recipes for copying ink in this period, as the "use of sugar in copying inks to slow their drying was already common." This practice would continue throughout the nineteenth century: "Ordinary iron-gall ink recipes published in arts and sciences journals and domestic encyclopedias throughout the nineteenth century often included a mention that the ink could be made to serve for copying by the addition of a little sugar" (33). Used slaves' clothing provided a basis for paper production during the period, and the sugar produced by slave labour also went into the production of ink. There thus appear to be few, if any, aspects of cultural production during the Romantic period that weren't in some way implicated in the Atlantic slave trade. And though Wollstonecraft refers to slavery in a much broader way in the *Letters* that is often insensitive to the realities of the Atlantic trade, her attention to the material offers a way of rethinking the connection between bodies and substances during this period. Bohls calls Wollstonecraft's "revisionist aesthetics" a call to "change the discourses and institutions that construct our bodies and senses" (142), and a closer consideration of historical bodies and their material relations supplies the content necessary for this critique.

In addition to this relation of text to the human enslaved body is a relation to non-human bodies. Gall, necessary to all ink production prior to synthetic inks, are growths produced on trees in response to the presence of insect eggs, usually those of the wasp. In ancient China, Greece, and Rome, animal glue was an important ingredient in ink, and as late as the nineteenth century burnt animal bones were an ingredient in the ink used in copperplate printing: "The ink ... is a composition made of stones of peaches and apricots, the bones of sheep, and ivory, all well burnt; and, as the best which is used in this business, comes from Frankfort on the Main, it is known by the name of Frankfort-black. It comes over in cakes, and being mixed with nut-oil, that has been well boiled, it is ground by the printer on a marble, after the same manner as painters do their colours" (*The Young Tradesman* 120–1). Though Wollstonecraft's work was not printed on copperplate, it is significant that many of the increasingly popular productions of landscape drawing and painting were. It is unlikely that the regular printing ink used for volumes like Wollstonecraft's was composed of animal parts, though animal glue was commonly used in the rollers of the press to prevent ink waste (Plant 322). Yet when lampblack, an essential component of printer's ink, became expensive in the nineteenth century, various other pigments served as substitutes, including "bituminous shale and schists (1856), bone oil (1866), and the tannin black from leather waste (1881)" (Plant 323). The human and non-human body inform the text in more ways than one, and the stone Wollstonecraft dwells upon would literally form the material presence of words on the page.

Conclusion: Glacial Erratics and Romantic Vagrancy

The various pressures that haunt the narrative and frustrate the Enlightenment plot of human exceptionalism deposit the narrator in an impossible position, caught between a model that promises an inevitable progress and a reality that everywhere demonstrates the inevitable destruction this "progress" produces. Like the stone carried by glacial movement known as the glacial erratic (from *errare*, to wander), Wollstonecraft moves across the Scandinavian landscape as one transported by forces beyond her immediate control. Wolfgang von Goethe was "one of the first to attribute the transport of erratic blocks to glaciers" (Cameron 751), identifying the phenomenon as one of many attributes of the natural world being unfolded during the period. There is a kind of existential homelessness, or a being at home everywhere and nowhere, developed in Wollstonecraft's narrative that would become a central motif in Romantic literature, a vagrancy that Celeste Langan calls "the framing issue of Romantic form and content" (14). The glacial erratic provides a geological analogy for the wandering of the *Letters*, which include Wollstonecraft's wandering, the movement of the text into cultural life, and the wandering figured in the act of reading. The glacial erratic is a stone that, like other stones, is expected to remain still and inert, voiceless and powerless. Wollstonecraft invests the stone with an agency and power that belies the increasing tendency of her time to identify the natural world primarily in terms of physical resource, and repeatedly entreats the reader to consider the stone, not as a metaphor or even as the subject of disinterested observation, but as an intimate material of lived experience that defies conventional categorization.

The appearance of stone at the beginning and end of the *Letters* coincides with an anxious awareness of the passing of time, which is not surprising given that stone undergoes metamorphosis at stages which make the human lifespan seem especially evanescent. The *Letters* open with "Eleven days of weariness on board a vessel not intended for the accommodation of passengers," then the "anxiety" with which she "watched two long hours for a boat to emancipate me," unsurprisingly resulting in a speaker "[w]eary of expectation" (5). In the final letter the narrator is "weary of changing the scene, and quitting people and places the moment they begin to interest me," and she wanders "around … to kill time" (130–1). As she arrives, she is weary of waiting for someone to arrive; as she waits to leave, she is weary of everyone leaving. As a response fails to appear, or continues to disappear, she wanders in a slow-moving trauma, like the glacial erratic, transported by epochal and incremental glacial movements. If, as Mary Jacobus indicates in relation to Wordsworth, "Rocks … serve to demarcate the porous boundaries and the erratic movements of selving" (164), then we can also read the *Letters*, as the narrator moves across borders and landforms, as demarcating these boundaries and movements. Glacial erratics are important in determining the direction of glacial flows and therefore in forming models of global climate, and the literary qualities of Wollstonecraft's text allows for an intimate understanding of material flows and their relation to the construction of models of subjectivity. The author narrates the stone as it narrates her.

It is an interesting coincidence that as Wollstonecraft, in her penultimate letter, contemplates the view of the Elbe from Altona, west of Hamburg, she is a few kilometres upstream from the site of Germany's most famous glacial erratic, known as Der Alte Schwede (The Old Swede), a stone moved from Sweden 400,000 years earlier and only discovered due to dredging west of Hamburg in 1999. Like the stone travelling from Sweden, Wollstonecraft gives no reason for her travel to Altona, and for the reader without outside knowledge her movements appear as erratic as those of the stone. Her description of the view of the river from Altona ties together the economic, ecological, and aesthetic once more: "The moving picture, consisting of large vessels and small-craft, which are continually changing their position with the tide, renders this noble river, the vital stream of Hamburg, very interesting; and the windings have sometimes a very fine effect, two or three turns being visible, at once, intersecting the flat meadows: a sudden bend often increasing the magnitude of the river; and the silvery expanse, scarcely gliding, though bearing on its bosom so much treasure, looks, for a moment, like a tranquil lake" (128–9). As she contemplates the beauty and tranquility of the Elbe, she also highlights the commercial activity in which it is involved. It is the "vital stream of Hamburg" at least in part because of its importance to commercial trade, and the "silvery expanse" not only evokes the coin that is the medium of this trade, it shares a metonymic relationship with the "treasure" that encompasses the vessels and their contents. The continual change in position of the boats is comparable to the fluctuation in market values, and even though this paragraph appears between two others highly critical of commercial practice, it appears to naturalize the very thing the larger passage seeks to critique, a contradiction emblematic of the *Letters* more broadly. The current of market forces pulls on things otherwise thought to be beyond its reach. Moving and being moved, motion and emotion, are caught in a market flow naturalized at the same pace it is abstracted from the substances on which it is based. Yet there is another pull here, represented by the glacial erratic that lies under this tranquil water, reminding us of deep time and a wandering with another current – the last of the *Letters* is "unfinished" as she is hurried to board the ship for Dover; they remain in transit and are figured as an act of wandering, as a kind of romantic vagrancy.

The cliffs of Dover, which she finds "insignificant" after those she "had seen in Sweden and Norway," yet capture something within their geological history that reminds the reader that the line between animal and stone is not as clear as it might seem. The famous white cliffs are made up of the deposits, over millions of years, of coccoliths, individual plates of calcium carbonate formed by single-celled algae. Wollstonecraft's "bones of the world" reveal the intrinsic connections between social and biological processes; they are more, finally, than what a metaphor can contain.

Chapter Two

Broken Arbour: Deforestation and the Cultural History of Trees in "The Ruined Cottage"

"Fell it!" exclaimed the yeoman, "I had rather fall on my knees and worship it."[1]
– Wordsworth (*Poetical Works*, 1910, 282)

When Wordsworth places us "mid all this mighty sum/Of things forever speaking" in the opening poem of the 1800 edition of *Lyrical Ballads*, he not only insists on the agency of things in human thought and culture, he inaugurates a practice within his own poetry that equates things with words.[2] Poems can also be things, "forever speaking" so long as they find a receptive ear. And because these things are incessant and omnipresent, they constantly exceed our ability to take in everything they express, no matter how carefully we listen and observe. Perhaps the most prominent natural object for Wordsworth, that which inspires him throughout his career and serves as a central symbol in his poetry, is the tree. The tree, like Wollstonecraft's stone, has both a literal and figurative connection to dwelling. As the growth lines of a tree reveal the climactic and atmospheric conditions under which they form, so the lines of a poem capture forces involved in their creation. This chapter will take a three-pronged approach to the appearance of the tree in Wordsworth's poetry, primarily attending to "The Ruined Cottage" (c. 1797). First, it will consider the "bare wide common" of this poem in terms of the widespread deforestation of Britain for the purpose of economic and imperial expansion. Second, it will take up the cultural history of the oak and elm, the two most prominent trees in "The Ruined Cottage." Finally, it will consider the importance of the tree and its disappearance in the places that Britain colonized. As the previous chapter read the multi-genre form of Wollstonecraft's text in terms of the stratigraphic layers of stone, this chapter will read Wordsworth's "The Ruined Cottage" in terms of a kind of dendrochronology, the practice of examining the growth of lines in terms of what they reveal about a larger narrative of atmospheric conditions. The poem narrates what Kurt Fosso calls "a disruption of mourning" (335), as Margaret pines and wastes away, deprived of the knowledge of her husband's fate. In terms of deforestation, we continue to inhabit a similar disruption, never having come to terms culturally with this transformation of the global ecosystem. Like Margaret, we continue to trace the same compulsive circles of nostalgia and neglect; we are left to "repeat/The same sad question" (475–6). When read through the history of deforestation, the historical loss and devastation depicted by "The Ruined Cottage" reveals a continuing agency of the thing in cultural production, despite its ghostly form.

In ancient Europe, trees were identified with the sacred and the oracular.[3] With the rise of monotheism, the oracle and its object became separated from one another. When Macbeth, close to his end, ignores the reports of the enemy's advance, he demonstrates a misunderstanding that is rooted in this separation:

> Bring me no more reports; let them fly all:
> Till Birnam wood remove to Dunsinane,
> I cannot taint with fear.   (1–3; Act 5, Scene 3)

Macbeth cannot turn so easily from the pressing encroachment of events. In scene five a messenger reports:

> As I did stand my watch upon the hill,
> I look'd toward Birnam, and anon, methought,
> The wood began to move.   (34–6; Act 5, Scene 5)

The oracular messenger says more than he can know: the wood was indeed beginning to move. The branch cutting of Malcolm's men reflects the accelerating destruction of the woodlands of Britain from the late sixteenth century onwards.[4] A 1608 tree census of six of England's royal forests showed 232,011 trees standing. A 1783 survey of the same forests found few more than 50,000 trees remaining.[5] "The Ruined Cottage," long recognized as a depopulation narrative, also registers the cultural and environmental effects of deforestation,[6] effects especially relevant to the Romantic era, since at its outset England had become one of the most deforested nations in the world.[7]

The tree is central both to the growth of capitalism and to the creation of poetry. In the first it must be cut down, and in the second it must be continually made anew in the mind of the reader. Though this suggests a distance between discourse and practice, it is one rapidly closing: by the time we read "objects are closer than they appear" it may already be too late. The past 200 years, which have seen the lionization of Wordsworth's poetry and the construction of Wordsworth as cultural icon, have also produced greater environmental destruction than any other period in human existence. The poet who announces the renewal of nature[8] does so at the dawn of the Capitalocene, and it is no longer possible to treat these phenomena as entirely distinct. Kate Rigby describes how this "romantic reframing … has once again acquired a new, and ambivalent significance in the contemporary era of ecocrisis" (11). And Scott Hess argues that this ambivalence is rooted in definitions of nature: "The meaning of nature … is deeply implicated in, even foundational to, the same modern social and economic systems that we often invoke such a nature to oppose" (3). Our social and economic structures are underpinned by conceptions of nature that often remain invisible. Nature and culture are inextricable, and as Timothy Morton claims, "To write about ecology is to write about society" (17). Laurence Buell indicates a more specific way this broader idea might apply to literary criticism: "Literature-and-environment studies must develop a 'social ecocriticism' that takes urban and degraded landscapes just as seriously as 'natural' landscapes" (22). The centrality of the tree to Western culture and the history of its removal offer the basis for a substance-based literary criticism that expands on the type of "social ecocriticism" in which these authors are engaged.

My procedure in this chapter will take "The Ruined Cottage" as its guide. I will start with the barren plain, move into the stand of elms, and then into the tale of Robert's enlistment and its ramifications. The first section: "Across a Bare Wide Common," will discuss the significance of the natural history of Dorset and Somerset and its influence on Wordsworth's poetry of the 1790s, particularly "The Ruined Cottage" but also "Goody Blake and Harry Gill" (1798). In the next section, "Beneath These Trees," I will be interested in the importance of the tree as a symbol in Wordsworth's poetry and in the broader culture of his time. The third section, "To a Distant Land," will focus on the deforestation of colonized nations and the response to environmental degradation in the poetry of these nations. These poets record the disastrous effects of colonization on the environment and evoke a pre-colonial landscape in defining national identity. Such a consideration is also made necessary by the global nature of deforestation and its relation to the advance of capital, a relationship that serves as the background for this chapter as a whole.

"Across a Bare Wide Common"

The uncanny nature of the vacant and huge space that spreads around the traveller in "The Ruined Cottage" and surrounds the elms in which Armytage narrates Margaret's story, illustrates a profound historical and ecological transformation, a vast taming of the land prior to that effected by the Enclosure Acts and the advent of industrial agriculture. The descriptor "bare"[9] describes a destitution which is enlarged by "wide" and extended by "common." This "common" has been eviscerated of its purpose, left a negative space in place of a formerly productive one. The traveller finds himself at the end of a development that has permanently transformed the physical environment and the culture on which it is based. His fatigue and discomfort disrupt the pastoral frame, and his restless solitude compounds the sense of being uprooted from a sustaining community and its memory of its past. In this sense his condition announces an alienation symptomatic of modernity: as his feet are "baffled" by "the slipp'ry ground" (20–1), he travels through what Antonin Artaud describes as "this slippery world which is committing suicide without noticing it" (32).[10] What the traveller lacks in terms of bodily needs, the landscape finds missing from its own body; his physical exhaustion mirrors the exhausted soil, while his mental suffering conveys a historical turbulence, erasing and redrawing identity in unexpected ways. Just as the deforested land, transformed by man, will again come to be viewed as natural, so too must the figures of the poem attempt to re-invent themselves in now unfamiliar circumstances ("their place knew them not" [144]). In this as in other such spaces in Wordsworth (the Salisbury Plain poems in particular) both the landscape and the subject are uprooted from their pasts and reinscribed upon an alien present, performing a dark parody of the pastoral plot, strangers to themselves and to each other.

The tragic story of Robert and Margaret evokes the intertwined social and ecological injustice that is carried out through legislating away the common rights of the poor and reshaping the land for the purpose of maximum profit. Despite the fact that Robert is "industrious ... Sober and steady" (120–1), crop failure, war, and disease drive him to idleness and despair. He enlists in the army for the bounty money it will provide his family. The years pass, Robert doesn't return, and Margaret falls into a distracted state, not able to mourn nor to give up hope. Her youngest child dies, and she passes away not long afterwards. The poem dramatizes the interrelation of ecology, war, changes in land use, and the circumstances of the working poor in the turbulent decade of the 1790s.

This dramatization questions not only where nature ends and the human begins but posits that categories of experience thought of as either human or non-human do not always agree to remain distinct. Armytage first appears merged with his surroundings: "His eyes were shut;/The shadows of the breezy elms above/Dappled his face" (46–8). At the poem's opening, the surface of the landscape is also described as dappled: "and all the northern downs/In clearer air ascending shewed far off/Their surfaces dappled o'er" (3–5). This not only identifies Armytage's face with the contours of the landscape but allows us to view the landscape also as like him, its surface a placid face it presents to the world. The pedlar becomes representative of the land itself; what Silvia Benso calls a "faciality" of things that enables them "to demand an ethical response" (xxx) is quite close to what Wordsworth evokes. Adam Potkay describes what Wordsworth's "giving face" to things effects, noting a slippage in Book V of *The Prelude* between "the speaking face of earth and heaven" (12) and the "ghastly face" of the drowned schoolmaster (472), that "reveals through disfiguration the living face that constitutes if not all identity then at least the identity of God or nature in a Stoic vein" (397). Spinoza, in the *Ethics*, proposes a "*facies totius Universi*," or "face of the whole universe,"[11] that chimes with lines Wordsworth would later add to "The Ruined Cottage" in its transformation into "The Pedlar," describing "the universal face/Of earth and sky" (ms. E, 179–80). And Marx suggests that "Nature is man's *inorganic body*"[12] (*Early Writings* 328), positing a merging of the natural and the human. Embedded within this mirrored face lies the traveller's restless journey, suggesting that the figure of Armytage provides a solution to the traveller's ontological dilemma, a putting to rest of doubts and fears about the nature of the relationship between the human and the natural that have a broad historical and philosophical context. In a way, the recognition of the figure of Armytage represents the poem's subtly realized anagnorisis; it is here, rather than the traveller's reaction to the story he tells, where one finds the poem's crucial moment, its dappled spot of time.[13]

Yet the story's affective resonance inevitably disrupts any attempt to reach an encompassing awareness removed from its particular historical context. Both social memory and material culture are transformed into an uncanny likeness of their former selves. The practices of the rural peasantry, formed over centuries in close communion with natural objects, would become unsettled by new methods of agricultural and industrial production. When Armytage conjures the practice of a collective memory, "The Poets in their elegies and songs/Lamenting the departed call the groves" (73–4), he avoids calling the groves himself, not simply out of a sense of decorum or Calvinist conviction but because the groves are to a great extent no longer there. Something disrupts the way generic forms appeal to particular cultural significations, and war and crop failure come to represent a darker witness, one intrinsically tied to the process of environmental degradation. Extensive deforestation leads to soil erosion and mineral depletion,[14] eventually creating a poor soil that will not support agricultural crops. According to the *Victoria County History*, "wholesale clearance and sale of timber turned many wooded parts of England into stretches of barren moor and heathy waste" (*Hampshire* ii, 429). The connection to war is perhaps even simpler. As Arthur Standish put it in 1611, "No wood, no kingdome."[15] Despite this stark necessity, Tim Fulford points out how "the gentry were clearing their parks and woods to raise cash to meet the burden of wartime taxation" ("Britannia's Heart of Oak" 192). In the eighteenth and well into the nineteenth century, Britain both imported wood from Baltic states and harvested it from its colonies[16] to build and maintain a growing empire. The need to control the flow of natural resources led inevitably to conflict, a cycle which is all too familiar today.[17] When Armytage describes "Two blighting seasons when the fields were left/With half a harvest" and "A worse affliction in the plague of war" he describes a blight and a plague both ecological and ideological that finds a basis of communicability in the slow violence[18] of deforestation. What Armytage says about Robert's and Margaret's fate might also be said of deforestation, that it was "scarcely palpable/ To him who does not think" (235–6).

Two studies of the region in which "The Ruined Cottage" is set demonstrate the plight of the landscape in stark terms. John Billingsley, in *A General View of the Agriculture in the County of Somerset, 1795*, counts 20,000 acres out of a total of 1,000,000 to be "woods or plantations," a total of 2 per cent. Billingsley feels even this to be excessive and suggests that the forest of Exmoor be transformed from a "useless, and void space" into "a fair a prospect as the surrounding country" (174). "A fair … prospect" references an eighteenth-century aesthetic appreciation of "landscape" or "view" but also evokes notions of speculation. An aesthetic that valued a smooth and bare landscape was particularly convenient, considering the vast selling off of woodlands that took place over the eighteenth and into the nineteenth century, to which the "surrounding country" inevitably attests.[19]

In *A General View of the Agriculture in the County of Dorset, 1793* John Claridge estimates that of 775,000 acres, only about 9,000 acres, or a little more than 1 per cent, are wooded (5). The two counties of Somerset and Dorset, an area that gave birth to much foundational British

Romantic poetry, appear as one of the most thoroughly deforested regions in England. According to Claridge, "the county finds a serious want of wood and it would be well worth the attention of those who have land proper for it to apply it to that purpose" (151). Both the land and its inhabitants have been rent of resources and in the process have lost something of their original character and purpose:

> It is a melancholy fact that, without any particular habits of oppression on the part of the farmers, or dissoluteness on the part of the poor, the labourers of many parts of this county, and particularly of South Wiltshire, may be truly said to be at this time in a wretched situation.
>
> The dearness of provision, the scarcity of fuel, and, above all, the failure of spinning work for the women and children, have put it almost out of the power of the village poor to live by their industry; and have, unfortunately, broken that independant spirit which in a very peculiar degree, formerly kept a Wiltshire labourer from the parish books. (Claridge 155)

"The Ruined Cottage" narrates just such a breaking of "that independant [sic] spirit" that Claridge describes. Robert carves "uncouth figures on the heads of sticks" (165), illustrating not only his alienation from his labour but the alienation of the natural object from its use by culture. This alienation is also apparent in "The useless fragment of a wooden bowl" (91) once used as a dipper. And while it is true, as Marjorie Levinson points out, that the poetic and imaginative value of the object increases as its practical, monetary value decreases (222), it is also true that the fragment takes part in a metonymic resonance with the other wooden objects of the poem, like Robert's stick, but also like Armytage's staff, the bench on which Armytage sits, Margaret's gardening tools, the door and casement, the chair, loom, and table, and that all these things share a relationship with the trees mentioned throughout the poem, pointing to a way of living in and with the world vanishing along with Britain's woodlands. As Armytage puts it, "a bond/Of brotherhood is broken" (84–5).[20] The relation between the human and the natural thing can no longer be what it once was.

The evidence of the trees that once blanketed the land is held in Robert's hand as a grotesque symbol of his own descent from industry into idleness. This absence of labour is a result of both crop failure and the "failure of spinning work," and there is little coincidence that the industrial and commercial forces that accelerated deforestation are also responsible for the fall in demand for hand-spun textiles. As Brian Inglis relates, "The wives of agricultural labourers or coal-miners might be employed in spinning wool or cotton, and they were seriously affected by the spinning-jenny, which reduced the number of spinners needed to sustain a weaver. In 1790, for example, a magistrate in Somerset was called to protect spinning machinery 'from the Depredations of a lawless Banditi of colliers and their wives, for the wives had lost their work to spinning engines'" (430). It is important to note that the type of household spinning described in "The Ruined Cottage" (and other Wordsworth poems) had been long established in rural England so that its disruption was not merely a matter of lost income but was an upheaval of customary communal and hereditary practice. Rather than a marauding band of "lawless Banditi," the group and others like it were attempting to assert the law of custom in the face of a historically unprecedented assault.[21]

Margaret is just such a wife of an agricultural labourer, and her spinning, like Armytage's wandering, is a tradition fast vanishing from the countryside.

> There to and fro she paced through many a day
> Of the warm summer, from a belt of flax
> That girt her waist spinning the long-drawn thread
> With backward steps.   (459–62)

Flax is the source material of linen that formed the sails on British ships, thus tying together Margaret's circuitous movement with Robert's, the "long-drawn thread" that runs through both their stories. But as indicated by the progress of the spinning-jenny and emphasized by Margaret's long, fruitless waiting, this thread was coming unravelled even as it was spun, mirrored in the decaying cottage and Margaret's "tattered clothes" (485). The threat to the expression of political opinion in the 1790s is also apparent here, as the connection between the line of the thread and the poetic line is enhanced by the relationship between the rhythmic steps of the spinner and the metric feet of the poem.

Claridge's mention of the "scarcity of fuel" in Dorset, an apparent result of the extensive deforestation of the county, is not only relevant to the general scarcity in "The Ruined Cottage," but is addressed directly by "Goody Blake and Harry Gill," a poem explicitly set "in Dorsetshire." In the poem, Goody, an elderly widow living alone, cannot make ends meet through spinning (like Margaret), and must find the wood she needs to warm her cottage. Not finding any fallen wood at hand, she approaches a neighbouring farmer's hedge to break off a few sticks. The poem reveals how deforestation is related to the changing enforcement of property rights and critiques this development. Because the poem uniquely brings to light the impact of deforestation on the plight of the poor, demonstrating how wood served as a medium for both everyday life and for the unprecedented assault on customary rights, it is central to my larger argument about "The Ruined Cottage." I will read the poem through Marx's "Debates on the Law on Thefts of Wood" of 1842, his first published work to take up the cause of the poor.

"Goody Blake" opens with a sense of urgency: "Oh! What's the matter? What's the matter?" The repetition, by not allowing for or not receiving an answer, suggests the rhetorical and performative nature of the question. It also mirrors the "incremental repetition" that is an essential element of the ballad form, a device meant to increase the power and nuance of the repeated material, here creating a sense of growing trouble or distress. The line also asks us to consider the subject matter of the poem, not only Harry's condition but the scarcity of wood and the subsequent plight of the poor, a subject of some urgency for the young Marx, who writes "We demand for the poor a *customary right*"[22] to wood (original emphasis). This urgency is unsurprising given that a large percentage of criminal prosecutions in Europe in the first part of the nineteenth century were for the "theft" of wood (Foster 66).[23]

Goody is described in the poem as "poor,/Ill fed ... and thinly clad" (21–2) and never able to store up enough wood "to warm her for three days" (56), despite her attempts to gather all the fallen wood she could find. While deforestation is never mentioned in the poem, it is clear that wood is scarce and that because of this it has increased in price and driven the poor to take wood where they could find it. Thomas Batchelor, in *General View of the Agriculture of the County of Bedford* (1813), reports: "There are always a considerable number in every parish whose firing consists entirely of broken hedges, which are conveyed home in dark nights, and such as have large families generally carry on the trade with impunity, as the farmers are not fond of providing entirely for a family of young children" (609–10). The firing got from broken hedges carried home under darkness fits the poem's description and demonstrates the increasing vigilance with which landowners attacked the customary rights of the poor.[24] Marx reports that during a meeting of a Rhineland assembly, one deputy argues, "It is precisely because the pilfering of wood is not regarded as theft that it occurs so often" and another, "the *value* of the stolen wood ... should be used as a measure for fixing the punishment" ("Debates"). It is significant that in these cases the argument is about fallen rather than living wood and demonstrates how as the century progressed the attack on common rights intensified.

In the above passage, Batchelor mentions "providing for a family" because after the head of the household was sent to prison or transported,[25] the children would fall on the parish for support, thus raising the farmer's rates.[26] This would also be in addition to whatever the farmer would have to pay to prosecute the case,[27] a factor that likely prevented many prosecutions in the first place. Batchelor implies, however archly, that the poor obtained some economic benefit in the theft because they "carry on the trade with impunity" when it seems likely that many who gathered from hedges did so in winter, like Goody, because "the frost was past enduring" (67). This helps to clarify the violence of Harry's seizing of Goody (a likely prelude to further violence), as prosecuting her would present too great an expense. The fact that his motive is described as "vengeance" rather than legal restitution further indicates landowners' attempts to bend the law to their will, regardless of what was considered just or permitted by custom. According to Marx: "Hence the legal nature of things cannot be regulated according to the law; on the contrary, the law must be regulated according to the legal nature of things. But if the law applies the term theft to an action that is scarcely even a violation of forest regulations, then the law *lies*, and the poor are sacrificed to a legal lie" ("Debates"). The poem justifies Goody's act against changing notions of property in the name of an older tradition, something like what Marx calls "the legal nature of things" (seemingly precipitous of a Darwinian web of relationships). Later, he indicates that the close relationship of the poor with the land is the basis for their legal rights: "By its act of *gathering*, the elemental class of human society appoints itself to introduce order among the products of the elemental power of nature" ("Debates"). Goody as a member of the rural poor at this time would have gathered many of her immediate needs from the surrounding countryside. She is the type of figure Alan Everitt has in mind when writing in *The Agrarian History of England and Wales*: "Almost every living thing in the parish, however insignificant, could be turned to some good use by the frugal peasant-labourer" (405; vol. 4). Thus economy and ecology meet in the essential interconnection between the operation of the individual home and "Almost every living thing in the parish."[28] The modern sense of "economy" as a system of purely financial exchange was just beginning to take shape in direct contradistinction to this ethos. As Thompson puts it, "non-monetary use-rights were being reified into capitalist property rights, by the mediation of the courts of law" (244). And as Marx writes, "The forest owner prevents the legislator from speaking, for walls have ears" ("Debates"). It is this mediation that enables the "denaturalization" of domestic economy.[29]

The repeated description of cold in the poem creates an atmosphere of dearth and discomfort, much like the "bare wide common" of "The

Ruined Cottage," which has been evacuated of its sustaining communal role. Harry's teeth, in a phrase repeated multiple times, "Chatter, chatter, chatter still" (3), despite his having "a blanket on his back,/ and coats enough to smother nine" (6–7). One thing Wordsworth appears to indicate by the repetition followed by "still" is that there is a poverty in Harry's thinking only in terms of monetary value, one that continues well into the future, in fact into our own time. There is an ominous note in "smother" that furthers this (this chatter cannot be smothered), as well as pointing towards the predicament of the voiceless poor.

The descriptions of the setting, including a "cold hill-side," the "ice," and "winds," the field "in frost and snow," the land "crisp with frost," and the "cold, cold moon" are all reflected in descriptions of Goody Blake, who "very cold" must "go to bed" and whose "old bones were cold and chill," and Harry Gill, who "icy-cold … turned away" after Goody's curse, and who "will never be warm again." The wood becomes the silent witness[30] to the story of Goody's suffering and Harry Gill's greed, and acts as a kind of medium of transference between Goody and Harry. A sympathy between Goody and the wood is created by describing them both as familiarly "old," (and therefore living testaments of a place and its history), by Goody's "shaking" bones resembling the limbs of a tree in the cold wind, and in the act of Goody "kneeling on the sticks" to deliver Harry's curse.[31] It is at this moment that Goody's cold transfers to Harry, reflecting what Marx writes about the punishments meted out for thefts of wood: "the objective defining element provided by the nature of the object itself must likewise be the objective and essential defining element for the punishment" ("Debates"). The wood becomes the medium through which the tale builds its tension and manifests its conclusion, on one hand a basic need, like air or water, necessary to support life, on the other, a commodity whose price is increasingly dictated by the urban-centred market and which is increasingly regulated by the urban-centred legislature.[32] And it is the attempt to regulate this basic right through "the law"[33] which the poem demonstrates as a crime not only against the poor but as one against humanity and the larger ecosystem in general.[34]

But in assigning punishment, Wordsworth goes much further than Marx, who only argues that the gathering of fallen wood be made a common right. Goody escapes punishment for what Marx allows is an act of theft. Not only is Goody miraculously delivered, it is the farmer who is struck down for daring to assert his ownership of the wood. Such a radical attack on property was dangerous in

1798 and likely influenced the subtitle "A True Story" and the emphatic insistence, in the original "Advertisement" to *Lyrical Ballads*, that the poem was "founded on a well-authenticated fact which happened in Warwickshire." The poem was after all one of many in the collection based in fact.

Though Harry places Goody under arrest, and liable to prosecution for trespass and theft, he becomes subject to an arrest of an altogether other kind. As what Lukács calls the "phantom objectivity" of commodity-based social relations fades away, the wood mysteriously takes part in Harry's affliction, as if some sudden but unshakeable recognition of its significance would leave him bare and skeleton-like against the wind, much like a solitary winter tree. As Marx puts it, "The fortuitous arbitrary action of privileged individuals is replaced by the fortuitous operation of elemental forces" ("Debates"). Goody, "Her bundle from her lap let fall;/ And kneeling on the sticks" (94–5) delivers the curse that sends Harry home shivering; this recalls the role of letting sticks fall in acts of divination. Herodotus records the ancient Scythian practice of bringing great bunches of willow wands, "which they lay on the ground and unfasten, and utter their divinations laying one rod on another" (*The Histories* 265: Vol.II). This is similar to a practice in ancient Germany, where according to Tacitus, "A little bough is lopped off a fruit-bearing tree, and cut into small pieces; these are distinguished by certain marks, and thrown carelessly at random over a white garment" (*The Complete Works* 713). In both cases the results are to be read as harbouring some clue as to future events. The white garment of the winter landscape and the intimacy with which the sticks take part in the recitation of an appeal to the supernatural, create an uncanny likeness between Goody and these diviners. The sticks fall on the winter ground like words onto the white garment of the page, their "certain marks" associated with an incantation not unlike that of the reciting of a poem.

"Beneath These Trees"

As the natural and social history of trees provides new context for Wordsworth's poetry, so his poetry clarifies the ways natural and social history are fundamentally imbricated. The symbolic importance of the tree for Wordsworth is ever related to its loss. Geoffrey Hartman opens *The Unremarkable Wordsworth* with the sentence: "When Wordsworth was fourteen, the ordinary sight of boughs silhouetted against a bright evening sky left so vivid an impression on his mind that it marked the beginning of his career as a poet" (3). In Book Four of *The Excursion* (1814),[35] Wordsworth describes a similar scene, in which the tree is a metaphor for an innate faculty:

> Within the soul a faculty abides,
> That with interpositions, which would hide
> And darken, so can deal that they become
> Contingencies of pomp; and serve to exalt
> Her native brightness. As the ample moon,
> In the deep stillness of a summer even
> Rising behind a thick and lofty grove,
> Burns, like an unconsuming fire of light,
> In the green trees; and, kindling on all sides
> Their leafy umbrage, turns the dusky veil
> Into a substance glorious as her own,
> Yea, with her own incorporated, by power
> Capacious and serene. Like power abides
> In man's celestial spirit.   (1058–71)

The tree, burning unconsumed and therefore endlessly symbolic, provides the setting for and enhances the experience of an essential light, a celestial spirit that like a mirror receives and reflects back the image of itself in the world. The dusky veil acts as a receiver and a frame, as the material body through which an incorporation of the spirit occurs. What is dark and obfuscating, the apparent barriers to transformative vision, are precisely what make such vision possible. Humans are also such an interposition in the world of nature, as receivers and framers of experience, offering a similar possibility of incorporation. Though they often act as to "hide/And darken," they also "so can deal that they become/Contingencies of pomp." There is a sense of both longing and belonging, of being and becoming, as if the incorporation the passage describes closes a distance and blurs lines of distinction. The tree narrates something of a life of the soul.

This identification with the tree is also apparent in *The Prelude*, where Wordsworth remembers his days at Cambridge in terms of time spent alone: "Oft have I stood/Foot-bound, uplooking at this lovely Tree/Beneath a frosty moon" (100–3; Book 6). In repeatedly standing thus, the viewer becomes like the tree itself: solitary, foot-bound, imaginatively branching:

> But scarcely Spenser's self
> Could have more tranquil visions in his youth,

> More bright appearances could scarcely see
> Of human Forms and superhuman Powers,
> Than I beheld, standing on winter nights
> Alone, beneath this fairy work of earth. (104–9; Book 6)

The verticality of the gaze, the open sky and quiet darkness evoke the transcendent imagery, anchored from below by the generic roots which Spenser represents and from which the poet hopes to offer a new growth. The ash offers an imposition between Wordsworth and an ethereal light that is intrinsically linked to his incipient conception of the form poetry should take in the world.

Wordsworth asserts the tree is "no doubt yet standing there" (91; Book 6), and this appears to have been true as he wrote this line, as Dorothy "found out William's ashtree" on her visit to Cambridge in 1810.[36] Yet as the years went by and Wordsworth continued to return to *The Prelude*, the certainty of its continued presence must have dimmed. The ash would eventually disappear, and his words, like the tree of the "Intimations Ode" (1807), would come to speak of "something that is gone." This is true of many other important trees in Wordsworth's life. The grove at the north end of Grasmere Lake where he composed "The Brothers" (1800), in which Leonard sits in a grove at the poem's climax, was "in a great measure destroyed."[37] The grove of fir trees known as "John's Grove" was also cut down, disturbing everyone in the Wordsworth circle.[38] In 1802 Dorothy reports on the environs of Grasmere: "They are making sad ravages in the woods – Benson's Wood is going & the wood above the River" (74). In "The Brothers," Leonard notes "Strange alteration wrought on every side" and at the close of "Michael" (1800) the narrator explains: "Great changes have been wrought/In all the neighbourhood" (487–8).

In so many Wordsworth poems, trees provide a place to dwell, and their destruction is a commentary on a method of dwelling. Heidegger writes, "poetry first causes dwelling to be dwelling" (89), but as in the above examples, the tree first causes poetry to be poetry. In addition to the long list of dire effects of deforestation on the biosphere, we must also consider how deforestation has affected culture, broadly defined as human discourse and practice. The removal of trees is therefore linked to a removal of cultural memory, to a forgetting of certain practices of dwelling. Though "The Ruined Cottage" tells a tale of irrevocable loss, it does so within the context of a certain kind of dwelling, "beneath these trees." The oak and elm are the most prominent trees described in the poem, and an examination of their cultural history in the context of the poem will help to recover the meaning of the type of dwelling the poem demonstrates.

The ash tree in the above passage from *The Prelude* is immediately preceded by a group of elms, that like those of "The Ruined Cottage," offer shelter to the weary and distracted traveller:

> Lofty elms,
> Inviting shades of opportune recess,
> Did give composure to a neighbourhood
> Unpeaceful in itself. (87–90)

"Inviting shades" offer both a welcome retreat as well as suggesting a movement to a nether-region where one might communicate with the dead. The welcome "cool shade" offered by the elms of "The Ruined Cottage" soon becomes a "heartfelt chillness" when the traveller learns the tale of its former inhabitants. Elms are often associated with death in myth, being placed on the tombs of dead soldiers in the *Iliad* and found near the entrance to the underworld in the *Aeneid*. The connection with funerary rites is most apparent in the widespread use of elms in coffins. As R.H. Richens writes, "The association of elm with burial has become irrevocable" (102). Yet by the Romantic period, elm was no longer the common material for coffin building, illustrating a growing class divide. As Richens relates, "In medieval times elm was used for coffins at any social level … In the centuries that followed elm lost out on both ends of the social spectrum" being replaced in the upper classes by oak and in the labouring classes, when a coffin could be afforded, by pine (101–2). It is the shades of trees, rather than those of the venerable institution, that give composure to the place and suggest a connection to the past. Yet, as Laurence Buell explains, place is "constituted simultaneously by subjective perception and by institutionalized social arrangements" (71). The "neighbourhood" that is unquiet is mind as much as place and is descriptive of the way in which the mind creates atmosphere within particular spaces.

In "The Ruined Cottage," elms provide the locus for the tale's events and the telling of the tale. They stand out in stark contrast from the wide bare common that encircles them and are the point to which we circle back around as Armytage tells his tale. They unfold a space for dwelling, not simply in the sense of occupation but in the poetic sense, in terms of being in the world. Elms are repeatedly referred to in the poem, drawing the line of vision upwards in distinct contrast to the horizontal plain on which the events of the poem unfold. Elms are also a regular sight in pastoral verse, offering shade for shepherds to sing beneath, as in the first Idyll of Theocritus:

> But, Thyrsis, thou canst sing of Daphnis' woes;
> High is thy name for woodland minstrelsy:
> Then rest we in the shadow of the elm
> Fronting Priapus and the Fountain-nymphs   (19–22)

The association of the elm with fertility is a tradition continued into European and English culture. According to Stephen Daniels, elms "were most closely tied to the working countryside" and "were used to signify farming interests" (50).

In ancient Ireland elms were classified as one of seven "Peasant trees" in terms of fines levied for unlawful felling.[39] Wordsworth also identifies them as tied to the peasantry and ancient fertility ritual in *The Excursion*:

> A wide-spread elm
> Stands in our valley, named THE JOYFUL TREE;
> From dateless usage which our peasants hold
> Of giving welcome to the first of May
> By dances round its trunk.   (831–5; book 6)

Elms first appear in "The Ruined Cottage" as "clustering elms that sprang from the same root" (32), similarly identified in terms of generation and community, reminding us of a way of life in which an elm tree was more than resource or commodity, more than aesthetic object, but something like the vine the ancients trained to grow around the elm, intertwined with human existence through habitual practice. The close association of this tradition with the May festivals Wordsworth witnessed and took part in during his trip to France in the 1790s evokes the "Tree of Liberty," one of the most prominent symbols of the revolution. The customs that surround the May Day festival involved carnivalesque practices, which, according to David Collings, register a "ritual assertion of communal counterpower" (48), asserting the peasantry as both an originary and a regulatory political and cultural force.[40] The depiction of the elm grove as a locus of disastrous loss, suggests a break down in a historical reciprocity that describes what is absent, a distant aristocracy, "determined and unmoved" regardless of the disaster unfolding on its hereditary lands. Yet the intertwining of the elm with the fundamental human endeavours of planting and harvesting suggests an underlying possibility of renewal and regeneration, a turning again of the earth's course, a revolutionary energy.

The dwelling offered by the group of shade-giving elms is a stark contrast from the imagined and solitary "huge oak" described earlier in the poem:

> Pleasant to him who on the soft cool moss
> Extends his careless limbs beside the root
> Of some huge oak whose aged branches make
> A twilight of their own, a dewy shade
> Where the wren warbles while the dreaming man,
> Half-conscious of that soothing melody,
> With side-long eye looks out upon the scene,
> By those impending branches made more soft,
> More soft and distant. (10–18)

The solitariness of the oak prefigures the traveller's own solitude, as its ghostly presence prefigures the haunted tale. The importance of the oak in European culture goes far back into prehistory, when "a god of the oak, the thunder, and the rain" was worshipped as "the chief deity" across Europe (Frazer 187). This identification of the oak with authority and power continued into the modern era, where it was identified in Britain with the monarchy, "protective of the subjects who sheltered beneath it" (Fulford, "The Politics of Trees" 47). The scene is imagined in such detail that it even includes a wren, long known in fable and folklore as "the king of birds" (Frazer 621–3). The imagined presence of the oak and wren in "The Ruined Cottage" signifies the actual absence of the protective, paternal force: it might be "pleasant" to have such protection, but as the speaker tells us,

> Other lot was mine.
> Across a bare wide Common I had toiled
> With languid feet which by the slipp'ry ground
> Were baffled still, and when I stretched myself
> On the brown earth my limbs from very heat
> Could find no rest nor my weak arm disperse
> The insect host which gathered round my face
> And joined their murmurs to the tedious noise
> Of seeds of bursting gorse that crackled round. (18–26)

The traveller's exhausted limbs "from very heat/Could find no rest," thus offering a commentary on the plight of tenants suffering increasing absenteeism among landlords and suggesting that Robert's and Margaret's fate could have been avoided had there been a landowner present and aware of his tenants' situation. What Fulford writes about Cowper and Clare's treatment of the oak is also relevant to the phantom oak of "The Ruined Cottage": "The sheltering oak had been used to naturalize landowners' monopoly on power ... Cowper and Clare showing trees cut down by landowners in the name of taste or profit depict the paternalist rhetoric as a sham" ("The Politics of Trees" 50). The way the oak is first presented and then demonstrated to be illusory demonstrates the broader phenomenon of the deforestation of Britain, which at the same time is the alienation of the oak as a symbol for monarchical power.[41]

An oak of several hundred years provides a sense of interconnectedness between events and practices within a given place, a kind of living memorial to the inhabitants of its locality. Robert Albion, in *Forests and Sea Power*, considers this interconnectedness in terms of family: "It required a large amount of patience and self-restraint to wait the hundred years, more or less, required for an oak to reach its prime; and a grove of full-grown oaks represented the English spirit of family continuity at its best" (112–13). When the narrator of "The Ruined Cottage" reveals the oak to be imaginary, he not only suggests a lack of patience and self-restraint among landowners of the period but the resulting breakdown of family continuity that the poem proceeds to narrate. According to Daniels, the oak was considered "venerable, patriarchal [and] stately," and was often associated with landed families. Burke describes the English aristocracy as "the great oaks which shade a country" (377). The oak appears to become increasingly iconic as it disappears from the landscape, and Wordsworth's illusory oak, "whose aged branches make a twilight of their own," whose "impending branches" make the scene "more soft,/More soft and distant," might describe not only the fading sense of responsibility and growing distance of the aristocracy towards the abject and struggling poor at the calamitous time the poem was being written[42] but also something slightly unsettling in their "impending" quality, a sense that their "aged branches" of ancient lineage may not be quite so secure after all. The revelation of the illusory nature of the icon suggests that the power traditionally held by the ruling class is based upon a naturalized structure that is likewise illusory. Cultural and ecological inheritances are both imbued with a sense of loss that struggles to name its object.

The oak also features prominently in the opening of the 1805 *Prelude* in a way that helps further illustrate the importance of its absence at the opening of "The Ruined Cottage." Here the traveller reclines "on the genial pillow of the earth" in stark contrast to the comfortless "brown earth" on which the traveller of "The Ruined Cottage" fitfully attempts to rest. And rather than the "tedious noise/Of seeds of bursting gorse that crackled round," the traveller of *The Prelude* hears the intermittent falling of acorns that "Fell audibly, and with a startling sound." "Audibly" and "sound" repeat their sense, emphasizing the sharp accent of their sounds. The stress pattern (fell AUDibLY and WITH a STARTling SOUND) and final alliteration, as well as the position at the end of the verse paragraph all further the impression. If the acorns here might be said to symbolize the genesis of poetic composition, the "fair seed time" of the soul, then the crackling gorse of "The Ruined Cottage" signifies a disturbance that threatens the independence of the psyche. In 1805 acorns mean more oaks, and therefore a symbolic continuity of British hegemony. In 1797 gorse only means more gorse, its exploding dehiscence testifying to the tension of war, catastrophic inflation, the fears of invasion, and to the agriculturally barren and morally bereft space of the open plain.

As with many other such Romantic disappearances, the absence of the object intensifies our feeling for what is left behind. The figures of the elms and of Armytage represent for the traveller a reconnection, through a living history, to a circulation of communal memory. The oral passing down of this memory from one generation to the next reflects Armytage's cyclical "way-wandering" movements through the landscape and is representative of the continuity of a particular form of social organization. Yet this continuity is expressed within a tale of calamity. The traveller's opening dismay is reflected in Margaret's despondent wandering, uneasily framing Armytage's circulation, positing a recognition of culture's repetitive and ongoing foundation in the ashes of its own destruction. In this sense the poem dramatizes an aspect of Hegel's negative dialectic, which, as Marx understood it: "includes in its positive understanding of what exists a simultaneous recognition of its negation, its inevitable destruction" (*Capital* 103). All the figures in the poem appear to be strangers in the landscape, even the seemingly at home Armytage, who as a pedlar is one of a group disappearing from the landscape as the poem is being written (c. 1797), as the increasing regulation of the distribution of goods turned pedlars from welcome aids to commerce into suspect and potentially nefarious characters who operated outside the laws of trade. The tale, like the landscape itself, narrates a removal and an emptying out that creates a present that is then reinscribed and renaturalized, that is "silvered o'er," camouflaging the act of its transformation. The monotony of the landscape conceals its past, and as Armytage explains, "Even of the good is no memorial left." The tale functions, through its framing and reinscription upon the landscape, as a memorial to this very fact.

Armytage opens Part Two of the poem with a justification for continuing his tale. Rather than directly appeal to underlying forces of conflict or ecological imbalance, Armytage insists on the local and the familiar: "'Tis a common tale,/By moving accidents uncharactered." However, moving accidents are precisely what undergird the tale, and the ambiguity of the phrase and its allusion to *Othello* suggest an underlying reference to broader historical developments (echoing, in this context, the "moving grove" of Act Five of *Macbeth*). The word "uncharactered" can also be read as ambiguous here, meaning not only "having no distinctive sign" (*OED* 1) but also "destitute of moral character" (*OED* 2). War and crop failure have removed not only the means of sustenance but have gradually undone the moral character of Robert and Margaret. In a historical irony, the *Oxford English Dictionary*'s first citation for this sense of "uncharactered" is from the military man, MP, essayist, and social reformer T.P. Thompson, a contemporary of Wordsworth's who was relieved from the governorship of Sierra Leone for his strong opposition to slavery there, himself uncharactered by forces blind and deaf to the suffering of the historically marginalized.[43] Language, of course, is also made up of characters, and Armytage's common tale and its pastoral frame are alike in danger of coming undone. The prominent linguistic theories of Wordsworth's day[44] often described language in organic terms, as to some extent influenced by the sounds of the natural world, the "sap that enlivens the roots of language" (Herder 135). One might well ask, given these perspectives, what happens to the roots when the sap stops flowing. This danger finds itself reflected in the knowledge that writing in itself was a potentially dangerous act, particularly in the 1790s. Just a few years before, a God and King mob had broken into Dr. Priestley's house and burned manuscripts of work in progress, along with his home, laboratory, and church, due to the perceived threat of his radical sympathies. It was not only the forest leaves that were threatened, and the example of Dr. Priestley is only one of many such acts of repression, submersion, and erasure enacted throughout the period.[45]

"To a Distant Land"

Thompson's experience in Sierra Leone is not merely coincidental to Wordsworth's poem; it evokes Britain's involvement abroad and Robert's deployment "to a distant land." Since Said has considered the many ways colonialism informs aesthetic production, it has been essential to consider the relationships between a perceived metropolitan centre and colonial periphery. In praising the work of Raymond Williams, Said makes an important proviso: "I sense a limitation in his feeling that English literature is mainly about England" (14). Alan Bewell has convincingly demonstrated how the colonized landscape reflects back upon the native English countryside. Yet work remains to be done in Romantic literary studies on the relevance of colonial environmental degradation. By exploring poetry that responds to this degradation, I will show how transformed landscapes play an important role in the way poets construct a national identity that recognizes the intimate ecological and economic underpinnings of physical oppression.

I use the word "intimate" for two reasons, first to signal the relationship that humans form with substances, and second, to stress what Lisa Lowe describes as "the links between 'free trade' policies, which expanded the trades in colonial commodities like tea, chintz, calico, silk, and opium, and the transformation of imperial governance and the emergence of a new international order" (15). This "new international order," formed through the intimacy of commodities and empire, compels new readings of substances like wood in the literature of the period. Like Lowe, I want to similarly consider "scenes of close connection in relation to a global geography that one more often conceives in terms of vast spatial distances" (18), but in the specific context of Wordsworth's poetry. Katherine Bergren argues reading in a global context "inspire[s] interpretations of Wordsworth's poetry that have previously been unclear or invisible" (9), and this section seeks to bring to light previously unconsidered aspects of Wordsworth by reading him alongside poets of colonized spaces. By focusing on the particular ecological and economic intimacy that people share with the tree and its products during the Romantic period, and how poetry uniquely brings this intimacy into focus, I hope to demonstrate that what appears distant is in fact much closer than it appears.

Deforestation in the colonial world between the seventeenth and nineteenth centuries was driven by European commercialism and transformed the land and the cultures on which it was based. Of this there are numerous examples. Daviken Studnicki-Gizbert and David Schecter describe the deforesting of Mexico by Spanish colonists: "By scouring the landscape of trees, mining set the stage for the development of colonial forms of land-use, especially the spread of agriculture and pastoralism, and the establishment of a new colonial society of indigenous, Afro-Mexican, and Iberian settlers" (105).[46] Portuguese mining operations created similar conditions in Brazil. Eduardo Galeano records the effects on the native population: "Of every ten that went up into the freezing wilderness, seven never returned" (51). J.R. McNeill details the far-ranging effects of deforestation in the Caribbean: "Broad areas were cleared for cane, for other crops, and for grazing. Sugar boiling consumed yet more forest ... Many local species dependent on the forest went extinct, while new plants and animals, suited to the emerging environment, prospered. Soil erosion and nutrient depletion accelerated rapidly with clearance and cultivation" (27).[47] This process changed the face of the cultural practices of nations just as it changed the relationship to the land. What Studnicki-Gizbert and Schecter say of New Spain is largely true of various colonies of this period: "the combination of deforestation, agricultural extension, and the development of colonial society marked the end of native peoples and life-ways" (112). Like many of the subjects of Wordsworth's poetry, but in ways that go beyond what he described, many native peoples became "the last of all their race."

The evisceration of native ways of life characteristic of empire is apparent in "The Solitary Reaper." The main figure of the poem "Reaping and singing by herself" demonstrates both a cultural and ecological result of forced changes to land use. Her melancholy song evokes the failed Jacobite rebellion of 1745 and the often brutal measures taken to pacify the region. Her singing and its setting reproduce a cultural loss, a communal memory that is now solitary and divided from its source. The Highland Clearances, in which thousands of tenants were forcefully cleared off their land to make way for more profitable imported sheep, left the Highlands (an area the size of Holland) one of the most sparsely populated areas in Europe. Regrettably, the area is often referred to as a "natural wilderness" today, de-historicized and re-naturalized; it is perhaps a recognition of the broader treatment of land and landscape of which the Clearances forms an important part that provides the uncanny quality to the vast plains of Wordsworth's poetry, including the bare common of "The Ruined Cottage."

"The Solitary Reaper" (1807) reflects this disturbance within its very structure. Lines 1 and 3, ending in "field" and "herself," and lines 25 and 27, ending in "sang" and "work," are the only unrhymed lines of the poem. In part, these lines serve to break up the monotony of the rhyme, as singing breaks up the monotony of work, or the figure breaks up the monotony of the landscape. But they also signify the greater lack of integrated experience the poem describes. This lack is discernible in the unrhymed words: both in what she sang and in the depopulated (and quite possibly deforested) field in which she does her work. "Natural sorrow" is not only social and cultural but insinuates a reaction of the land itself at its transformation.

Deforestation reduced the habitat of bird species, and the absence of trees in the landscape contribute to the sense of the reaper's song as being under threat of disappearance. The poem insists on the absence of birds ("No Nightingale" and no "Cuckoo-bird") as enhancing the resonating pathos of the song. As the song leaves its listener without closure, so too birdsong "has no ending in this sense, as also certain types of human feeling and memory that will not come to closure" (Prynne 87). Yet birdsong and memory are quite directly affected by the changing landscape. Without a song post, there is no song, and the fragment the poem presents is indicative of the fragility of both cultural memory and natural habitat.

Attitudes towards land and peoples that produced solitary reapers were mirrored elsewhere in the period. A little more than a year before Jean-Jacques Dessalines declared Haiti a free republic, Wordsworth was writing "To Toussaint L'Overture" (1803). The sonnet equates L'Overture's legacy with the objects of nature, "air, earth, and skies," reminding the reader that his memory would long outlive his imprisonment. Yet the poem remains quietist in its political thrust, stressing "patience" and urging the sufferer to find "comfort" in his distress. A generation later Ignace Nau, in "Dessalines" (1839), imagines, in contrast, a Haiti rejuvenated by revolution:

> L'oiseau nous chantera des chants d'amour encore,
> La voix de nos forêts redeviendra sonore,
> Et nos fleuves taris jailliront en torrents,
> Et nos lacs rouleront des flots plus transparents,
> Et toi, peuple héroïque, et toi, mon beau génie,
> Demain vous saluerez une ère d'harmonie!…
>
> The birds once more shall sing of love; the trees
> Shall fill our forests with deep harmonies.
> Our arid riverbeds shall gush and pour;
> Our lakes shall, crystalline, shine shore to shore.
> And you, heroic folk, and you, my pen,
> Shall hail an era, blessèd once again!…   (Norman R. Shapiro, trans., 35–40)

The restoration of a natural heritage represents a future social unity brought about by revolutionary struggle. The insistent future tense points to the current reality: no birds sing, the voice of the forests no longer resounds, the arid riverbeds do not gush. The process of colonization is also a process of desertification, one that can still be read in the landscape of Haiti today. As McNeill explains, the forests of the

Caribbean were cleared by colonists partially for the profit-motivated purpose of growing sugar but also in part out of aesthetic and health concerns: "Settlers on these and other islands cleared far more land than they intended to use for sugarcane. They tried to recreate the open vistas of the British Isles (or France or Spain) for aesthetic reasons. They needed room for their livestock to roam. And they thought that cleared land would be less conducive to disease because it had less in the way of rotting vegetation, humidity, and other factors thought to create "'miasmas,'" from which fevers emanated" (30).

Deforestation led not only to soil erosion but to the extinction of local species.[48] Nau's birdsong, like the song of the reaper, or indeed the Gaelic in which she sings, exists as an ungraspable haunting of the landscape for the listener, who lacks the necessary historical and cultural experience, while for the singer it represents the memory of a shared inheritance of a natural history that forms an essential basis of a sense of community and identity.

In 1928 Aldous Huxley imagined "Wordsworth in the Tropics," claiming that had Wordsworth experienced a more raw and less tamed form of nature, he could never have formalized the universalizing "great recompense" so essential to the inception of Romanticism. When one gets past the rather broad nature of Huxley's point, it becomes increasingly obvious that his various characterizations of the "tropics" and its natives are disquietingly colonialist. To begin to imagine Wordsworth in the tropics, one would first need to imagine the "tropics" as an area consisting of many nations, each of which formed unique notions of nationality based on its unique physical surroundings. The process by which cultural formations produce national identity comes to look, from this perspective, quite similar to the one described by Wordsworth.

The destruction of woodlands caused by European colonial expansion is, like in Haiti, also apparent in the British attempts in Jamaica to defeat the Maroons, who used forest cover and terrain to their advantage in a strikingly successful resistance to British empire. For the Maroons, the forest was home and therefore represents a space of resistance to colonial hegemony. As Robert Charles Dallas reported in 1803: "All internal danger ... arises from gradual collections of fugitives, their flying to the recesses of the woods, and becoming a rallying point for the discontented." Dallas proposed to solve this resistance in a way typical of the colonial mindset: "The grand object, then, of the inhabitants of Jamaica, should be the settlement of white people in the interior of the island" (457).

Frustrated by the inability to penetrate into the thick woods inland, the British eventually enlisted savage methods[49] to finally overcome over a century of Maroon resistance. Honor Ford Smith's lines from "A Message from Nian" (1997) are especially pertinent:

> Blinded by a future
> I could not vision, my old words meaningless,
> choked to silence in a forest of trees
> I had no names for, I fell and fell,
> was lost, bled, marooned in a landscape
> that grew stranger with each discovery I made. (12–17)

The future, rather than the subject of vision or a looking forward, becomes instead a blinding and choking smoke. The words relive a long and painful struggle. "I fell and fell" recalls the many who died in the struggle for independence, and the "landscape/that grew stranger" describes the gradual and painful changes made to the natural world under British occupation. The "old words" of Smith's poem suggest a dispossession of language went hand in hand with a dispossession of land, and trees appear to become much like these words in the way they establish or undermine a sense of social belonging. The trees are "uncharactered" here, a former basis for understanding the world that now there are "no names for."

The landscape "grew stranger" here because it was being transformed, as in many British colonies, for both the purpose of plantation farming and to make the land look more like Britain. This attempt to imprint British values onto the land would later find a parallel in the attempt to imprint these values onto native populations, as apparent in school curriculums throughout the Caribbean. This sense of strangeness is present in many writing from the colonies when expressing their experience with Wordsworth's poetry. Jamaica Kincaid, Lorna Goodison, V.S. Naipaul, Michelle Cliff, Stuart Hall, and Shirley Lim, to name a few,[50] have all responded to the experience of having to memorize and recite "I Wandered Lonely…," and all report the experience as strange largely because they had no idea what a daffodil was. Language fails in two directions in this colonial context. It introduces things which there are "no names for," and it introduces words that there are no things for. The perversity of memorizing Wordsworth in this context is directly related to the transformation of landscapes and ecologies occurring across the globe in the wake of empire.

A language shift is also taking place in Ireland at this time, in a way also directly related to the destruction of the forests for both the profit of English or Anglo-Irish landlords and the prevention of guerrilla resistance. That Wordsworth was sympathetic in the early 1790s to the cause of Irish self-rule is implied in a letter of June 1794 to his friend William Matthews, with whom he was planning the production of a radical journal,[51] and in Wordsworth's offer "to go personally to Dublin to find an agent to disseminate the magazine" (Barker 100). Stephen Behrendt indicates the important timing of this language shift: "That the apparent watershed moment of this language shift (and submersion) lies precisely within the Romantic period should interest us more than it historically has done, given the critical and cultural interest in the rise and flowering of all aspects of nationalism ... during these years" (209–10). It is likely no coincidence that deforestation in Ireland appears to occur simultaneously with the enforced disappearing of the Irish language. Letters in the old Irish alphabet known as Ogham are named for trees: *alim*, meaning "elm"; *beith*, "birch"; *coll*, "hazel"; *dair*, "oak"; and so on. The letters are collectively known as "feda," or singularly as "fid," meaning "wood" or "tree."

The poem *Cill Chais* (Kilcash) (1855), likely written in the early nineteenth century but not published until later, laments a cultural disappearance that is intrinsically tied to the loss of trees:

Cad a dhéanfaimid feasta gan adhmad?
Tá deireadh na gcoillte ar lár...

Níl ceol binn milis na n-éan ann
le hamharc an lae a dhul uainn,
náan chuaichín i mbarra na ngéag ann,
ós í chuirfeadh an saol chun suain.

Now what will we do for timber,
With the last of the woods laid low...

No birdsong there, sweet and delightful,
As we watch the sun go down,
Nor cuckoo[52] on top of the branches
Settling the world to rest.

(Thomas Kinsella, trans. qtd. in Flood and Flood, 1–2, 13–16)

It is worth noting here, in considering the importance of song to these encounters with absence, that "By its very nature, Cill Chaise was intended to be sung" (Flood and Flood 85). This links the poem to the song of the solitary reaper and to the importance of birdsong in many accounts of place-identity. If Ireland lost its woods, the poem or the song serves as a reminder of this lost heritage, a precarious monument to the invisible in a society ever more focused on the public visibility and display of the commodity form.

The felling of trees represented the imposition of a mass forgetting, both of a pre-colonial culture and the history of resistance to colonization. John Perlin relates "Although once a great source of timber for England, Ireland had so little wood left by the eighteenth century that Irish tanners had to rely on Great Britain for bark" (329).[53] The English language came alongside the bark, and by 1800 Gaelic was no longer the dominant tongue in Ireland, pushed to remote rural areas (much like in the Scottish Highlands). The loss of language becomes representative of a collective consciousness robbed of its very basis in the land itself. The violence of an enforced cultural amnesia is buried in the deforested landscape, and the ground upon which the traveller of "The Ruined Cottage" inarticulately suffers represents a sense of loss transcending borders and nationalities.

The effects of European imperialism on language, landscape, and cultural practice is also visible in the experience of the indigenous inhabitants of North America. As Robin Wall Kimmerer relates:

> The word *pecan* – the fruit of the tree known as the pecan hickory (*Carya illinoensis*) – comes to English from indigenous languages. *Pigan* is a nut, any nut. The hickories, black walnuts and butternuts of our northern homelands have their own specific names. But those trees, like the homelands, were lost to my people … In the span of a single generation my ancestors were "removed" three times … I wonder if they looked back for a last glimpse of the lakes, glimmering like a mirage. Did they touch the trees in remembrance as they became fewer and fewer, until there was only grass? (12–13)

This account shares a number of parallels with those discussed so far, highlighting the debt to which empire was in to those peoples and places they colonized, a debt that has never been paid and one that is rarely acknowledged. The removal of trees is part of a broader removal, and the grass that remains cannot speak of former presence, just as those who have benefited from the legacy of empire continue to pretend as if the places empire conquered had always been as empty as they are now.

Various attempts, including Wordsworth's own (in later revisions), at ameliorating the tragedy of the pedlar's tale through either a transcendent nature or through religious belief seem inevitably unsatisfying. There is, however, in the presence of the linnet and thrush at the poem's close, an indication that the natural world can still speak its meaning to those who would listen:

> A linnet warbled from those lofty elms,
> A thrush sang loud, and other melodies,
> At distance heard, peopled the milder air. (531–3)

These birds feature prominently in "The Tables Turned" (1800) and in doing so offer a telling contrast to the absent wren, the "king of birds" from the poem's opening, suggesting a more egalitarian song:

> Books! 'tis a dull and endless strife,
> Come, hear the woodland linnet
> How sweet his music; on my life
>
> There's more of wisdom in it.
> And hark! how blithe the throstle sings!
> And he is no mean preacher;
> Come forth into the light of things,
> Let Nature be your teacher. (9–16)

Despite the reassurance that the presence of these birds would seem to offer in the closing lines of "The Ruined Cottage," what has been done cannot be undone, and the effects, like deforestation, cannot be elided, as "silvered o'er" as they may be. This is even more true in our own time than it was in Wordsworth's. Nature is the sign under which capital has transformed the earth. It is like the tree in that haunting song at the close of Orwell's *1984*:

> *Under the spreading chestnut tree*
> *I sold you and you sold me* (77)

If tragedy cannot become catharsis, it is possible to recognize, in the failure of society that "The Ruined Cottage" narrates and the utter devastation it presents, the necessity of finding new ways to conceive of social and natural arrangements that depart from prevalent attitudes and inherited notions. Armytage's final recollection of Margaret is based on what others observe in his absence, blurring and dislocating received conceptions of authority. The "tedious years/She lingered in unquiet widowhood" recalls the "tedious noise of seeds of bursting gorse" and the psychic disturbance of the exhausted traveller on the plain. The progressive process of deforestation lies at the heart of the desperate scene:

"I have heard, my friend,/That in that broken arbour she would sit/ The idle length of half a sabbath day" (449–51). The ministry offered by the natural world is now idle, and the broken arbour illustrates the broken bond between the human and the natural, reflected in Margaret's anguished attempt to remember and reshape the past. In a way the reader and the traveller alike are a late-returning husband, turning towards a group of trees that are ever disappearing, repeating the words that crack with the senseless sound of grief.

Chapter Three

"Strange Look'd it There!": The Paradox of the Palm in the Poetry of Felicia Hemans

In her poetry what appears as substance is imagined on the brink of dissolution, just as what comes as shadow continually refuses to evaporate.
— Jerome McGann (1994, 220)

As then figure is nothing else than determination, and determination is negation, figure … can be nothing but negation.
— Spinoza (2006, 375)

As the strata of stone or the growth rings of the tree provide subtexts for reading Romantic literature, the palm and its derivative palm oil offer another key locus for investigating how this literature captures the intermingling of human and nonhuman agency amidst a tectonic cultural shift brought about by political, economic, ecological and technological change. The palm gets its name from the similarity of leaves of the order *Palmae* to the fingers of the human hand. This dual assignation suggests a connection between the fate of human artefacts and that of natural objects that gains new significance when considering the future of the biosphere. The word derives from the Latin *palma*, which in addition to these two meanings could also denote the blade of an oar, victory (figuratively), and in medieval Latin, a linear measure. This etymology, evoking an interrelation of the empirical and the naval, is well suited to a consideration of the role empire played in the Romantic period and the role it continues to play, in a different guise, today. It also evokes the literary, the notion of the hand as a unit of measure suggests poetic meter and the physical act of composition. As poetry is produced by the human hand, so palm oil is produced from the palm. Derived from the *Elaeis guineensis*, large quantities were first imported into Britain from West Africa during the Romantic period, and it is today the most consumed vegetable oil on the planet.

Palms appear more often in the poetry of Felicia Hemans, the best-selling English poet of the nineteenth century (Curran 190), than any other major poet of the period. Hemans is possibly attracted to the palm due to its classical and biblical association with femininity,[1] as, according to Marlon Ross, "Hemans sees her goal as the feminization of culture at large" (292). This is not, as many of her Victorian readers assumed,[2] simply to champion a moralizing "angel in the house" sort of domesticity, but rather to subtly bring normative notions of gender and empire (and their interrelation[3]) into question. A host of recent critics,[4] beginning with Stuart Curran's groundbreaking "The 'I' Altered," have found a strong undercurrent in Hemans's work that problematizes conventional depictions of Hemans as a poetess of "hearth and home." According to Curran, close examination reveals "a focus on exile and failure, a celebration of female genius frustrated, a haunting omnipresence of death – that seem to subvert the role [she] claimed and invite a sophisticated reconsideration of [her] work" (189). Hemans's use of the palm, I argue, should be seen in light of this re-envisioning of the poet; that is, we hear in Hemans's verse not only the call to far off classical and biblical sources, but a subtler, yet insistent, note that speaks to nineteenth-century Britain's colonial and industrial endeavours, and understanding the palm through these opposing lines demonstrates the power its imagery conveys. This note is even more insistent today, when the global dependence on palm oil and the ecological and social upheaval associated with its production once again force us to come to terms with uncomfortable realities of the global marketplace. The "haunting omnipresence of death" that Curran finds in her poetry is particularly relevant to the catastrophic ecological destruction currently underway (including what is being called a sixth mass extinction event) as a result of the desperate race for profit and limited natural resources.

Recent critical attention to the nuanced aspects of Hemans's work have revealed a voice attuned to women's position in society and to the costs and complexity that the spread of empire brought with it. Marlon Ross takes up the claim that Hemans's poetry lacks a "struggle toward self-discovery," demonstrating that assumptions about gender-based "cultural rituals of maturation" (234) and "masculine forms of poetry" (235) have clouded the subtle yet insistent forms of introspection in her work. Describing the "music" of women's poetry of the period, Isobel Armstrong finds a double register, "an affective mode, often simple, often pious, often conventional" which becomes "subjected to investigation, questioned, or used for unexpected purposes" (316–17). This tendency to ironize culminates, as Jerome McGann points out, in a form of ideological critique (225). The palm in Hemans's poetry can be read, I claim, in terms of this critique, both "reclaiming the power of the 'feminine' within literature" (Ross 292), and revealing the interwoven relations of social, environmental, and colonial constructs; the palm, like Hemans's verse, is "filled with unexpected surprises and juxtapositions" (Wolfson xxv), and I will be exploring a number of these in the following pages.

This chapter will address the appearances of the palm in Hemans's work in terms of the symbolic qualities of the palm and the history of the palm oil trade. Hemans's multilayered depiction of the palm is reflected in the expanding commercial and industrial uses of palm oil during the late Romantic period. As her poetry reached a wide audience, so palm oil became an everyday substance in Britain, serving both national and domestic purposes as an industrial lubricant and essential ingredient in body soap. Hemans's identification with the palm as a symbol of female interiority[5] and a female-defined space of self-possession makes possible a reading of her work that challenges both patriarchal structures of meaning and the exploitative practices, both social and ecological, of British colonial and industrial endeavour.

Each of the sections that follow will focus on a particular way Hemans deploys the palm, addressing the palm's commercial and cultural history in terms of these deployments to bring into sharper focus the force of Hemans's use of this imagery. The first two sections are brief and meant to provide background for the later readings of Hemans's poems. "The Palm: Ecology and Commerce" lays out some basic facts about the palm and the palm oil trade, and "Hemans's Nineteenth-Century Readers" deals with the consistent identification through the nineteenth century of Hemans's work with an exotic atmosphere of botanical lushness. "The Palm as Image of Female Interiority" considers the use of the palm in creating a sense of inner space, showing how Hemans argues for a female identity defined by independence from patriarchal domination. This section will also examine palm oil production in West Africa as a labour-intensive practice carried out largely by women and how the palm oil trade was rooted in the Atlantic slave trade. As I have pointed out in the preceding chapters, the "Black Atlantic" is inseparable from the development of Western wealth and geopolitical power, and this chapter furthers this argument. "Palm as Domestic Space," will consider the way Hemans identifies the palm with the domestic space and motherhood and the contrast this sense of closeness creates with the distant source of palm oil and its invisible presence within British culture.

"The Palm and Changing Attitudes towards the Body," addresses the increasing consumption of palm oil as an ingredient in soap and how this is tied to changing cultural practice. The symbolic employment of soap by European missionaries in West Africa is addressed here as a kind of ironic coming full circle of the commodity. The final section consolidates these different points through a close reading of Hemans's "The Palm Tree," considering, in addition, what relevance this poem has to the contemporary ecological significance of the global dependence on palm oil. The palm, as botanists have long noted, is an ideal site for interdisciplinary study. As P.B. Tomlinson writes, "They can be used to illustrate the way in which tissues and organs, normally considered independently of each other by plant anatomists, are capable of being understood in a highly integrated way so that the several major functional processes that plants exhibit ... can be seen to be interrelated" (3). This chapter seeks to illustrate a similar relationship between the tissues and organs of cultural and historical processes of the Romantic era to bring out a sense of the integrated function of the palm and its products in the work of Felicia Hemans. The palm is central to British constructions of origins, just as the vast increase in palm oil importation signifies a shifting economic and cultural landscape. Rather than a mere evocation of an exotic orientalism, Hemans's use of the palm offers an alternative site for identity formation that troubles Enlightenment accounts of the liberal subject and associated notions of human purpose.

The Palm: Ecology and Commerce

The literary and ecological history of the palm evoke the unexpected and the unexplored. At the opening of *Frankenstein*, Walton imagines a kind of tropical paradise at the pole, a "country of eternal light." The hope of finding the geographical location of Eden was still active in the Romantic period, combining the accelerated exploitation of the globe with a nostalgia for a lost paradise. But as the world became smaller, so did the conviction that such a place would be found. By the Romantic period it had become something, in J.P. Hunter's words, "more hoped for than believed in"[6] (8). Though Walton, or Shelley for that matter, could not have known, there was a time in earth's history when the poles enjoyed near tropical conditions. Fossils recently found in Antarctica indicate that palm trees grew there 50 million years ago (Pross et al.). And given that the Arctic is currently warming at twice the rate of the rest of the planet,[7] palms might be found there again within a much shorter time span. Walton was off, but he wasn't all wrong.

Palm trees were not always confined to tropical places, and they are predicted to increasingly inhabit the temperate zones as the earth warms, found today in the foothills of the Swiss Alps, among other unexpected locales (Reichgelt et al.). England may itself be covered in palms in the not too distant future. The work done under the auspices of empire to transform colonial landscapes is creeping back towards the home territory, where the English landscape will be remade by an ecological change instigated by Romantic industrial and imperial development. And though palms aren't yet ubiquitous in Britain, they already infused everyday life in the Romantic period in the form of palm oil.

Hemans's popularity grew as palm oil became an everyday presence in Britain. The origin of our modern dependence on palm oil, now the most popular vegetable oil in the world,[8] is located in the surge in its importation into Britain during the Romantic period. As detailed by Martin Lynn, the two most significant periods of increased importation occur directly following the Slave Trade Act of 1807. The 1810s saw "the sharpest growth of British imports at any time in the nineteenth century" and the late 1820s/early 1830s saw "sharp increases in volume … and even greater increases in value" amounting to the "most significant" span (in terms of volume) of increased importation in the century (15–16). The first decades of the nineteenth century also saw a vast expansion of the literary marketplace, and the "late 1820s/early 1830s" is precisely the period in which Hemans's "fame was clinched" (Wolfson and Fay 9). The palm and her poetry intersect in these growing markets, utilized by middle classes eager for "improvement," and to elide the ways this "improvement" was at the expense of both human and non-human others. To take up a history of the palm is also to delve into the construction of modern Western societies and subjectivities formed out of a hyper exploitative and extractive relation to human and non-human "resources."

Romantic depictions of the palm have classical and biblical sources veiled by an exoticism resulting from the legacy of colonialism. The palm is central to Western cultural constructions of origin and to constructions of a newly defined other. To its associations with victory and the idyllic is added a fetishistic desire for the distant and different. A doubling is also apparent when considering the gap between the palm's depiction and its use. Palm oil was increasingly important in late Romantic period Britain, most notably as an industrial lubricant ("vital to [Britain's] industrial expansion" [Crowder 27]) and as an essential ingredient in body soap (to meet the demand of the new trend of washing the body). And the palm was already becoming a cliché for tropical paradises, a signified increasingly emptied of its meaning at the historical moment when its oil is increasingly emptied into vessels for British use. The space between the contrasting meanings of the palm offer rich ground for understanding its appearance in Hemans's poetry and for appreciating her employment of the tree in seemingly contradictory yet subtle purposes.

Hemans's Nineteenth-Century Readers

The relation of palm to palm oil comes to resemble that of poet to poetry in the nineteenth-century reception of Hemans's work. These assessments consistently evoke plant-based metaphors that often include associations with the exotic and the east. *The British Critic* of July 1823 praises her work for its "luxuriance of feeling, and splendor of language" and its "richness and fertility of description" (*Felicia Hemans: Selected Poems* 538). A few years later Francis Jeffrey, in *The Edinburgh Review*, would offer an influential assessment of her work, which includes this observation: "All her pomps have a meaning, and her flowers and gems are arranged, as they are said to be among Eastern lovers, so as to speak the language of truth and of passion ... This is particularly remarkable in some little pieces, which seem at first sight to be purely descriptive–but are soon found to tell upon the heart with a deep moral and pathetic impression" (37). Jeffrey goes on to give Hemans's "The Palm Tree" (1827) as an exemplar, printing it in full. In an anonymous preface to *The Poetical Works of Mrs. Felicia Hemans*, published the year after her death, we find a similar assessment (likely following Jeffrey's lead): "All her imagery ... is made like oriental flowers, to mean something and to utter it in a language of its own. It is a sort of trellis-work, for thought and affection to climb upon. The Palm Tree, for example is laden ... with a moral, as with clusters of golden grapes" (x). A generation later, Jane Williams records the indelible impression made on the young Hemans by her early reading of the Scriptures, describing "the pastoral images of patriarchal life, the tents, the palm-trees, the fountains of the desert, the rocks, the reposing flocks, and the slow procession of the loaded camels ... out of those words her mind made pictures, vivid and durable enough to serve in after years as the basis of accurate descriptions" (*Felicia Hemans: Selected Poems* 599). And in 1878 W. M. Rossetti describes the atmosphere of her verse as "Balmy" (608). The association of her work with fertile growth is important here in that the palm was relied on in several parts of the world as an important foodstuff, whether it produced oil, dates, or nuts. Given the consensus that emerges over the course of nineteenth-century assessment of her work is that of a luxuriant growth, often associated with an exoticized east, it is unsurprising that more than one reader saw her work as aptly represented by such a poem as "The Palm Tree." What is surprising, perhaps, is that a poet lauded for her apparent nationalism and emulation of domestic affection should be Orientalized in such a recurrent and reliable fashion. This is meant, at least superficially, to lend Hemans's work an air of ornate beauty, delicacy, rarity, and timelessness (like that suggested by porcelain or japanned furniture); in the same way the well-to-do decorated their homes in the fashion of chinoiserie, they could consume Hemans's verse (in the superficial nationalist and sentimental way) with the satisfaction of thinking themselves readers of taste. But there is a darker undercurrent to this fashioning of the poet that draws on the fear of the foreign, the complexity of Britain's dependence on its colonies for its wealth, and the perceived erosion of traditional mores in the wake of consumer culture. Though they certainly didn't intend it, these critics evoke submerged developments that are central to understanding Hemans as much more than a poetess of hearth and home.

The Palm as Image of Female Interiority

In "The Image in the Heart" (1829), a poem addressed to a woman grieving the death of her husband, Hemans creates a sense of interiority in terms of a tropical scene:

> For in thy heart there is a holy spot,
> As 'mid the waste an Isle of fount and palm,
> For ever green! – the world's breath enters not,
> The passion-tempests may not break its calm;
>   'Tis thine, all thine! (11–15)

The pious and devotional tone of the poem is reinforced by the stanza structure of four iambic pentameter lines followed by the indented four-syllable dimetric line, creating the feeling of a call and response prayer. Yet, in Armstrong's words, there is a "second and more difficult poem" (317) beneath this surface piety that has to do with the complexity surrounding the palm as an image for female interiority.

When besieged by grief and/or worldly troubles, there is a safe haven within the self, the poem suggests, a kind of second Eden, identified with the palm through its idyllic associations. Though "waste" refers to the ocean, it is more broadly relevant to the process of imagining a female interiority in a society that denied women a complex inner life. As Luce Irigaray in *This Sex Which is Not One* explains: "The rejection, the exclusion of a female imaginary certainly puts woman in the position of experiencing herself only fragmentarily, in the little-structured margins of a dominant ideology, as waste, or excess" (30). In framing the poem as a woman speaking to women, "'mid the waste" (developing a woman-centred value that comments on the Wordsworthian formula of the poet as a man speaking to men), and developing this inner space, Hemans attempts to develop this "female imaginary" from the margins and remains of social experience.

Hemans therefore meaningfully questions dominant forms of subject identification through a redefinition of what intimacy can mean. According to Lowe, "the dominant meaning of intimacy, as sexual or reproductive relations of the individual person within the liberal private sphere, is a defining property of the modern citizen in civil society" (21). While Hemans does construct the subject in terms of an intimacy, it is with a natural object in a situation in which the expected male subject is literally eliminated. This redefines the notion of intimacy, removing it from the "liberal private sphere," which is replaced by, it is true, a "waste," but one that presents possibility as well as despondency. This in turn suggests a different take on the "modern citizen" that is less about normative gender relations and more invested in an identification with the natural object and in a nascent cosmopolitanism.

The landscape Hemans describes is also much like the "country of eternal light" that Walton dreams of at the opening of *Frankenstein*, and one that was actively searched for, a kind of origin myth for Britain's imperial and commercial exploitation of the globe. At the centre of this myth stands the palm. As Katherine Manthorne writes of European depictions of the palm in Latin America, "The stately palm became a *genius loci* of these southern regions; its nearly ubiquitous presence in the painted and verbal imagery indicated transport to the torrid zone ... The palm offers the key to isolating within the larger body of tropical scenes an iconographic program associated with the Edenic landscape" (376). Associated with this iconographic program was an ideological one, in which "torrid zones" were mapped onto the "southern regions" of female bodies in a way that underpinned a larger imperial project, as detailed by Felicity Nussbaum. What Hemans's poem effects, in its use of the palm as emblem of interiority, is a remapping of the Edenic space from the torrid zone into the female psyche, to represent not a sexualized exoticism but a complex inner life and a resilient female subjectivity. In this way we might think of the space of interiority as the space of the poem itself, that read along its margins and excesses elicits precisely the kind of interiority described. Yet this attempt to describe a reliable and unchanging basis for subjectivity is complicated by the very gender, class, and colonial discourses into which it enters.

The repetition of "thine" at the close of the third stanza, with its emphatic insistence on possession suggests the development of bourgeois subjectivity and the growth of imperial dominions. Yet this possession also stands in stark contrast to a legal system that denied women the right to property upon marriage and treated women themselves as property. Two questions asked by Irigaray seem potentially answered by this poem: "How can this object of transaction claim a right to pleasure without removing her/itself from established commerce ... How could material substance enjoy her/itself without provoking the consumer's anxiety over the disappearance of his nurturing ground?" (32). One way of reading this poem is to conclude, as does Irigaray, that the answer is to remove the male from the picture[9] (which Hemans does repeatedly – see the discussion of "Repose of a Holy Family" below for another example). This is the only way to assure the development of a truly female subjectivity outside of patriarchal social structures. In the context of a woman speaking to women, the turbulence and calm the poem negotiates can be read in terms of the married state and how the speaker encourages the reader to consider its aftermath. "I call thee bless'd!" opens the poem and is repeated at the end of the second stanza, towards the end of the sixth, and again, simply as "Bless'd" at the opening of the seventh. This insistence seems odd in a poem meant to console the addressed for the loss of her husband and combined with other aspects of the poem, suggests another meaning, one which allows woman to claim a right to pleasure because she is no longer an "object of transaction" under a patriarchal gaze.

"'Tis thine, all thine!" could refer, in other words, to more than just an inner calm, but to a self-possession (and material possession) only made possible by freedom from the married state (the release into a pastoral ease that is "forever green"). The archaism appears to distract from the associations of class, empire, and inheritance, or throw over them a softer light, one associated, perhaps, with the language of the King James Bible (chiming with "holy" and with the Edenic scene). In its insistence on female self-possession and subject-hood, the stanza, and the poem as a whole, can be read as both registering and resisting the ideological twinning of colonial and sexual possession, as well as common social strictures on female participation in the public realm, including the denial of property ownership in marriage.

The sense of interiority Hemans develops through the image of the palm becomes historically relevant when we consider the interiority of the palm itself, from which a valuable commodity is produced in the form of palm oil. At the time Hemans is writing, this production is largely female work. According to Lynn, "production of oil in nineteenth-century West Africa was women's work" (52) and was labour-intensive, involving a process of fermentation, boiling, crushing, and boiling again (47–8). The work the palm does in Hemans's poetry should be considered in terms of this work done on the palm historically. This applies to the gendered production of both literary and commercial products within a male-dominated market. In West Africa, it was men who generally "kept the resulting proceeds" (53) from palm oil sales, as in Britain literary production was controlled by men. This male domination of the market not only affected the control of wealth, it also carried into the content of the products themselves. As Hemans, for many of her readers, produced a certain kind of domestic space, women in West Africa produced a product, like their labour, invisible, that made this notion of domestic space possible. And as Stephen Behrendt has noted, "The increasing critical unanimity suggest that a literary – *but also ideological* – pressure was exerted on Hemans and her work through the medium of the reviewing press" (108, original emphasis). The market's need for a female poetry of domesticity appears something like its need for palm oil. Both function to lubricate the groaning wheels of empire and offer to cleanse the social body from the moral taint associated with those human groans.

This sense of the palm as a distant and exotic interiority is important to the way consumption of foreign goods like palm oil were becoming an integral part of Western identity during the period. What is perhaps less expected is the parallel this offers to the presence of palm oil in West African cultures, where it was both an important staple in the diet and increasingly a commodity for export. The growth of palm oil's importance as an export drove a change in the way it came onto the market, and individual family units became the largest producers. According to Lynn: "This shift to individual units of production has been seen by scholars as marking the start of 'modernity' in West Africa's economic history" (56). The importance of the palm to the development of modern identity continues today, as the palm oil industry has burgeoned into an enormous economic engine. On the one hand the palm oil industry is blamed for deforestation, habitat loss, and the destruction of sacred indigenous spaces in Southeast Asia, and on the other it continues to operate as a defining aspect of West African culture.[10] This industry creates new and unpredictable relationships that are increasingly global in nature. Danielle Gallegos describes how palm oil can make the everyday newly legible for West Africans living in Australia: "Palm oil acts … as an Arendtian bridge, offering the promise of arrival to islands of predictability and certainty" (30). By contrast, in Malaysia, the second-largest palm oil producer in the world, much of the labour required in palm oil plantations is carried out by migrants, who are "not well received by sections of the population that view their presence as politically or economically threatening" (Cooke and Mulia 141). The ambiguity and paradox surrounding the palm is apparent in the poetry of Hemans, in its cultural significance, and, then as now, in its commercial exchange. To paraphrase Gallegos, the palm has multivalent meanings and as such produces fluid identities (19).

The Palm as Domestic Space

Interiority is ever connected to notions of home, and it is striking that Hemans should so often evoke the exotic and distant palm to define this interiority. Palms again and again are identified with dwelling and the domestic, almost always in the context of the maternal:

> In your own land
> Doth no fond mother, from the tents, beneath
> Your native palms, look o'er the deserts out,
> To greet your homeward step? (132)

These lines, from the drama *The Siege of Valencia* (1823), are spoken by a mother in a desperate appeal to save her sons from the fatal decree of a Moorish chief besieging the city of Valencia. The "native palms" are appealed to as the dwelling space of human culture, identified here with a sheltering maternal influence that is meant to transcend nationality. Though set in the thirteenth century, the play comments on a more recent siege of Valencia in 1812 by French forces and a later invasion of Spain by France in 1823, the year the poem was written. The up-to-dateness of the poem's subject calls attention to the contemporary place of the palm in structuring ideas of nation. Though not as visible as tea or sugar, the palm entered into and shaped the development of British culture and economy in the Romantic period, either as literary symbol of a reclaimed Eden or as a literal substance applied to industrial machines and to bodies.

Palm oil is present but invisible both in Hemans's time and in our own. Today palm oil is an ingredient in such varied products as livestock feed, pharmaceutical products, detergents, cooking oils, prepared foods,[11] cosmetics, lubricants, and fuels, not to mention its various industrial applications[12] (Sassen 111, Aghalino 19, "Palm Oil"). Greg Critser tells the story of how palm oil became essential to the growth of the fast-food industry in the United States (7–19). Though not as ubiquitous, it was the surge of the importation of palm oil into Britain when Hemans was writing that forms the basis for our contemporary use of the substance. Another poem that features the palm also treats the theme of the hidden away that becomes a ubiquitous presence.

In "Repose of a Holy Family" (1833), Hemans describes an "old Italian picture," beginning with these lines:

> Under a palm tree, by the green old Nile,
> Lull'd on his mother's breast, the fair Child lies.

This scene, known as "The Flight into Egypt," was a popular one for artists, and many paintings depict it, particularly during the Renaissance. It was painted by Titian (c. 1508), El Greco (c. 1570), Rembrandt (1627), and Poussin (1657), among many others. Though Hemans appears to be offering an ekphrastic poem, her description varies significantly from the general treatment of this theme. All the paintings mentioned depict Joseph, as well as Mary and the baby Jesus. He is significantly absent in the poem. Also, none of the above paintings include the Egyptian architecture described in the poem. Hemans's form of ekphrasis emphasizes the engendering power of the female figure and heightens its Orientalist import. The green of the palm is metonymically connected to the oxymoronic "green old Nile," which reinforces the pastoral[13] import of "Lull'd," implying a lullaby, or the music of the poem itself. One of the apocryphal legends of the flight, also recorded in the Quran, includes a miracle involving a date palm,[14] in which Jesus orders the palm to lower its branches so that Joseph may pick the fruit. In Hemans's poem, however, fruitfulness is identified solely with the female.

This identification has further implications when we consider another important biblical iteration of the palm associated with generation – Tamar, the daughter of Judah, whose name can mean "date," "date palm," or simply "palm tree," and who was responsible for the continuation of Judah's line. There was an association of the palm with female beauty (as in Homer), that the name represents. The story of Tamar, one of the most assertive women depicted in the Hebrew Bible, interestingly involves identity, and the establishment of identity through clandestine (necessarily so, one could argue) yet bold means, a claiming of identity as a right when that identity would not be recognized in any other way due to gender distinctions. Hemans's poetry, as many critics have shown, often works through a clandestine veil of outward piety that is then ironized or otherwise undermined. Hemans was fluent in several languages, and it is possible she was aware that "Tamar" could mean "palm." But even without this direct knowledge, the biblical account shares many parallels with Hemans's general approach and to her use of the palm in particular.

Hemans's poetry often, as described above, develops both a superficial and a clandestine meaning, and along with the setting of the poem in Africa, this suggests both the invisible nature of palm oil in its daily use and the source of that substance. That the commodity should step in in this way to a religious poem appears dissonant but not when considering that the commercial and colonial powers of Europe ever justified themselves by veiling their motives in religion. What Hemans writes of the spread of Christianity could just as easily be said of the future of palm oil (especially in that Tamar is considered an ancestor of Jesus):

> A new born spirit, mighty, and yet meek,
> O'er the whole world like vernal air will spread! (11–12)

Palm oil might thus be considered as representative of the influx of foreign goods into Europe that presaged a global economy and the types of relationships that developed as a result of this commerce. One way this can be seen today is the use of palm oil to replace synthetic materials and animal fat in the production of personal care products. Palm oil acts as a surfactant, or foaming agent, and today "70% of personal care items contain one or more palm oil derivatives" (Tullis). Roland Barthes, in "Soap-powders and Detergents" comments on the metaphorical qualities of foam: "As for foam, it is well known that it signifies luxury. To begin with, it appears to lack any usefulness; then, its abundant, easy, almost infinite proliferation allows one to suppose there is in the substance from which it issues a vigorous germ, a healthy and powerful essence, a great wealth of active elements in a small original volume. Finally, it gratifies in the consumer a tendency to imagine matter as something airy" (37). This luxury and seeming never-ending abundance belies its dependence, not so much on a "vigorous germ" as on a fragile and increasingly compromised ecosystem, not to mention the social inequalities involved in maintaining the palm oil industry. As Gallegos puts it, "Palm oil epitomises the globalisation of commodities and their increasing role in the relationships between nation states and their influence on the food supply and livelihoods of marginalised groups" (28). Rather than "something airy," this substance partakes in weighty historical and geopolitical issues. Though it remains hidden, palm oil is a ubiquitous agent in shaping the living conditions of the modern world.

The likely embellished, if not outright invented, ekphrastic account, in an English poem of an unnamed Italian painting, referring to an apocryphal story based on a brief mention in one of the four gospels, dislocates the reader a number of times. We are asked to consider what it means to be both present and absent, here and elsewhere, just as increasing colonial territory and exploration situated British imperial identity in an always elsewhere. The palm is the figure for such a doubling, especially as it could represent not only the history of Christianity but also its future, as it increasingly spread into tropical locales.

The Palm and Changing Attitudes to the Body

Just as in the previous poems cited, the palm here is associated with a maternal domestic space. The way the palm creates the domestic space complicates Hemans's characterization as a kind of priestess to a "cult of domesticity" (Behrendt 105). That is, the domestic becomes defined by the foreign object, which itself comes into intimate contact with the body, as close as the baby with his mother. Palm oil was a necessary ingredient in body soap, the use of which was growing in popularity under new middle-class notions of hygiene and morality. And according to Anne McClintock: "Both the cult of domesticity and the new imperialism found in soap an exemplary mediating form" (208). The same might be said of Hemans's verse. If the palm in Hemans's poetry represents both the foreign and the domestic, then the palm oil in soap mediates changing domestic rituals and growing imperial desire. As McClintock puts it, "Domestic ritual became a technology of discipline and dispossession" (227), and Hemans's complex depiction of the domestic offers a glimpse of the inner workings of that technology.

In another poem that features a mother and son without a father[15] in a domestic setting, "The Crusader's Return" (1825), the palm plays a significant role. The titular figure, who easily suggests the British soldiers and sailors returning to England from distant conflicts in Hemans's day, bears a "long-withered palm branch" (3), the sign that though he may have left as a crusader, he returns as a pilgrim. The victory associated with the palm, is here "long-withered" and thus implicitly empty and useless, which is one way of viewing the violent "victories" of British imperial expansion. The crusader has rather oddly hung onto the palm over the course of many years, suggesting it is more than just the leaf of a plant to him, but has taken on symbolic significance – it tells a story.

The withered palm parallels the pilgrim's "wan cheek and brow" (63). This likeness between skin (which also is described in the poem's epigraph) and the leaf of the palm is suggestive of the relationship between palm oil (as a necessary[16] ingredient in soap) and bathing. Bathing, of course, is a key practice that was part of the changing role of the domestic in everyday life in Britain, "indispensable to the consolidation of British national identity" (McClintock 209). The pilgrim doesn't bathe in the poem, though he is metonymically bathed in tears throughout, and as Mary Douglas has noted, "tears are naturally pre-empted by the symbolism of washing" (126). At the time the poem is set, bathing would have been seen as possibly deadly (it was thought to open the pores and make one susceptible to disease) as well as sinful (long considered so by the Catholic Church). These ideas were changing during Hemans's day, as more and more of the population took up the practice. Writing in 1824, the radical and reformer Francis Place compares the current state of the populace with his childhood experience: "The increased cleanliness of the people is particularly striking ... [in the past] [t]he wives and grown daughters of tradesmen and gentlemen even wore petticoats of camblet ... stuffed with wool or horsehair and quilted these were also worn day by day until they were rotten, and never washed" (51). The palm leaf he carries in this sense can be considered in terms of the palm oil that was being brought back from Africa to make body soap. Just as it occupies a prominent place in the domestic scene of the poem, so too does soap stand "at the center of the domestic cult" (McClintock 209).

One of the reasons bathing was becoming more common was the new definition of skin as an organ.[17] The notion that one could be contaminated by dirt, that it could be reabsorbed into the blood through the skin, was beginning to gain traction. Soap early on was seen both as a method to avoid contamination by dirt as well as a method to maintain notions of racial superiority. As McClintock puts it, "Soap offered the promise of spiritual salvation and regeneration through commodity consumption, a regime of domestic hygiene that could restore the threatened potency of the imperial body politic and the race" (211). The palm that the crusader turned pilgrim carries is also meant to be a sign of spiritual salvation and victory, though these associations are implicitly questioned by the poem. The mother, at the poem's close, finally recognizes the aged and weathered form of the pilgrim as her son, in terms that capture the ambivalence of the palm's appearance in the poem: "Is it – alas! yet joy! – my son, my son!" (64).

The palm presents a double aspect historically as well. Not only was palm oil brought in increasing amounts from West Africa, but it would be brought back to West Africa later in the century in the form of soap by missionaries.[18] The use of soap provided a metaphor for the cleansing of sin from the soul. According to David Hardiman, "any Godly person who understood the rudimentary principles of hygiene and sanitation was in a position to bring health to the 'native' by cleansing their bodies with soap and their minds with the Gospel" (11). That soap would perform both physical and spiritual duty is not surprising given its importance in Victorian England, where, McClintock writes, it "was invested with magical, fetish powers" (207), offering "the promise of spiritual salvation and regeneration through commodity consumption" (211). If the increasingly widespread use of soap could represent "The Birth of Civilization" (223), then it carried with it all the brutality inherent to that civilization. What the palm had been for Christianity is something like what palm oil would become for Western capitalism. If for Origen, the palm was "the symbol of victory in that war waged by the spirit against flesh" (Hassett), then in Hemans's England, soap was increasingly the symbol of victory of the commodity over the individual subject.

The repeated reference to the pilgrim's appearance is especially ironic in that the mother does not, until the poem's close, recognize her son. Her first mention of "the darkness of thy sunburnt brow" recalls the Ancient Mariner's "long, and lank, and brown" body, and his "brown hand." According to Debbie Lee, the wedding guest fears the Mariner in part because his brown body "links him to British sailors who had been yellow fever victims" (53). We might imagine reticence on the part of the mother for a similar reason. Fear of contamination was also one of the major reasons motivating the growing practice of bathing with soap, which as McClintock notes, had racial overtones.[19] And as Lee details, the Mariner can also be identified as a slave, not only through his description, but through the fact that he doesn't drop down from the same illness that affects the rest of the crew (just as Africans were resistant to many of the colonial diseases that affected Europeans). Therefore, Lee explains, the wedding guest's fear "also demonstrates a fear of 'losing self in another,' of being infected and thus profoundly changed by the alterity carried in the blood under dark skin" (54). When the mother asks her son, in the last stanza of the poem "– what art thou?" it doesn't feel very far from the hermit's question, at the close of *The Rime*, "What manner of man art thou?" The "what" rather than "who" in the mother's question reveals another similarity to the Mariner, who we know is identified in the first word of the poem by an "It." The palm leaf, in this context, appears something like an albatross, a dead, wilted penitential sign, carried across continents, full of an enigmatic significance.

What Lee calls the "boundary-dissolving" (54) aspects of *The Rime*, when considered in terms of "The Crusader's Return," bring out another important aspect of the palm. The palm oil and slave trades were closely related: "Slaves and oil were exported together in a symbiotic relationship, as indeed had been the case from the days when palm oil provided the foodstuff for the middle passage ... [A]s far as the heart of the oil trade – the Bight of Biafra – is concerned, slave exports continued to increase alongside oil exports for several decades after 1807" (Lynn 32). This symbiotic relationship is at the heart of the development of Western capitalism and is particularly important to representations of the palm in Hemans's work. Though the pilgrim in "The Crusader's Return" does not return with barrels of palm oil, there were many others who did, and the withered palm he carries can be read as a sign of the explosion of this industry in Britain.[20] It is also important that even after the slave trade ended, a form of slavery continued in West Africa: "Those who were formerly exported to the New World as slaves were now employed in the production or porterage of the palm-oil and groundnuts European traders now required in place of slaves" (Crowder 56). Lynn concurs, "in many parts of the [Niger River Delta] region palm oil production for the market was accompanied by a considerable increase in slave labour" (51). And as a missionary travelling in the region in the 1840s describes, "Their palm oil, as well as their slaves, are said to be taken down the Benin branch, to a place called Egabo" (Schon and Crowther 45). Palm oil was also an important foodstuff on the middle passage. Writing in the 1780s, Alexander Falconbridge observes that captured Africans on board slave ships "sometimes make use of a sauce, composed of palm-oil, mixed with flour, water, and pepper" (21). This is likely a simplified version of traditional soups of West African cultures (see n83, above). But what Falconbridge also observes, and that connects palm oil with the skin in a different way than it did in Europe, was the use of it as a cosmetic: "[T]he purchased negroes are cleaned, and oiled with palm-oil" (16). The trade of palm oil was not only rooted in the slave trade, but palm oil was a substance permeating the historical practice of that trade and demonstrating in stark terms the interconnection of capitalist expansion with the commodification of human beings. When Olaudah Equiano describes his fear as a child, on first seeing Europeans (as sailors aboard a ship) that they would eat him (47), he not only reverses the trope of the savage, he conveys a widely held folk belief about European cannibalism in West and Central Africa from the seventeenth century onwards (Piersen 147) and connects, in a disturbingly direct way, to the use of palm oil on Black bodies to enhance the appeal of their flesh for the market.

Palm oil, in its historical production and use, is a figure of contrasts. This is captured in "The Crusader's Return" by the striking juxtaposition of the exoticized object and the formative mother/child relation. The palm leaf held between the two figures can be read as the sign of Britain's overseas investments. The regions in which palms grew were regularly identified not with the home and the mother, however, but with a sexualized other. As Felicity Nussbaum argues, "the contrasts among the torrid, temperate, and frigid zones of the globe were formative in imagining that a sexualized woman of empire was distinct from domestic English womanhood" (7). But as she goes on to say, "because the women in both torrid and frigid regions possess bodily torrid zones, women of all regions threaten to inject sexuality into the most temperate geographical domains, even as imperial discourse strains to confine it to certain areas" (10). The palm can be read as an identifying marker of these "torrid zones," both geographical and bodily, adding a further layer to the presence of the foreign at the heart of the domestic in "The Crusader's Return."

The sexuality that appears elided or sublimated by the absence of the father can be read as returning through the deployment of the palm and its place in the commodification of the orient. As Nussbaum notes, "Colonial enterprises contributed to eroticizing and commodifying the female body, and unlicensed public sexuality in the London streets connected to the rest of the world, especially the 'torrid zones'" (95). The palm, and especially its oil, which was a prized commodity and, potentially, a moral danger through the sensuality historically associated with bathing,[21] operates as a sign of this elision, bringing the "torrid zones" back into the domestic spaces of Hemans's broad readership.

The palm leaf carried by the male traveller in "The Crusader's Return" is held out as a sign of an interiority that the carrier cannot otherwise convey. It communicates something about Britain's newfound relationships with various distant parts of the globe and appears to ask what place these relationships have within the context of a nostalgic image of the past as more insular and uniform in its structure and its traditions. The history of palm oil importation into Britain also asks this question, as palm oil becomes necessary to both Britain's self-image as an industrious and innovative world leader and to the increasing personal connection between bodily and moral cleanliness.

"The Palm Tree"

When the literary, historical, and ecological qualities of the palm and its oil are considered together, they emerge as a key to the intersection of diverse relationships, including Britain and its colonies, gender and domesticity, the body and dirt, and, as I discuss below, textuality and the archive. The versatility of palm oil is reflected in the varying discourses and practices of which it became part. Perhaps more than any other poem of the Romantic period, these developments and their relationship to each other are expressed in Hemans's poem "The Palm Tree."

"The Palm Tree" opens with a description of imagined distances that are negated in turn:

> IT wav'd not thro' an Eastern sky,
> Beside a fount of Araby;
> It was not fann'd by southern breeze
> In some green isle of Indian seas,
> Nor did its graceful shadow sleep
> O'er stream of Afric, lone and deep.

The first two words of the poem, "It wav'd," seem ordinary enough until we remember that this tree is named for the resemblance of its leaves to the human hand. We are hailed and not hailed by a distance that is illusory, by an object that should not have the agency to hail us. This double "palm," along with the sensuality of the stanza, evoke the sense of touch. The depth of the waters here effectively communicate this depth of touching and its relation to female identity, as Irigaray explains: "They do not have the interiority that you have, the one you suppose they have. Within themselves means *within the intimacy of that silent, multiple, diffuse touch*" (29 original emphasis). The poem is both acoustic and tactile event, touching both our ears and through what the words evoke, our sense of touch. The palm, through its derivation from the human palm, reaches out to us, its waving suggesting a familiarity, even an intimate knowledge.

The sensuality of the stanza besets us, regardless of the negation that attempts to create distance. The fluid imagery with which the tree is associated (fount, seas, stream) suggests the flowing of its oil into Britain. The negations point to the removal of the commodity from the distant land and its importation, through the water, into Britain, which is where we learn the tree in this poem is located. And it should not escape our attention that it is in the act of bathing (another evocation of touch) that these two fluids, water and palm oil, are brought together. One thing the poem does by evoking and negating the exotic locales is to cleanse and inoculate the commodity to make it safe for consumption – to make the foreign domestic.

The connection between these leaves and the human hand suggests the act of composition. Poetic lines stripe the page as, in Elaine Scarry's words, "palm leaves stripe the light" (24). This gives the palm a kind of textuality. As in "The Crusader's Return," the protagonist, now from India, never speaks in the poem, and the tree in effect speaks for him. Palms have a long history of being used as writing surfaces on the Indian subcontinent and in Southeast Asia, both for the writing of poetry[22] and for copying religious texts, and though its precise date of origin is unknown, scholars believe a Tamil poetic tradition dates back at least two millennia (Houben and Rath 1), and a Sanskrit one even earlier (Lienhard 53). Scarry describes these leaves in terms of their "pliancy designed to capture and restructure light" (18), and the same might be said for how, in these Asian traditions, poets use them to capture and restructure language. "The Palm Tree," in reuniting a (apparently) young Indian man with the palm in an English garden, negotiates a relationship between Britain and India. Yet in its cultural importance for India and Southeast Asia, the palm represents far more than what the poem can contain.

The devotional nature of many of the texts written onto palm leaves is relevant to the palm as a sign of pilgrimage. The withered state of the palm in "The Crusader's Return" also indicates something about these texts: if not carefully maintained, they don't tend to survive for long periods due to improper handling, climate, insects, and other causes (Samuel 298). The repeated negations in the first stanza of "The Palm Tree" also gesture to the increasingly global nature of trade and the way cultures were transformed by this development. Palm leaves continued to be used as writing material until the arrival of the printing press in the early nineteenth century. Writing on the development of the Tamil language, which was one of many written onto palm leaves, Sanford Steever indicates that the characters "evolved from angular to cursive characters, as angular strokes tend to rip leaves" (426). Here the material directly shapes the form of the archive, even the very shape of thought itself. One example of classical Indian poetry in the Tamil language,[23] originally written on palm leaf, provided here in translation, displays a distinctively maternal point of view:

> You stand against the pillar
> Of my hut and ask:
> Where is your son?
> I don't really know.
> My womb was once
> a lair
> for that tiger.
> You can see him now
> Only in battlefields.   (Puram[24] 86. A.K. Ramanujan, trans. 265)

This short poem, moving from the domestic space, identified with the female body, out into the world and its battlefields, shares several themes with the poetry of Hemans examined in this chapter: distance, the absence of the father, the centrality of the mother-and-son relationship, war, and loss all illuminate the speaker's words. The palm here makes the text and its survival possible; it *is* the text, in an important material sense. This shares something with "The Palm Tree" which on the surface tells a story, but also works as a figure for the tree itself. The spaces of imperial desire dissolve into the palm, blurring beauty with exile:

> But fair the exil'd Palm-tree grew
> Midst foliage of no kindred hue;
> Thro' the laburnum's dropping gold
> Rose the light shaft of orient mould,
> And Europe's violets, faintly sweet,
> Purpled the moss-beds at its feet.   (7–12)

That the palm is "exil'd" is appropriate, given the dislocation that went hand in hand with British imperial expansion. "No kindred hue" in this context suggests a racialized landscape, all the more relevant due to the close connection between the palm oil and slave trade, as detailed by Lynn and discussed above. Palm oil, a traditional foodstuff in West Africa, and a staple during the middle passage, becomes a staple import necessary to lubricate the British industrial machine and to wash the bodies of the aspiring middle classes. In our own period it has become again an important, though hidden, foodstuff in its inclusion in a host of packaged foods.[25] The reader is hailed here again at the point of this symbiosis. The "Bight of Biafra" is the area along the coast of West Africa that contains the Niger river delta, where much of the palm oil trade was plied, (which, more recently, has been replaced by the petroleum industry, to disastrous ecological effect) recalling the "stream of Afric" at the end of the first stanza. Though the palm tree is the ostensible subject of the poem, its oil is what illuminates the historical flows the tree and the poem partake in.

Set amid violets and moss-beds, the palm is made over into a recognizable form of nature, now situated securely within the home territory, just as many products from overseas were becoming an integral part of the British domestic scene. Hemans foresees the way the natural world would come to be consumed. As Alan Bewell writes, "In our new, post-natural world, 'nature' is primarily marketed as an 'event' or 'experience' for consumers" (4). The treatment of the palm in this poem as an experience or encounter we are led towards appears to put the reader in a similar position to the contemporary consumer led towards a fetishized "nature."

The other plant in this stanza, the laburnum is, like the violets and moss-beds, ubiquitous in the four nations. The laburnum has an interesting history within the context of the movement of plants in the eighteenth century, as it was the wood traditionally used to make bagpipes until it was replaced by ebony and African blackwood in the nineteenth century (Dickson 50). The fact that an instrument so central to Scottish and British identity came to be constructed with imported African wood is emblematic of the types of changes the transnational movement of plants introduced into the world during this period.

The violets and moss in this stanza also recall Wordsworth's "She Dwelt Among the Untrodden Ways" (1798), where Lucy is described as: "A violet by a mossy stone/Half hidden from the eye!" In both Wordsworth and Hemans plant life is mobilized to signify a type of interiority. Yet in the Hemans poem the changing natures of the types of plant life used and consumed complicate how this interiority is constructed. The presence of palm oil in our contemporary products is similarly hidden, and in this way reflects the structure of global trade wherein consumers remain largely ignorant of who produces their products, where they come from, and with what they are made. Hemans captures a process in which the familiar is saturated with strangeness:

> Strange look'd it there! – the willow stream'd
> Where silvery waters near it gleam'd;
> The lime-bough lured the honey-bee
> To murmur by the Desert's Tree,
> And showers of snowy roses made
> A lustre in its fan-like shade. (13–18)

The willow streaming into silvery waters lures us, like the honeybee, to luxuriate in the multi-sensory showers of snowy roses, a pastoral excess which appears to ameliorate but only enhances the strangeness of the scene. What Mary Favret writes of distant violence is also true of the palm: it "becomes at once strange and familiar, intimate and remote, present and yet not really here" (15). The palm is in motion both in the poem and historically, capable of imaginatively representing a deep past[26] at the point of its relation to a troubling future. Two stanzas later, the poem conflates the non-human and the human by representing a figure as the palm tree's double, who is similarly presented as a stranger, now at an English garden party:

> But one, a lone one, midst the throng,
> Seem'd reckless all of dance or song:
> He was a youth of dusky mien,
> Whereon the Indian sun had been,
> Of crested brow, and long black hair –
> A stranger, like the Palm-tree, there.   (25–30)

Hemans's characterization leaves open whether this figure is a native of India or someone who has spent a good deal of time there. This fits with the ambiguity and double-ness presented throughout the poem in relation to the palm. He seems "reckless all," though that phrase might better describe the way palm oil is produced today.[27] His "crested brow" and long hair are suggestive of the animalistic and feminine qualities typically attributed to the east in European representations. Yet the figure's feeling for the tree later in the poem is compared to that of "The patriot" who "girds himself to die." As in "The Image in the Heart," Hemans meaningfully challenges her society's gender roles and sex-specific assignment of particular feelings, expressions, and appearances. By describing a young (likely) Indian man in an English garden in terms of one preparing to face death at the hands of an enemy, Hemans also meaningfully challenges imperial assumptions about power and its use. It is not very difficult, that is, to see how a young Indian man could see the English as the enemy in this scenario.

The penultimate stanza forms a direct connection between the tree and the domestic, maternal scene:

> His mother's cabin home, that lay
> Where feathery cocoas fring'd the bay;
> The dashing of his brethren's oar,
> The conch-note heard along the shore; –
> All thro' his wakening bosom swept:
> He clasp'd his country's Tree and wept!

The father is again absent or unmentioned here, and it is the mother who possesses the "cabin home" that is closely associated, as in other Hemans poems, with the palm (this time a coconut palm[28]). This is not an unimportant detail, as it is connected to how love of nation is defined in the poem, and this, as other poems by Hemans, is suggestive of a much larger role for women in the public sphere than allowed at the time. Like the negated locations of the palm, the mother is both present and not present, intimate and remote. This female presence has important relevance to the palm oil arriving on Britain's shores because, as discussed above, it was women who did most of the labour in the production of palm oil in West Africa.

The mention of death in "The Palm Tree" and its relation to patriotism, for which the tree becomes the symbolic object, is present in several other Hemans poems where the palm is designated as a grave marker. The relationship between the growth of nationalism and the rise of global trade can be seen in this figuration of the palm. In "The Abencerrage" (1819) we find the lines "Fair is that scene where palm and cypress wave/On high o'er many an Aben-Zurrah's grave" (419–20; canto 1). In "The Siege of Valencia" there are multiple such references, such as in the lyrics to Theresa's song: "And none but strangers pass the tomb/Which the Palm of Judah shades" (52–3; scene 5). This turns out to be a piece of foreshadowing, for as the battle for the city is at its height, the most frenzied activity takes place "beneath the lonely tuft of palms" (142; vol. 9), which Gonzalez immediately recognizes as the spot where the children of the city's leader had been executed by Abdullah. "Death and the Warrior" (1827) also figures the palm as grave marker: "And the palm-tree wave o'er my noble grave,/Under the Syrian sky" (19–20). "England's Dead" (1822) is a poem which imagines the global extent of Britain's empire in terms of its sons' dead bodies, and one of these locations, Egypt, is described as a place where "the palm-trees yield no shade" (12). In "Forest Sanctuary" (1825) there is a reference to the destruction of an enemy force besieging Jerusalem: "When the Most High, on Syria's palmy plains/Had quell'd her foes" (436–7; part 1). "The Indian City" (1828) reverses the typical trend in the period of condemning Muslim aggression towards Hindus in India, by describing the execution of a Muslim boy by a Hindu mob. The mother of the executed boy raises an armed force that overruns the city, and in her dying words exclaims: "Give him proud burial at my side!/There, by yon lake, where the palm-boughs wave,/When the temples are fallen, make there our grave" (208–10).

All these references to the palm as marking sites of death and destruction are particularly relevant to issues raised by palm oil production today. According to recent studies, the boom in the palm oil industry in Malaysia and Indonesia has not come without social and environmental costs:

> [I]ntensive farming practices and unplanned land use have led to deforestation, loss of species and social conflict between local community and

plantation companies … synthetic chemicals … [have] caused land contamination, soil and water pollution … increased dependence on fossil fuel for processing and farming operations … [has had a] resulting global warming impact … Drainage and burning of peatland forest for palm oil production alone released about 2 billion tons of CO2 equivalent GHG emissions each year, contributing to 4% of global annual emissions … [Indigenous peoples have lost] native customary land to large plantation companies … many cultural sites e.g. the sacred ancestral burial ground, were destroyed and replaced by palm oil plantations. (Lim et al. 14–15)

These are issues that grow more exacerbated with each passing year, and the palm increasingly becomes a sign, as Hemans intimates, of a violence submerged within the everyday, as well as of the destruction of a cultural and environmental heritage that first took place during the age of European imperialism and whose work is now continued through the ecological disaster brought about through capitalist modes of production. This destruction is today carried out in part due to an insatiable global demand for this oil, particularly on the part of "developed" nations whose citizens are far from the sites of production and who are often oblivious to the practical effects of their commercial purchases. In the various ways Hemans uses the palm in her work, we can witness a host of developments crucial to our understanding of our current moment. If palms are sensitive indicators of changing climates (Aronsohn), and Hemans displays a "keen sense of the changing cultural climate" (Berendt 108), then a reading of palms in her work provides the opportunity to draw together culture and climate, text and environment, in ways that have not yet been considered. The palm participates in us, in our literary and environmental history, and through the wide variety of products in which it is consumed today. As such, it provides a locus for an alternative construction of self that draws together such threads as female interiority, the Atlantic slave trade, the birth of the body soap industry, and modern ecological crises into an interconnected assemblage that challenges normative forms of liberal subjecthood and the shape of the cultural institutions that have arisen therefrom.

Chapter Four

Preserver and Destroyer: Salt in *The History of Mary Prince*

In the forced alliances with the inhuman, a different mode of subjective relation is formed …

– Kathryn Yusoff (2018, 19)

Material flows help to productively rethink the human, simultaneously opening possibilities for the interpretation of cultural production. Romantic period authors maintained a peculiar sensitivity to these flows, demonstrating an interpenetration of the material of agency and the agency of the material, their texts offering an opportunity to experience these flows within their own moment and into our own. The history of this period takes on more nuanced significance when understood not as a purely social concern but as an ongoing trans-corporeal exchange between forces "human" and "non-human." I use quotes here to indicate the malleability[1] of these categories, or the need, as Paul Youngquist indicates, to invent "new genres of the human" (6) in the face of an historically hegemonic definition of "Man" that has all too often been used as a conceptual weapon to both assimilate and to marginalize and dehumanize those "consigned to the Other of history" (Spivak 408). A recognition of the agency of the non-human in our histories and our philosophies is, I argue, integral to thinking about what "new genres of the human" might be. Such a recognition enables an understanding of social structures as saturated by substance, both on a fundamental level (the role of substance in human evolution), and in terms of a historical shift in cultural values signified by the rise of the commodity.

As the previous chapter pointed to the nuanced relationship between the palm oil trade and the slave trade, in which "slaves and oil were exported together in a symbiotic relationship: as indeed had been the case from the days when palm oil provided the foodstuff for the middle passage" (Lynn, *Commerce* 32), so this chapter will consider the salt trade, one also intimately bound with the slave trade, as British salt was traded for people in West Africa, and cheap salted foods were an important part of the diet for those brought from Africa, with implications for the health of the diasporic community today. Like salt, Prince's text preserves, making a living meaning possible in the face of overwhelming historical hostility, and despite the editorial incursions that claim authority over her narrative. It also acts like salt on an open wound, narrating a history of pain that continues into our moment. *The History of Mary Prince* (1831) offers a kind of doubly conscious text, facing in two directions at once, not only in terms of the journey from enslavement[2] it describes and perspectives from the Caribbean and from England but also in terms of the history of a modernity saturated with violence and loss, like the bodies saturated with salt that Prince describes. To navigate the question of how colonialism and the history of the African diaspora saturate Western modernity it is necessary to consider the role substances play in the various exchanges, everyday uses, and symbolic gestures of a variety of historical actors. Prince's text, in its illustration of what Yusoff calls "forced alliances with the inhuman" (19), provides just such an opportunity.

As the vast oceans that covered the planet gradually receded, they left behind them huge deposits of salt, a substance that has ineluctably shaped the geography, biology, and culture of our world. Salt plays an essential role in regulating the metabolism and brain function of the human body. No long-distance travel, whether commercial, scientific, or military, could take place without it due to its key role as a preservative. The British empire, or the American republic, would have been impossible without regular supplies of huge quantities of the substance. Salt has been used as currency, has provided the word "salary" (from the Latin *sal*), has played an important role in religion and ritual, and has been for millennia symbolic of the permanence of oaths and covenants. It contributes, through salt tectonics, to the shape of the earth's surface. An examination of a substance ubiquitous to both the structure of the biosphere and the construction of the present reveals important and unexplored aspects of material and cultural practices and productions. The importance of salt in creating the conditions of the modern is exemplified by the Romantic-era autobiography *The History of Mary Prince*, which details the physical and psychological conditions of Turks Island salt production in the early nineteenth century. The qualities and movements of salt, both within Prince's text and among the broader history of the diaspora, emblematize the corrosive impact of colonial contact and the preservative capability of text. By examining Prince's narrative in conjunction with the scientific, cultural, and economic history of salt,[3] this chapter seeks to reveal a largely untold[4] story about the place of a commodity in the making of Romantic life and consider the importance of this history to our contemporary moment.

This chapter is divided into six sections, the more readily to address the variety of registers in which salt takes part. "The Whiteness of Salt" addresses the invasive presence of salt in Prince's narrative in relation to the vexed issue of the white editorial intervention into the text. "Rupture" takes up Prince's repeated use of the imagery of swelling, bursting, and cracking that depicts a metonymic relationship between emotional stress, swelling and bursting bodies, the cracking of objects and landscapes, and the dramatic changes to the social landscape occurring during the period. "Governing Salt," details the ways in which salt influenced governance on Turks Island before and during the time of Prince's residence there, as well as how specific officials shaped policy on Turks Island. Colonial Office archival materials are employed here for the first time to reveal this important background to Prince's narrative. "Salt as Text/Text as Salt" examines some of the ways text and salt present similar qualities, exploring another important figure of the Black Atlantic, Booker T. Washington, who details his experience as a child in the salt works of modern-day West Virginia. In "Global Salt," I further my attention to the history of salt in the diaspora by attending to the folklore of West Africa and consider this folklore within the context of the growth of global trade and the way this trade ties together disparate narratives. Finally, "Salted Away" briefly considers the archival qualities of salt, wherein now defunct salt mines are being used to store papers from the UK national archives along with hundreds of thousands of tons of toxic ash. The diversity of subjects treated is necessary, I argue, to understand how Prince's narrative offers a commentary on the multifaceted agency of this substance in the development of modern Western culture and history.

The Whiteness of Salt

Though salt in its solid form does not appear in Prince's narrative until her adult life, it is already present in its opening words: "I was born in Brackish-Pond, Bermuda" (57). Just as salt makes fresh water brackish, so it invades the narrative from its outset. This brackish birthplace also indicates the way the larger history of the Black Atlantic is a key component to the hybrid structure of Western modernity. This hybridity can be seen in the importance of the slave trade to broader economic development, a trade Joseph Inikori calls "central to the development of industrial capitalism in England in the eighteenth century" (100).[5] Salt has always been central to the Atlantic slave trade, as it was commonly used as ballast on ships leaving Liverpool and was one of the commodities used to purchase people. In this way salt is present in Prince's narrative long before the moment of her birth. Salt was also one of the major exports of the West Indies at this time, a highly prized commodity sold mainly to the American colonies and smuggled into North America during the Revolutionary War. Cynthia Kennedy has demonstrated that by the nineteenth century, salt "outranked sugar, molasses, and rum as the leading cargo, as measured in tonnage shipped, carried from the West Indies to North America" (219). The majority of this salt came from the Turks Islands[6] (229), where Mary Prince spent approximately ten years (1802–12) working in the salt ponds (Maddison-MacFadyen). Her narrative interrogates the historical relation between substance and society, its text both a preservative and a salted wound.

In the years Prince spent on Turks Island, salt is a ubiquitous presence, not only in the landscape but in Prince's mind and body and the minds and bodies of those she worked alongside. Prince relates working in the salt ponds from four in the morning until "dark at night" and explains how standing in the salt ponds would cause the salt to eat into the body, "in some cases, to the very bone" (72). Sickness was treated with "a great bowl of hot salt water, with salt mixed with it, which made us very sick" (73). Ubiquitous and invasive, salt becomes invested with a psychic and symbolic energy similar to what Freud called *Besetzung*, a strong identification of the self with an object. *Besetzung* is often translated as "occupation"[7] and thus usefully connects Prince's relationship with salt to the British presence in the Caribbean.

Prince's text operates, narratively and historically, along the line of this occupation, in which the object becomes assimilated into the self in a process of crystallization.[8] First, salt is an essential component of the human body, present in intracellular fluid that makes possible the communication of electrical signals though the body. It is thought that when life emerged from the oceans, it took with it a kind of internal sea, represented in humans by the necessity of salt to bodily function. Second, there is a psychological identification of self with place, including the objects habitually encountered in this place. These two identifications become combined in a third, which is a recognition, largely lost to us today, of the subjection and prostration of the human before the forces of the natural world. And finally, Prince experiences these last identifications under conditions of extreme duress and against her will. This illustrates the pathology associated with the history of racialized landscape, one which continues today in the form of environmental racism. The occupying force of *Besetzung* proves appropriate to both Prince's relation to the mechanisms of colonial power, the "white people's law" (2), and her relationship to salt.

The invasive whiteness of salt in Prince's narrative also provides a way of understanding the vexed issue of the whiteness of the editorial intervention in its production. This invasiveness extends beyond whatever emendations were made to Prince's narrative to the way the text continues to be presented to audiences. A.M. Rauwerda describes the various "appendices, editorial prefaces, and introductions" (397) that overshadow most editions of the text, making it "as much about the editors" (399) as about Prince. These intrusions reflect the history of European colonialism, both affecting the legibility of a larger historical record. When Prince says of the salt that it "eats down in some cases to the very bone" (72), she describes the broader invasiveness of whiteness historically. The salt that eats into the bodies of those working in the salt ponds is shipped to North America to be eaten, reflecting a cannibalizing aspect of capitalist imperialism. This also inevitably reflects on the ways Prince's text was consumed as it went through three printings in its first year, whether dismissed as abolitionist propaganda or co-opted by abolitionists whose notions of freedom were, according to Jenny Sharpe, "racially coded": "The antislavery position, like its proslavery counterpart, articulated a racial hierarchy, but one that was culturally rather than biologically determined" ("Something Akin to Freedom").[9] The invasive whiteness described by Prince reflects both aspects of the writing and of the reception of Prince's narrative.

These interventions are further related to the whiteness of salt through the curative qualities associated with whiteness.[10] This is true whether we mean "cure" as the process of preserving meat or that of healing sickness. In *The Poetics of Spice*, Timothy Morton describes a "blancmange effect," so named due to the all-white ingredients of this supposedly curative dish. According to Sidney Mintz, curative dishes such as blancmange "strongly suggest that whiteness itself may have been thought to be inherently curative" (106). The supposed curative quality of white foods also extends to salt, which was used to treat a number of ailments.[11] Salt was also figured as medicine for the soul. The *Rituale Romanum*, a seventeenth-century text that codifies Catholic practice, is full of references to salt, and its use in baptism is particularly relevant here: "we beg you, Lord, our God, to sanctify and to bless this creature, salt, thus providing a perfect remedy for all who receive it, one that will permeate their inmost being." It gives pause that this foundational Christian ritual becomes completely reversed in Prince's narrative, where salt, though it permeates the minds and bodies of those producing it, is a curse and a source of illness.

This sense of permeation and its relation to sickness and remedy is explicitly captured by Prince: "When we were ill, let our complaint be what it might, the only medicine given to us was a great bowl of hot salt water, with salt mixed with it, which made us very sick" (73). If we consider Prince's depiction of salt in terms of broader literary depictions of whiteness, her narrative comes to demonstrate a rare departure from a theme which permeates Western cultural production. Examining several canonical texts, Toni Morrison discovers "figurations of impenetrable whiteness that surface in American literature whenever an Africanist presence is engaged," which serve as "both antidote and mediation on the shadow that is companion to this whiteness" (32–3). Prince's text meaningfully interrogates this antidote and mediation and demonstrates its pathology, its direct impact on the bodies of those to which it is raised in response. Morrison's observations further draw attention to the power of literary language to reinforce social prejudice. In this context, Prince's depiction of the whiteness of salt itself serves, to some degree, as antidote and mediation to the dominant literary treatment of the Africanist presence in the Western canon. She speaks against the grain, in this sense, of a whiteness that resists definition, that must remain pristine, blank, meaningless, precluding the possibility of meaning. This whiteness dulls the vision by withholding the possibility of an object, as Prince's failing eyesight at the time of her narration was at least in part caused by the damaging effects of the tropical sun reflected thousands of times off the innumerable crystals of salt and their inescapable glare, the "dislocating dazzle" of whiteness (Gilroy 9). Yet her narrative continues to speak, to counter a hegemony that may make it difficult to see but cannot take away our ability to hear.

The whiteness of salt can accrue and debilitate over time, as a type of slow violence, or can create horror in an instant, as in one of the most horrific descriptions in Prince's narrative, concerning the treatment of Daniel: "our master would order him to be stripped and laid down on the ground, and have him beaten … till his skin was quite red and raw. He would then call for a bucket of salt, and fling upon the raw flesh" (74). The "would order" and "would … call" indicate that these actions were not one-time occurrences but were habitual and repeated, not moments that pass and can be recovered from but a process that is ongoing and continual (not only in this case but in the broader historical sense). The salt, directly identified with the agency of the white "master," bears a further metonymic relation to the creatures on Daniel's body, signs of his ongoing suffering: "This poor man's wounds were never healed, and I have often seen them full of maggots, which increased his torments to an intolerable degree" (74). The living creatures described here are representative of the life that whiteness takes on as an institutionalized quality and its historical effects upon Black bodies.

It is of further importance to recognize that the horror produced by whiteness that this scene reflects is in direct contradistinction to that figured by Blackness in Western literature of the period. One influential example of this is in Burke's discussion of the sublime, where a boy that is born blind regains his sight through an operation as a teenager: "Cheselden tells us that the first time the boy saw a black object, it gave him great uneasiness; and that some time after, upon accidentally seeing a negro woman, he was struck with great horror at the sight" (131). Prince's increasing blindness, likely due to an inescapable whiteness, begs for a rereading of the sudden return to vision in Burke's famous passage, with implications for the historical construction of the sublime as aesthetic category of experience, and the place of such categories in the development of Western institutions, including, as Gilroy notes, the field of cultural studies itself (10).

A recognition of the trauma associated with salt and its relation to constructions of race might be read in the episode in which Prince is reunited with her mother. Prince describes seeing "a sloop brought in with slaves to work in the salt water." When Prince is first told that her mother is on board, she responds with disbelief:

> I could scarcely believe them for joy; but when I saw my poor mammy my joy was turned to sorrow, for she had gone from her senses. "Mammy," I said, "is this you?" She did not know me. "Mammy," I said, "what's the matter?" She began to talk foolishly, and said that she had been under the vessel's bottom. They had been overtaken by a violent storm at sea. My poor mother had never been on the sea before, and she was so ill, that she lost her senses, and it was long before she came quite to herself again. (76)

Prince's mother suffers a sea change that is more broadly related to the millions of Africans who suffered the middle passage, "overtaken by a violent storm" of another kind. But her eventual recovery points to the importance of the ship to the diasporic experience in other ways, including the lives of figures such as Olaudah Equiano and William Davidson, among others, seagoing men who, among their accomplishments, became important figures within English radical movements. It reminds us that "it has been estimated that at the end of the eighteenth century a quarter of the British navy was composed of Africans for whom the experience of slavery was a powerful orientation to the ideologies of liberty and justice" (Gilroy 13). Prince's father, we are told at the narrative's opening, is a "sawyer" working for a shipbuilder (57), and Prince sells "provisions to the captains of ships" to "earn money to buy my freedom" (82). And it is eventually her journey aboard a ship to England that would result in her earning her independence from the Woods. Like her mother, we might say, "it was long before she came quite to herself again," but she does earn some modicum of freedom, even if only later in life. In Prince's *History*, the ship offers a site for reconfiguring modernity through the lens of the Black Atlantic.

Rupture

In their book *Rupture: On the Emergence of the Political*, Paul Eisenstein and Todd McGowan define their titular concept as "an interruption of the flow of social life whose force remains in the wake of revolutionary changes" (3). Prince's text, I argue, offers just such a rupture: reprinted three times in the first year of its publication, it not only acted as an interrogation of the framework upon which British social life was built, its force remained in the revolutionary changes of the Abolition Act of 1833 and continues to inform our own moment. What is even more astounding is how Prince's imagery offers literal and metaphoric figures for this rupture, long before the theorization of the concept. Its repeated deployment of images of swelling, bursting, and cracking make it a text that both contains and is about rupture. This imagery conceptualizes a larger historical change that includes the racial violence evident in the nearly continual uprisings throughout European colonies in the Caribbean, the most successful of which, the Haitian Revolution, served as an impetus for many enslaved on Turks Island to escape to Haiti during this time. I evaluate Prince's imagery of rupture in terms of this broader eruption on the global stage.

Throughout Prince's narrative, we come across swelling and bursting hearts and bodies. Early in the *History*, Prince "burst out a crying" (60) on learning she would be sold and separated from her sisters. When at auction she tells us, "I thought my heart would burst" (61) and "My heart ... continued to leap as though it would burst out my body" (62). Shortly afterwards she summarizes her situation thus: "Oh, the trials! the trials! they make the salt water come into my eyes" (64). These outbursts would become literalized in the bursting bodies that appear later in the narrative. After Hetty is beaten to the point that she miscarries, we are given this description: "Ere long her body and limbs swelled to a great size ... till the water burst out of her body and she died" (67).

After Sarah is beaten and thrown onto some thorn bushes, "her naked flesh was so grievously wounded, that her body swelled and festered all over, and she died a few days after" (75). Prince's descriptions of her own failing health reinforce these descriptions. She contracts rheumatism, which she describes in terms of the swelling of her joints. She also contracts "St. Anthony's Fire" or erysipelas, a condition marked by the swelling of the skin. The approach to England towards the *History*'s end causes a violent physical reaction, as if she drew closer to the source of her disease: "When we drew near England, the rheumatism seized all my limbs worse than ever, and my body was dreadfully swelled" (86). These repeated swellings and burstings have implications to the larger theoretical work of rupture.

Rupture is present in the way the history of the Black Atlantic disrupts conventional formations of Western culture. As Axelle Karera writes, "Blackness ruptures the spaces of ethics and throw its most revered concepts … into crisis" (47), prompting a radical revision of fundamental aspects of Western thought. Siraj Ahmed's exploration, in *Archaeology of Babel*, of how the humanities have arisen from colonial philology is a further example of a violence residing within the archive. Debbie Lee details the narrative's "abortive cracks" in a threefold manner, first in terms of the way words fail Prince in describing the enormity of certain events, where these cracks are "sites where Prince finds English words and sentiment inadequate. She simply cannot describe some of the abuse she underwent because it is 'too, too bad to speak in England'. Her loss to 'find words to tell you all I then felt and suffered' proves a sharp contrast to the abolitionist poet's repetitive descriptions of the brutality of slavery" (216). These cracks in the narrative are secondly visible in the *History*'s "peculiar status as oral narrative" and the mediation involved in textualizing this narrative and thirdly, and "Perhaps most impressively," in Prince's own rupturing of the forms imposed upon her (216). Prince's narrative, the first known publication by an enslaved woman, is also among the first to provide an imagery for the rupture that lies at the heart of the revolutionary developments of the late eighteenth and early nineteenth centuries and for the intersecting rupture that Blackness presents to the history of Western modernity.

Prince's imagery of swelling and bursting links together environmental and bodily trauma in a way that continues to be relevant to our own moment. Edema, or bodily swelling, is caused by the excess retention of salt and is a symptom of hypertension, itself a condition brought about by salt sensitivity. The huge amount of salt that was part of the diet of the enslaved for centuries is a generally unrecognized, but likely central, cause of the epidemic of hypertension amongst members of the African diaspora today. The debate within the scientific community over the causes of salt sensitivity[12] is evidence of changing ideas about race and racialized views of disease. Studies which have focused on a genetic cause for salt sensitivity have tended to reinforce unhistorical conceptions of race and overlook environmental and psychosocial factors, such as the large amounts of salt that were part of the diet of slaves for generations in the West Indies and North America. The fluid retention that occurs due to excess salt retention and the disastrous effects of hypertension are represented in Prince's swelling and bursting imagery.

Finally, these swellings, crackings, and burstings and their relation to salt production and consumption extend well beyond the geographical location of Turks Island into England itself. The salt carried as ballast on slave ships was produced in Cheshire and floated on barges to be loaded in Liverpool[13] for its transcontinental voyage. One of the results of the exploitative methods of producing salt in Cheshire were the disastrous subsidences that occurred there throughout the nineteenth century. These sudden and violent alterations of the landscape offer further evidence of a rupture caused by the exploitative extraction of salt in the service of empire. The continual pumping of brine over generations caused the land to give way, leading to whole city blocks precariously slanted, lakes suddenly appearing overnight, and the landscape permanently transformed. One subsidence in Dunkirk unfolds a series of events which include a "rumbling subterranean noise, the violent bubbling of the water in all the surrounding pools, and the uprising of air and foul gas through rifts which its passage tore in the ground … A series of alarming, but comparatively small displacements caused extensive rifts in the ground about Ashton Salt-works, and these were followed by a sudden explosion in a neighboring pool, which ejected a geyser of mud and water some 30 feet into the air" (Calvert 122). The pastoral landscape of the English countryside was for many emblematic of the value and purpose of the nation itself during this period, and its violent transformation through exploitative practices (salt production one of many) has ramifications for this landscape as a site of the formation of a national consciousness.

Governing Salt

Prince demonstrates an understanding that West Indies societies are largely structured and regulated by the "white people's law." However, the mechanisms of colonial power as laid out in the colonial archive, including the government of Turks Island and the flow of salt from this island, have not yet been fully addressed in studies of Prince's *History*.

I will, like Lisa Lowe, be treating this archival material "not as transparent data, but as an archive of *colonial uncertainty* in which one observes British imperial desire and ambition" (78; author's emphasis). This uncertainty and its relation to imperial desire is particularly apparent in the case of Turks Island, for centuries under the control of Bermuda, but by the time of Prince's residence there under the rule of the Bahamas, a colony some 500 miles distant. Far from the objective, consistent, and transparent model it was often held up as being, the "white people's law" was, in the case of Turks Island, often opaque, whimsical, and feckless.

One way this is made clear is when Prince's owner is physically abusing his daughter and Prince defends the girl with her own body and the words "Sir, this is not Turk's Island" (77). Prince highlights the relative lawlessness of Turks Island in comparison to the norms of Bermuda, and her point appears to be immediately recognized. Though technically under the government of the Bahama Islands, seated in New Providence, the owners of the salt ponds on Turks Island were nearly all from Bermuda, which was its own colony and had its own government (Bermuda was originally a colony of Virginia, and many Bermudans therefore had sympathized with the American rebels[14]). These Turks Islanders had no choice but to officially recognize the authority of the Bahamian government, though in practice they defied it. The remoteness of the Turks Islands, some 500 miles from the seat of government in New Providence, the Governor's lack of means to enforce his rule without a nod from the Colonial Office, and the British government's unwillingness to get involved in a spat between colonies (especially if this would affect the collection of duties on salt) all contributed to the unique social structure of Turks Island.

The governor of the Turks Islands during Mary Prince's residence there was Alexander Murray, the second son of John Murray (4th Earl of Dunmore), and he almost certainly obtained his position as King's Agent on the Turks Islands due to his father having been governor of the Bahamas from 1787 to 1796.[15] Murray's correspondence with the successive governors of the Bahamas and with the Colonial Office, and what others wrote of Murray's tenure, provide a record of colonial desire necessary to the understanding of the material agency of salt during this period. Like the salt which seeps into everything on Turks Island, the "white people's law" is an inescapable agent with which Prince must everywhere contend.

Soon after Murray is appointed King's Agent, the then governor of the Bahamas is writing breathlessly to the Colonial Office, "Nothing but anarchy has existed at the Turk's islands since the appointment of an agent there" (CO 23/44). Governor Haklett also writes to Lord Hobart in the same year (1802) that "smuggling of every description is carried on with impunity" (CO 23/41). It is believed that Prince was brought to Turks Island in 1802. Whatever may have been the truth of these assertions, Murray's aristocratic connections, the greatly increasing salt duty flowing into British coffers, and a Colonial Office whose resources were stretched thin appears to have been more than enough to protect him from any investigation. Murray, in the same year, suggests to Lord Hobart that Halkett be removed, and by 1805 he has been replaced by Charles Cameron (CO 23/44). In 1807, when the Assembly of the Bahamas requests the "recall of the Commission of His Majesty's Agent at Turk Island ... as illegal, and mischievous" (CO 23/52), again no action whatever is taken by the Colonial Office.

Murray himself boasted of doubling salt production in a short period, despite complaining that Turks Island was an inhospitable, comfortless place and the salary meager (CO 23/42). Just what methods Murray employed to achieve such an increase are unspoken, but Mary Prince's narrative appears to offer a first-hand account: "The people in England, I am sure, have never found out what is carried on there" (11), illustrating the covert nature in which much of the production of commodities in the colonies took place. In the same memorial, Murray argues that the Turks Islands should be made an independent colony and makes the case that though the Bahamian government wishes to exert their control over the islands, the inhabitants have no use for this government, for they resort to Bermuda for their legal needs, claiming only once in twenty years to have had use of the Bahamian courts, for the "alleged murder of a slave" (CO 23/42). The memorial concludes with a list of signatories, among them one Robert Darrell. Mary Prince gives a memorable description of Darrell, her likely[16] owner on Turks Island: "[M]y former master used to beat me while raging and foaming with passion; Mr. D – was usually quite calm. He would stand by and give orders for a slave to be cruelly whipped, and assist in the punishment, without moving a muscle of his face; walking about and taking snuff with the greatest composure" (72). The coldness and heard-heartedness of Darrell, like many other whites Prince encounters, is often contrasted in Prince's narrative with images of the soft and yielding, such as the long grass Prince and others use to wrap their legs in, makeshift bandages to cover the ravages of the salt and make sleep a little more possible. This contrast between the soft and hard is precisely what the production of solar salt consists of – a process of hardening through crystallization.

Such hardness of heart is overtly performed by Murray himself when he later becomes the collector of duty in Nassau. Here he agrees to take on the task, for one guinea per head, of "apprenticing out and taking charge" of a group of 440 Africans. He neglects his duty and then writes aggrievedly of himself as victim when he says that their complaints, "when unattended to, [have] caused attempts at suicide," and he requests the task be given to someone else (CO 23/62). When he receives no response, he complains again in a letter to Governor Cameron (CO 23/63). Murray's callous disregard and sense of entitlement are not merely the flaws of a single individual but are part and parcel of a system that flows from the very centre of British government and the hierarchical systems of class and race upon which it is built.

The owners of the salt ponds, who had been coming from Bermuda for centuries, felt any involvement of the Bahamian government in their affairs to be oppressive and unjust. One way their defiance expressed itself was through smuggling. Secreting away substances from the eyes of authority is also evidenced in slave resistance towards the demands of forced labour. One of the meanings of the verb "to smuggle" is to "make off stealthily" (*OED* 3c), and this clandestine act is related to the strategies of slave resistance. In a practice Saidiya Hartman terms "stealing away,"[17] those enslaved not only removed themselves from the conditions of their bondage, they also re-appropriated the time meted out for their labour. The smuggling of salt offers a multi-inflected site of resistance to definitions of property on which colonial ideology depended. Prince's various ways of repurposing and withholding her labour takes part in a figurative smuggling as well. Indeed, her narrative may be read as something smuggled from colonized space into the metropole, in the sense that such representations of Black experience were exceptional, the growing European bourgeoisie relying almost solely on accounts of the colonies written by fellow Europeans. Many colonial parties had a vested economic and social interest in keeping the truth from reaching the European capitals and did their utmost to attempt to discredit any narrative that leaked through, as was most certainly the case with *The History of Mary Prince*, which long after its publication was claimed to be an abolitionist invention.

Salt smuggling was a global phenomenon during the period, largely due to the high taxes[18] placed on it, and it was smuggled into England and Scotland from Ireland from the eighteenth to the early nineteenth centuries (when the salt duty was eventually repealed in 1823).[19] In a 1779 letter, the governor of the Bahamas, Montfort Browne, writes to the Colonial Secretary Lord George Germain that "The Trade and Intercourse with the Rebels from this place I find has been extensively carried on," and in another letter a month later, "This Colony must at present be considered in a state of open rebellion" (CO 23/9). Though

Browne was recalled by the British government in the same year he wrote these letters, other sources verify that salt was making its way from the Turks Islands through Bermuda to American rebels (see, for example, Williams and McEachern 9 and n21).

Attempting to quantify the extent to which smuggling salt was a general practice, Archibald Cochrane,[20] in *The Present State of the Manufacture of Salt Explained* (1785), writes: "Thus it appears, that the sum actually produced from the duties of salt in this country, is deficient to the amount of above *three hundred thousand pounds* sterling of the sum which these duties ought to produce if there were no smuggling" (52; author's emphasis). Given the duty of five shillings per bushel at the time Cochrane wrote, this indicates a widespread and lucrative business involving over a million bushels of salt. Though salt was primarily used during this period to preserve the dead bodies of animals for human consumption, it was also used in the process of mummification in ancient Egypt, and seventeenth-century prisoners in France who died before their court date were salted and brought to trial (Kurlansky 227). All these methods recall the close relationship of salt with dead matter and the power of salt, like text, to preserve beyond the grave.

Those working in the salt ponds of Turks Island often attempted to smuggle themselves off the island. Charles Cameron, governor of the Bahamas from 1804 until 1820, writes in 1807, "I am sorry to inform you that the negroes at the Turk's Islands ... have availed themselves of the vicinity of St. Domingo to desert to it" (CO 23/52), likely to the newly minted republic of Haiti. The nearby island of North Caicos was the site of the largest such escape recorded, in which fourteen slaves escaped in 1800. Wade Stubbs, the proprietor of the plantation from which these slaves escaped, was one of the largest slave owners in the West Indies at the time and was from a family that "had salt works all over Cheshire" (Kurlansky 327).

Salt acts as a bridge connecting the metropole and the colony, and as this metaphor suggests, it was a tenuous and fraught structure. Smuggled, used, and discarded, and inhabiting the space of disease and failed curation, the bodies of exploited workers exhibit the same material status as the island's most ubiquitous commodity. Salt thus becomes throughout Prince's narrative a consummate figure of, and for, the material and psychological effects of the colonial condition.

Salt as Text/Text as Salt

Whether smuggled or stolen away, the reappropriation of time and substance beyond the accepted uses of colonial ideology becomes essential to the production of text across the Black Atlantic world. Prince details several ways she "steals" time to pursue her own initiatives in the pursuit of freedom from bondage, from attending Moravian meetings to selling produce while her owners are away. Even getting married is an act she is forced to complete furtively, rightly fearing that it would enrage her owners. Prince's narrative is part of a larger pan-African literature that demonstrates not only this particular relation between text and reappropriated labour but also does so in specific reference to salt. One prominent example is the Antebellum American autobiography of Booker T. Washington, who as a child worked in the salt furnaces of Kanawha in current-day West Virginia:

> My step-father seemed to be over careful that I should continue my work in the salt furnace until nine o'clock each day. This practice made me late at school, and often caused me to miss my lessons. To overcome this I resorted to a practice of which I am not now very proud, and it is one of the few things I did as a child of which I am now ashamed. There was a large clock in the salt furnace that kept the time for hundreds of workmen connected with the salt furnace and coal mine. But, as I found myself continually late at school, and after missing some of my lessons, I yielded to the temptation to move forward the hands on the dial of the clock so as to give enough time to permit me to get to school in time. This went on for several days, until the manager found the time so unreliable that the clock was locked up in a case. (25)

Here salt and text both appear as irreducible substances that spill over into each other, as the minutes stolen from industrial clock-time are taken directly from the production of salt to advance the acquisition of knowledge. Washington's movement of the hands of the clock also represents a resistance to the transformation of time instantiated by industrial timekeeping. The description of the clock being locked up in a case is an apt metaphor for the carceral nature of labour experienced by African Americans and is a prophetic image of the incarceration of African Americans today, often seen as a kind of enslavement by another name. It also demonstrates more broadly how, as industry and technology spurred each other on over the nineteenth and into the twentieth centuries, the passing of time increasingly came to be experienced by working people across the Western world.

It was Washington's stepfather who had brought the family to Kanawha, where he had formerly been enslaved and forced to produce salt. Washington's stepfather's experience in Kanawha has several parallels with Mary Prince's on Grand Turk. Like salt production on Turks Island, Kanawha relied heavily on slave labour, which was unusual in salt-works in the early United States. Kanawha was also physically remote from other settlements and therefore not subject to the same social restraints, as Prince notes of Turks Island. Both salt-works were seen as places to be avoided at all costs, and slaves made various efforts to avoid being sent there. As one manager and overseer describes the Kanawha salt-works, echoing the comments of Alexander Murray on Turks Island, "They all despise this place as much as I do, & more they cannot" (Stealey 134). The slaves who worked at Kanawha were mostly leased out by their owners, a practice comparable to the system in place on Prince's Turks Island. And those who worked at these salt-works made constant escape attempts, not to St. Domingo but to the free state of Ohio (Stealey 145).

It is in the salt furnaces of Kanawha,[21] before he obtains permission to attend school, that Washington has his first experiences with text: "Every barrel of salt that was packed in the mines was marked, and by watching the letters that were put on the salt barrels I soon learned to read" (23). The crystallization of the basis for all of Washington's later learning is saturated with the crystallization of salt.

Washington's own precarious smuggling of time and knowledge from the salt furnaces is indicative of the continuing necessity of such an effort in the face of a historiography that elides the history of those who worked in Kanawha. As Cyrus Forman has noted, the tale that continues to garner the most attention is the abduction of a white settler, Mary Ingles, by Native Americans in 1755 and her brief time being forced to labour in the production of salt: "While her story of salt slavery is commemorated in a play that is annually performed in the state of West Virginia, a mass-market paperback, and two feature films, the public memory rarely acknowledges the thousands of enslaved people who replaced her as slaves in the Kanawha Valley salt works" (3).

This history, like that of Mary Prince, deserves to be recovered and restored to its rightful place. We will never arrive at a more accurate understanding of the larger history of modernity without access to such lost narratives. Luckily, a trove of documents that record the use of slaves in the salt trade in West Virginia have currently come to light and are at the time of writing being archived in the Huntington library after a recent sale at auction. This discovery will no doubt help clarify a picture that has for far too long remained in the blind spot of history.

Global Salt

The movement of salt crystallizes a number of global developments and brings a new urgency to the function of this substance in *The History of Mary Prince*. Because Prince's *History* plays out on a global stage, moving around the Caribbean before terminating in London, it is a cosmopolitan work that requires, I argue, that it be interpreted in the context of the larger pan-African diaspora and its history. Because salt plays an important role in this larger history it offers a touchstone that links seemingly disparate narratives, demonstrating economic, colonial, and cultural ties in common. This section will consider an African perspective on the salt trade between Britain and West Africa through the tale "Jĕki and His Ozâzi" to better comprehend the role of salt within the history of the diaspora and within Prince's text. "Jĕki and His Ozâzi" further details the global ramifications of the salt trade by bringing salt from Europe to the equatorial coast of West Africa, the same area from which Mary Prince's ancestors had likely been brought west. A reading of salt in this tale, with its complex entanglements with traditional and postcolonial West African life, demonstrates the global reach of salt and its fundamental role as a bridge across various diasporic traditions.

The folktale "Jĕki and His Ozâzi" that I discuss here was collected by the Rev. Robert Hamill Nassau in *Fetichism in West Africa: Forty Years' Observation of Native Customs and Superstitions* (1904) and is therefore mediated through its collection and translation by a white male missionary. While this mediation complicates an understanding of the tale's source, it does not erase this source, and indeed the tale has enough elements of folktales in the West African tradition that it should, I argue, be understood as partaking of that tradition, if not on a word-for-word basis, then in the spirit in which it is expressed and in the elements of the tale which can be verified as belonging to a larger body of cultural expression. Like *The History of Mary Prince*, there is much valuable material to be recovered, even despite, and at times even because of, the nature of the text's mediation.

The protagonist of this tale, Jeki, obtains a magical object, an *ozâzi*, from his grandfather. He is told that this object will grant his every wish: "But there is one orunda (taboo) connected with it: no one must pronounce the word "salt" in your hearing. You may see and use salt, but may not speak its name nor hear it spoken, for if you do things will turn out bad for you" (381).

The grandfather goes on to provide Jeki with a secret which will be of help to him in case the taboo is broken. The pronunciation of salt as taboo has compelling ties with the spiritual associations of salt in various African diasporic traditions. Meredith Gadsby demonstrates how salt has a unique role in the ritual life of the diaspora: "In several belief systems (Shango, Condomble, Santeria) foods prepared for the ancestors never contain salt … This belief in the spiritual benefits of the avoidance of salt is also held by Rastafarians and participants in the Kamina tradition" (26). This avoidance of salt was thought to provide special abilities, including the ability to fly back to Africa. Salt was thought to weigh down the soul and thus make escape from the plantation more difficult. According to one account recorded by the ethnomusicologist Lorna McDaniel from the island of Carriacou: "The Africans who were brought here didn't like it. They just walked to the sea. They all began to sing as they spread their arms. And a few rose to the sky. Only those who did not eat salt left the ground. The Africans flew home" (qtd. in Gadsby 25–6). This notion of the "flying African" is retold in various ways, times, and places, and it shares historical links with "Jĕki and His Ozâzi."

Jeki uses his *ozâzi* to summon ships full of merchandise. It is important that the *ozâzi* doesn't merely grant the immediate appearance of the desired object but mediates this appearance through the agency of the ship. The *ozâzi* and its use thus functions in several intersecting ways: as a commentary on the slave trade (in that it's holder has power to command ships and their contents), as a comment on the salt/palm oil trade between Britain and West Africa in the aftermath of the Slave Trade Act, and as a symbol of the social effects accompanying the influx of exotic products into West Africa.

Through the use of the *ozâzi*, Jeki becomes a powerful and benevolent ruler, which in turn incites envy among some of his relations: "to prove things, Jeki thought he would try his half-brothers, and see what were their real feelings toward him. So the next time he caused ships to come with a cargo of salt only ... The half-brothers came close to him, and exclaimed, 'Dâgula [Sir], the ships are loaded with nothing but salt, salt, salt, and the captain is waiting for you.'" This mysterious captain, who we never hear of again, undoubtedly represents the European merchant trader, no longer loading a human cargo but now seeking palm oil for use as an industrial lubricant and in the making of soap (as discussed in the previous chapter). We might think of this trader in terms of the historical figure John Tobin, who Martin Lynn describes as "the person behind the initial expansion of the trade in palm oil from the Niger Delta during the 1810s and early 1820s. He did this ... through the export of large quantities of Cheshire salt from Liverpool." Tobin was formerly in the slave trade, so it is unsurprising that "the techniques and practices developed for this [salt/palm oil] commerce ... owed much to the slaving era" ("Trade and Politics" 105). Tobin's situation wasn't unique, for "of the seventeen African traders in Liverpool in 1809, all were former slavers" (Lynn, "Liverpool and Africa" 34). The vessels full of salt arriving on the coast of West Africa in the early nineteenth century must have often been the same that had formerly carried slaves. Another reason for the taboo in Jeki's tale becomes apparent. Now that the word "salt" has been pronounced and the taboo broken, Jeki must prepare himself to face the consequences, and he must have recourse to his grandfather's secret to do so.

Jeki boards one of the vessels and begins a performance:

> He raised a death song, "Ilendo! Ilendo![22] Give me skill for a dance! Ilendo! Ilendo! Give me skill for a play!" This he sang on the way, jumping from boat to boat. He said he would go on board the ships, but ordered all his brothers not to come ... He boarded one of the ships, and went over the deck singing and dancing with that same Ilendo song. Then he jumped to the deck of the next vessel.
>
> As he did so, the first one sank instantly. On the second ship he sang and danced, and jumped hence on the third, the second sinking as the first. On the third ship he continued the song and dance; he remained on it a long while, for he caused it to sink slowly.
>
> When it sank, the boats went ashore wailing, and took the news to the town. (384)

Jeki's half-brothers pretend to mourn but actively seek to seize Jeki's possessions and his rule. However, Jeki had prepared everything so that he could, employing his grandfather's secret, return to the living, victorious over the half-brothers challenging his position as the rightful ruler of the province, but also, and perhaps more importantly, victorious in claiming an independence from European trade and its effects, first in terms of slavery and then in terms of an influx of newfangled European commodities. The hero's resurrection through traditional modes of ancestral knowledge rejuvenates the community and returns it not to an imaginary precolonial paradise but to the envisioning of a postcolonial state.

Jeki's self-sacrifice suggests the Igbo landing, in which seventy-five enslaved Igbo walked into a creek on the Georgia coast and drowned in a mass suicide in 1803, the likely source of the "Flying Africans" folktale. Terri Snyder explains the historical background:

> The flying African folktale probably has its historical roots in an 1803 collective suicide by newly imported slaves. A group of Igbo (variously, Ebo or Ibo) captives who had survived the middle passage were sold near Savannah, Georgia, and reloaded onto a small ship bound for St. Simon's Island. Off the coast of the island, the enslaved cargo, who had "suffered much by mismanagement," "rose" from their confinement in the small vessel, and revolted against the crew, forcing them into the water where

they drowned. After the ship ran aground, the Igbos "took to the marsh" and drowned themselves – an act that most scholars have understood as a deliberate, collective suicide. The site of their fatal immersion was named Ebos Landing.

   The fate of those Igbo in 1803 gave rise to a distinctive regional folklore and a place name. (162)

Any historical consideration of the Atlantic slave trade must necessarily consider the three continents that were integral to its practice. Salt provides a unique vehicle for considering these complex relationships. Jeki's tale illustrates the fact that the connection between Britain and West Africa remained well after the slave trade ended and that one can read in salt the ongoing legacy of this trade, both in West Africa and in Mary Prince's West Indies, where the salt trade also continued after abolition. At the same time, both tales are also committed to historical narratives of freedom. Though Prince is saturated with salt, she obtains some freedom from bondage, and though Jeki may sink with the salt, his resurrection insists on the power of traditional modes of knowing as resistance in the face of seemingly insurmountable compulsion.

Salted Away

Salt, then, has historical resonances that raise questions as to its foundational role in the development of Western society, the larger movement towards the globalization of commerce, and the hybrid nature of modern identity. Prince's narrative captures the violence underlying the production and sale of this commodity, a violence which parallels the way the archive is itself haunted. In *Slavery and the Culture of Taste*, Gikandi claims that his goal is "to find a language for reading what lies buried in the crypt, what survives in the 'secret tomb' of modern subjectivity" (x). The history of salt offers a commentary on this "crypt-ic" nature of the archive, especially when considering the common nature of this archival substance, which holds out a promise that there are yet experiences that survive and wait to be recovered and transmitted.

   Salt mines have long been used as archival spaces, due to their location far underground and their ability to maintain steady temperature and humidity year-round. This history develops another strand in considering the larger function of salt. A wide variety of materials have made their way into salt mines and caverns. A large proportion of the developed world's strategic petroleum reserves is located in underground salt caverns (Shi et al. 1). A salt mine in Hutchinson, Kansas, stores original film negatives "of *Gone with the Wind, The Wizard of Oz,* and thousands of other Hollywood films" ("Strataca"). The same mine also hosts seventeen minutes of deleted scenes from Stanley Kubrick's *2001: A Space Odyssey*, and an unpublished film script by Samuel Beckett, Harold Pinter, and Eugene Ionesco (Galloway). The famous stained glass of Strasbourg Cathedral was stored in a salt mine near Heilbronn, Germany, to protect it from Allied bombing during the Second World War. A large mine in Winsford, Cheshire, now operated by a private storage company, currently holds a vast variety of archival material, from documents belonging to Britain's national archives,[23] to several hundred thousand tons of toxic ash[24] (Gray). The salt mine has become a place to store cultural memory, whether treasured, indifferent, or unwanted, and to think about cultural futures, whether in terms of natural resources or toxic waste.

This contemporary history of the salt mine reflects back on the production and use of salt during the Romantic period, as it was the digging out of these mines over the course of centuries that made them the valued archival spaces they are today. Just as Turks Island was the centre of salt production in the Americas, so Cheshire was the centre of salt production in Britain. The discovery of immense deposits of rock salt in Cheshire at the end of the seventeenth century would lead to Britain's independence from foreign salt, and according to John Holt, writing in the 1790s, the salt trade was generally recognized as the central force behind the rapid rise of Liverpool in the eighteenth century (Barker 83), as this was the port through which Cheshire salt moved. Of course, the rapid rise of Liverpool at this time was also due to its central role in the British slave trade. Even with the prohibition on this trade in 1807, Liverpool would maintain a relationship with West Africa, conducting a lucrative business in the trade of salt for palm oil. The same mine in Winsford that now houses material from the national archives produced the salt sent to West Africa, where it arrived at Lagos, a port city raised on the slave trade.[25] Prince's narrative achieves an enhanced relevance when we consider that the relationship between salt, slavery, and the development of capitalism extends from the salt ponds of Turks Island to the shores of Great Britain and beyond, revealing both a corrosive and preservative facet of Romantic life.

Chapter Five

"Lin'd with Moss": John Clare's Rhizomatic Poetics

Moss is easy to ignore. It is often associated with damp and gloomy places, with disuse and decay. It arouses sensations very different than the sleek, ultra-efficient, and shiny objects with which people in wealthier parts of the world surround themselves today. The atmosphere it evokes is almost a pre-human one, in stark contrast to those things meant to remind us of the supposed long march of human progress and serve as proof of human exceptionality. The growth of moss presents a different timeline from the one used to measure the history of human civilizations. Its slow, clinging, incremental progress seems, from this later measure, a form of backwards growth, one that constantly threatens to pull the developments and achievements of civilization back into the primordial landscape (if it is not a sign of that inevitability, an evolutionary destiny run full circle). Yet there is another way of thinking about moss, one that recognizes its place in human life and culture and in the history of life in general.

Moss is the most widespread plant on the planet. It inhabits nearly every ecosystem on earth and numbers as many as 22,000 species (Kimmerer 15). It is thought to be the first land plant to emerge from the water during the Devonian era, 350 million years ago (23), providing the base ecological conditions for the evolution of all other terrestrial life forms. It is so much a base for the development of life that we generally don't even notice it's there, or when we do we rarely consider its evolutionary or ecological significance. Moss has been used in a surprising number of ways throughout human history,[1] most of them lost to our own era, apart from a few places where peat is still burned as fuel or its smoke used to flavour whiskey. Peat moss is, however, of considerable importance as a carbon sink, a precarious storehouse of huge amounts of carbon, and as a palaeoecological archive, one that tells the long and varied story of the earth and from which scientists today find evidence of human-induced change to the biosphere. The harvesting of peat over thousands of years has transformed the face of the four nations,[2] with unexplored implications for the cultural forms that grew out of these landscapes. Peat also fueled the Dutch Golden Age and thus played a complex role, one that has been largely understudied, in the history of European colonial and commercial growth. And peat bogs have turned up both relics and bodies that have served as a link to a distant past for which there is often little other record. Though we may have few common applications for moss today, it has an outsized relevance to our cultural past and ecological future.[3]

Poetry of a certain age shares several characteristics with moss. It is generally ignored, at odds with the goals and desires of contemporary society, associated with the (supposed) backwardness of bygone ages, lacking in practical use and interest to the greater part of the "developed" world. It raises the same questions for many of the same reasons. The relationship between moss and poetry, I argue, is nowhere better represented than in the work of John Clare.[4] This project as a whole has demonstrated a relation between language and specific common things as central to reconceiving our histories and subjectivities by decentring a traditional understanding of the human and refocusing on the agency of the common natural object. In this chapter, I argue that Clare figures the cultural resilience of poetry in terms of the ecological resilience of moss; like a cool bed of moss on a hot summer's day, this relation offers a place to dwell and to contemplate dwelling.

Moss takes an unprecedented role in the poetry of Clare, who looked past its seeming insignificance to excavate its profound importance. This chapter will examine the economy of moss in the poetry of John Clare primarily through a close reading of three "middle period" poems in which moss plays a central role. A consideration of the economic, ecological, and cultural qualities of moss in terms of the qualities of Clare's verse will provide a method of reading the imbrication of human culture and the natural environment at a moment of historical change at the root of contemporary ecological crisis. This chapter will explore the reciprocal topography shared by the qualities of moss and those of Clare's poetics. While there have been studies that examine Clare's "botanical aesthetics,"[5] this is the first to give sustained attention to moss in his work. As in previous chapters, I will be interested in both how substance infiltrates the literary and how the literary infiltrates substance.

The chapter examines how moss provides a way of understanding the imbrication of poetry and the ecological, cultural, and economic systems of the Romantic period. It is organized in four sections. The first deals primarily with the ballad "On Seeing Some Moss in Flower

Early in Spring" (c. 1832). Here I consider how moss provides a habitat for various types of life and its human use as a building material and fuel. I examine particular formal strategies of Clare's work in terms of the biological qualities of moss. "The Flitting" (1833) deals with the explicit comparison this poem makes between the qualities of moss and those of poetry. Here I consider the capillary action of water in moss in terms of Clare's imagery and his evocation of the enduring quality of moss in terms of what is known as "cryptobiosis," or the ability of certain life forms to endure despite displaying no discernible metabolic functions. "Clare's Fen Aesthetic" deals with the way Clare champions a peaty, boggy landscape in the face of a long tradition in English verse and culture that denigrated these types of places. I discuss this landscape in terms of the history of those who dwelled in boggy places as well as the history of fen drainage, the importance of peat as a commodity and as a source of energy, especially to the Dutch Golden Age, and the discovery of artefacts and bodies in bogs. I draw here on "The Flitting," "Song" ("Swamps of wild rush beds & sloughs squashy traces" [1821]), and "To the Snipe" (1832) as illustrative of these developments. This section concludes by proposing a reading of Clare in terms of contemporary ecocrises. The final section provides a close reading of "The Robin's Nest" (c. 1832) as a way of putting to work the findings of the first three sections and demonstrating the centrality of the "common thing" to Clare's work.

"On Seeing Some Moss in Flower Early in Spring"

The title of this chapter is taken from one of Clare's earliest poems, "Noon":[6]

> Seek the spring-head lin'd with moss
> There your little feet may stand,
> Safely printing on the sand; (58–60)

Clare's facetious direction to birds on a day of "hot relentless sun" (50) is inevitably connected to the poet's printed work, from where it flows and what it seeks, and the birds' habitation in this mossy spot is analogous to the poet's own a few lines later:

> There, aside some mossy bank,
> …
> Shall be where I'll choose to lie;
> Fearless of the things that creep,
> There I'll think and there I'll sleep; (71–6)

And there perhaps he will compose as well. In understanding Clare's poetry as "lin'd with moss," I wish to exploit "lin'd" in a double sense as both archivally creating a space (if contentious) for dwelling and as describing the lines of the poetry itself. Moss not only "lines" Clare's poetry in this double sense, it also everywhere inhabits his native Helpston as both a cultural and ecological object.

In the ballad "On Seeing Some Moss in Flower Early in Spring," Clare hails moss as representative of the "common things" that are celebrated everywhere in his verse. The poem begins,

> Wood walks are pleasant every day
> Where thought so full of talk
> Through autumn brown & winter grey
> Meets pleasure in the walk.

The stanza contains the plan of the poem within it, as the poet will take us on a walk where, towards the end we will meet the titular moss as thought meets (and "metes") pleasure through poetry. "[T]hought so full of talk" reminds us of the sociability contained within this supposedly lone walk and within the shape of thought itself. Also on display here is the diffuseness of Clare's style (which mirrors the diffuse habitats of moss): the "Where" of the second line might refer to the woods, the walks, to every day, to all of these, or to the where-ness of the mind, with its own branches and paths and continuities, and this grammatical openness demonstrates the connection between these things in a kind of distributed consciousness. We move "through" seasons here as well as a landscape, and Clare frames this dual movement as one towards spring and fructification, for which moss serves as the mediating figure.

The ballad[7] is a form particularly suited to a poem about moss, due to its reliance on paratactic linking and on repetition. That is, the concept of placing side by side in a nonhierarchical structure, and the repetition of this process, is precisely what the growth of moss figures. Mosses do not have roots, and thus no centralized organizing system, but are a series of distributed individuals, each attached to the earth by tiny hair-like rhizomes. One small patch of moss can contain thousands of individual plants. The growth of moss might be thought of as an incremental repetition which in the ballad "shows a compositional unity between repetition and the paratactic linkages inherent in ballad structure" (Green 82). This incremental repetition, in the growth of moss and within the poem (of both "common things" and "every" in "every where," "every body," and "every place"), provides a way of thinking about how a common substance like moss can establish a relation between passing through space and cycling through seasonality.

The "Wood walks" are teeming with life here, and moss reflects this proliferation in miniature, harbouring a rich variety of living things. Moss beds are often described as scaled-down versions of the forest canopy, habitats for a variety of life. As little as a gram of moss "would harbor 150,000 protozoa, 132,000 tardigrades, 3,000 springtails, 800 rotifers, 500 nematodes, 400 mites, and 200 fly larvae" (Kimmerer 55). And as Clare knew well from his fascination with birds' nests, moss was commonly used for nest building by a variety of birds. Not only birds, however, use moss as cushioning. Flying squirrels, voles, chipmunks, bears, and others line their burrows with the substance (Kimmerer 147). And as Clare reminds us in "Noon," moss could also provide a human habitat ("There I'll think and there I'll sleep"). And this was true not only for the itinerant poet. H.N. Dixon, writing towards the end of the nineteenth century, reports: "Polytrichum commune is used in the North of England for making mattresses, for which purpose it is said to be superior to straw ... Linneaus speaks from experience most highly of the comforts of such a bed" (240–1). Various forms of moss were used as building materials: "Bog moss was used extensively during the Post-Medieval Period and probably earlier, for insulating roofs and walls of dwellings" (Ardon 37), and as Brunksill writes, "peat or turf roofs were used regularly to cover walled farmsteads and cottages in western parts of the British Isles, including Ireland, Scotland, Wales, and the Isle of Man, during the Medieval Period, through to present times" (47). And, as mentioned, peat also warmed these cottages (Wordsworth attests to the comfort of a "warm peat fire" in *The Prelude* 535; Book 1). Moss provides a dwelling space within itself for various life forms, and without itself through its various uses by animals and humans. Clare's poetry also describes a double sense of dwelling, both within the text and within the specific spaces he describes.

In addition to the way this poem makes use of the interrelation of its subject matter and its form, it further hides within itself another poetic form: the sonnet. The fourteen stanzas of the poem correspond to the fourteen-line sonnet, and the turn occurs at the last line of the eighth stanza, which would be the last line of the octave in a Petrarchan sonnet. This line reads "The coming of the spring." This is where the poem has brought us from its first stanza "Through autumn brown & winter grey" so that we can now "turn" our heads to witness the moss in flower, the sign of new growth, or as Phillis Levin writes of the volta, the "possibility for transformation" (xxxix). In the late poem, "Sonnet to x.x.x.," Clare compares his early poetry and his mature poetry in terms of poetic form. In his youth, he "walked with poesy in the sonnet's bounds," but later his "stretching" journeys "found no resting place." In this poem, set in early spring, also representative of the season of childhood, Clare finds a way to combine both the diffusive sense of wandering freely into the countryside with the contained and secure circuits through the village. In this way Clare makes new use of both the ballad and sonnet forms, revolutionizing the ballad while holding to its roots in a commonly held culture. For Eavan Boland, the octave/sestet formula of proposition and rebuttal has allowed poets "to replicate over and over again the magic of inner argument" (46–7). Clare's poem offers several points of inner tension in this context, between youth and adulthood, the general ("common things") and the specific ("this moss"), between time (the "every day" of the opening line) and space (the "every where" of its closing), between the mind and the natural world, between the ballad (as popular form) and the sonnet (as high art), and finally between poetry and its object.

The next stanza explicitly connects the journey of the walk to the journey of the seasons:

> O natures pleasant moods & dreams
> In every journey lies
> Gladding my heart with simple themes
> & cheers & gratifyes

Moods and dreams may appear to anthropomorphize nature, but they have a direct relation to the movement through the seasons evoked in the first stanza, where seasons mediate between thought and sensation. In choosing states beyond the direct control of the conscious mind, Clare points to a similarity between the behaviour of the natural world and that of the human, who is, in this context, a part of that world. The verb "lies," along with "dreams," further suggests the imagery of the unconscious. The ampersand of the first line returns to visually dominate the closing line of the stanza. It connects "themes" to "cheers" and "gratifyes," turning verbs into nouns, akin to how "Gladding" changes an adjective into a verb. As with other instances of anthimeria, these changed forms hold onto something of their former state; the nouns hold onto a part of their verb-ness and become, as it were, active things. The ampersand also joins the seasons in the first stanza and the "moods & dreams" of the second, which are also seasons, if not quite in the same way.

Ampersands do important work in this poem, and in Clare's work in general. There are fifteen of them in this fourteen-stanza poem, an average of one per stanza, plus one extra, which we might take as representing the additive, paratactic character of the verse. Simon Kovesi convincingly relates Clare's ampersands to the rhizome as described by Deleuze and Guattari: "Clare's predominant use of the ampersand … shows affinity with the rhizome in terms of its coordinated, levelled, planar, anti-hierarchical shape … it destabilizes and problematizes not just subject/object relations, but also subject/object definitions" (85). At the same time as the rhizome destabilizes hierarchical relations, it generates new possibilities for meaning. The ampersand is both cohesive and adhesive, it both connects and makes generation possible. The kind of productive and reproductive presence of moss in Clare's poetry becomes comparable to the way a vast array of images and objects become intimately interconnected; that is, the ability of moss to form and reform allows for unity in the poetry's symbolic input. The rhizome, I argue, has implications beyond the ampersand to the various ways Clare's poetics creates non-hierarchical connections between subjects. As Deleuze and Guattari claim, the synaptic networks of the brain behave in a non-hierarchical, mutually supporting (or rhizomatic) way (15), and Clare's particular style may be read as not only the development of an aesthetic but as a representation of the underlying material basis for embedded structures of consciousness. Put another way, Clare's rhizomatic links provide a way of seeing the development of a unified consciousness from a multiplicity of independent affects.

Clare's treatment of the relation between poetic imagery and the human unconscious, detailed in the third stanza, also addresses the relation between poetry and mental functioning:

> Though poesys woods & vales & streams
> Grow up within the mind
> Like beauty seen in pleasant dreams
> We no where else can find

The process of the formation of poetic imagery is related to that of the formation of dream imagery, suggesting an innate relationship that is at the same time paradoxical, as the parallel established by "Like" is then seemingly deconstructed by "no where else." In psychoanalytic terms, the dream image is not beautiful because of its particular appearance (its manifest content) but because of the associations and ideas with which the image is laden (or its latent content). The dream state is uniquely able to attach these meanings to images in a way that the waking state cannot, under normal circumstances, thus "We no where else can find" this particular type of beauty. Freud describes the formation of dream thoughts as a rhizomatic development, and his description of this process is useful to understanding Clare's comparison: "The dream-thoughts to which we are led by interpretation cannot, from the nature of things, have any definite endings; they are bound to branch out in every direction into the intricate network of our world of thought. It is at some point where this meshwork is particularly close that the dream-wish grows up, like a mushroom out of its mycelium" (525). These mycelium are rhizomorphic and thus behave in a similar way to the rhizomes of moss. We can witness in Clare's rhizomatic poetics, in their open-ended unpunctuated (without "definite endings") branching out, a similarity with the formation of the dream thoughts as articulated by Freud. "[P]oesys woods & vales & streams" are the "meshwork" where "the dream-wish grows up." As Clare points out again and again, the growth of poetry is akin to the growth of the natural objects of his poems.

The next stanza introduces "common things" as a potential source of human gratification, and the following indicates that by this Clare means native, local objects, demonstrating his awareness that new commodities were transforming a traditional way of life: "Some value things for being new/Yet nature keeps the old." To "keep" is not to possess materially, but to hold to, to continue, to value. The next two stanzas set up a refrain – stanza six beginning "The common things of every day" and stanza seven, "The common things of every place," again reiterating the poem's employment of the common thing as the mediator between the passage of time and the contingencies of location. The "daisey" of stanza seven is both a harbinger of spring and of the moss which will first appear in stanza ten. It is as if we are walking through the landscape, on one of the "wood walks" of the opening stanza and coming across these "common things" as we go, and the daisy thus leads us to violets, which in turn bring us to moss.

The turn that "The coming of the spring" represents is foregrounded by the daisy, which is reflected in the opening of stanza nine: "& violets." M.M. Mahood, writing of a late Clare poem, "Spring Violets," makes this comment: "This is a poem that could be summarised in three words; violets? yes, *violets*" (136). To begin the stanza (and the sestet) with "& violets" is a similarly emphatic gesture, both insisting on the violets themselves as a kind of release (following the "tension/release" form of the sonnet) and insisting on a principle of an additive profusion through the ampersand. Following the logic of the sonnet (not to mention the close observation of both seasonality and environment that this ordering of daisy, violet, moss entails), the ampersand is the hinge upon

John Clare's Rhizomatic Poetics 131

which the octave and sestet swing, framed by these two "common" flowers. But Clare is not writing a poem about flowers:

> But the sweetest yet that grows
> Is that which every hedgrow owns
> & every body knows

We pass by the flowers to find our real subject, moss.[8] It is sweetest partly due to its appearance, partly for its intrinsic qualities, and partly because of the age it confers on objects (a sign, as in stanza five, that "nature keeps the old"), but largely for its commonness. "The common things" that have been the refrain up to this point in the poem, have found their exemplar in the move to this specific plant, and it is as if we have stopped upon our walk to take in the scene:

> This moss upon the sallow roots
> Of this secluded spot
> Finds seasons that its station suits
> & blossoms unforgot   (37–40)

The querying "w" sound of the first stanza ("Wood walks," "Where," "winter," "walk") has flowered into the satisfying plurality of the "s" sound here (like winter into spring, another sign of the tension and release, or question and answer form of the Petrarchan sonnet). The image of moss upon roots, and the contrast of the bright new moss with the dark old root, is a very common one in Clare's work, and this commonness is one way his poetry mimics the objects he treats. That the moss "finds seasons that its station suits," echoed in the next stanza's "Finds seasons of its own," is remarkable in how it defines "seasons." Moss is not passively subject to a general unchanging rotation here, but it "finds" its own seasons (like the "moods & dreams" of the second stanza). Clare not only demonstrates his knowledge of the reproductive strategies of moss, many varieties of which can reproduce throughout the year,[9] he also asks us to think about an ecological niche as itself a kind of season, and to understand that there are different ways of dwelling in the world. The mosses' seasons are not those of the tree, for instance, and this makes up part of its unique identity. That it "blossoms unforgot" does not simply mean it is remembered by the poet; the passive structure makes it available to the passerby, or indeed the reader, and through this network this blossoming achieves a kind of mnemonic resilience. "Unforgot" also suggests the fragility of this memory by raising an echo of its potential loss. Clare has directed us to "This moss" in "this secluded spot," and this specificity is essential to understanding its beauty. As Elaine Scarry writes, and Clare exemplifies, "Beauty always takes place in the particular" (18). If we recall Clare's description of certain dream imagery as being unavailable elsewhere, we can further understand that Clare sees each poetic image as a unique instance, even when acting as a group in the larger service of the poem. A bed of moss appears to form a unified object but is in fact made up of thousands of individual plants.

Stanza eleven extends the precarious, and thus all the more necessary, nature of remembering, as the moss is "so hid from view" and "To heedless crowds unknown." But, as if to remind us that the moss is not merely a subject for human consumption, whether literally, when burned as peat, or figuratively, through its aesthetic appreciation, stanza twelve focuses on its agency:

> It peeps among the fallen leaves
> On every stoven grows
> Sufficient sun its shade receives
> & so it buds & blows

"Peep" is used here in the sense of to emerge or protrude, also used to refer to sunrise ("To emerge or protrude a very short distance into view; to begin to appear; spec. [of a day, morning, etc.] to dawn [now English regional]" ([*OED* 1a]). There is also a sense that the moss returns our gaze here, "among the fallen leaves," which suggest pages, and along with "They teach my heart lifes good to trace" of the next stanza, explain a relationship between the agency of the moss and the tracing of the poem. "Sufficient sun its shade receives" reminds us that moss requires some sunlight in order to photosynthesize but that too much direct sun will deprive it of the moisture it requires, as well as hinting towards a self-sufficiency, the possibility of human freedom from debilitating labour and want. The line "& so it buds & blows" again ends a stanza where the ampersand is prominent and here describes the progression between when the plant "buds" and when it "blows," or comes into full flower.[10] Blowing might also describe one method of reproduction in which spores[11] are ejected to be taken on the wind and deposited randomly. Spores can survive long periods in unfavourable conditions, not unlike Clare's poetry, which languished for over a century until sustained critical interest revived. Moreover, spore derives from the Greek σπορά (spora), meaning "seed, sowing," which is an excellent metaphor for the potential that poetry presents. When mosses use this strategy, the seta (stem supporting the capsule which contains spores) grows particularly long (up to twenty centimetres) so that its spores can catch the air currents that don't reach the surface (Raven). Clare brings us down to this surface where the earth meets the atmosphere, a realm known as the bryosphere.

Air generally behaves differently closer to the surface of the earth than it does above it: "As the laminar flow is disrupted by the drag of the surface, the air stream becomes separated into different layers of speed ... Down towards the surface the air becomes progressively slower and slower until, immediately adjacent to the surface, the air is perfectly still, captured by the friction with the surface itself" (Kimmerer 16–17). By directing our attention to the miniscule and trifling, Clare asks us to become slower and more deliberate in our observations. Clare's verse captures this friction with the surface that becomes a rhizomatic friction between words, able to convey both what Seamus Heaney calls "the inexorable one-thing-after-anotherness of the world" ("John Clare" 137) and that slowing to a nearly perfect stillness, "That quiet peace & calm content" of this poem's penultimate line. The very redundancy of the descriptors "quiet" and "calm" are what give them additive force when we remember the importance of incremental repetition both to the ballad and to moss.

"The Flitting"

The movement through the landscape and its accompanying movement through the seasons are essentially the same to Clare as the movement from one line to another. Yet certain types of mobility at work during the period, such as the "improvement" of the landscape through enclosure, cut off the traditional paths and connections these paths made available. In addition, the movement of particular plants disrupted a sense of continuity in the landscape that was connected, for Clare, to communal rural life.

Mobility thus has a split function in Clare's work: in one way it enables a relation to time and place, while in another, it alienates him from his environment and its connection to the past. As Alan Vardy succinctly puts it, "His poetry addresses the problem of his divided self" (1). The same basic formula is at work in Gary Harrison's comment: "Clare who is usually thought of as the poet of place might more precisely be called the poet of between places" (149). His poetry mediates between places and between selves and remains a constant presence though everything around him changes. One feature of the landscape not as prone to change is moss, mostly because it thrives in the "between places." Even in moments of painful loss, moss is an enduring presence with which he identifies his own poetry. The relationship between the form of Clare's verse and the biological form of moss discernible in "On First Seeing Some Moss in Flower Early in Spring," is made explicit in "The Flitting" (1833):

> Where moss did into cushions spring
> Forming a seat of velvet hue
> A small unnoticed trifling thing
> To all but heavens hailing dew
> & Davids crown hath passed away
> Yet poesy breaths his shepherd skill
> His palace lost – & to this day
> The little moss is blooming still (80–8)

Moss and poetry partake of the same qualities here, offering a space for dwelling that outlasts the symbols and structures of empire. Even from within this poem about loss,[12] Clare asks us to consider the relationship between the ecological and the poetic and how this relationship comments on what it means to dwell within a specific historical moment. Both his poetry and moss produce and reproduce a rhizomatic growth, a sense of rootedness without roots that connect back to a sense of biological and cultural origin.

The "small unnoticed trifling thing/To all but heavens hailing dew" captures something of Clare's sustained attention to the minute and the delicate. The role of this dew in the reproductive life of moss helps to demonstrate the way moss operates in Clare's poetry. "As a result of … strong cohesion and adhesion, water can form a transparent bridge between two plant surfaces. The tensile strength of this bridge is sufficient to span small spaces, but collapses if the gulf is too broad. The delicate leaves and small stature of mosses provide spaces of just the right size for these bridges to form by the capillary forces of water … Every cell of every leaf is in intimate contact with the atmosphere, so that a raindrop soaks immediately into the cell" (Kimmerer 39). This intimate contact is predicated by a radical openness that allows the moss, or the mind, to be suffused with its surroundings. Clare's poetry too has a tensile strength, it enables a capillary stemflow of verse into small and secluded spaces. Each line is a tiny bridge forming intimate contact with its surroundings.

"The Flitting" forms a metonymic connection between moss, weeds, and grass, forming lines related to those of his verse, this relation commenting on the form of consciousness itself: "Many people have a tree growing in their heads, but the brain is much more a grass than a tree" (Deleuze and Guattari 15). These connections are formed at moments in the poem that turn away from loss and towards the relationship between poetry and the natural world. As he writes in lines that predict the stanza quoted above: "& still my thoughts like weedlings wild/Grow up to blossom where they can" (59–60). "& still" suggests that not only does Clare endure and continue to produce poetry during this removal but that his words continue and others can take this example of resiliency for their own benefit. This sentiment is repeated later in the poem, when "may blooms with its little threads/Still comes upon the thorny bowers" (141–2), "& still they bloom" a few lines later, "& nature still can make amends" (206), and finally "& still the grass eternal springs" in the penultimate line. The ampersands here connect a sense of continuity with an irresistible fecundity. Weeds come up again several times in "The Flitting": "I feel at times a love & joy/For every weed & every thing" (189–90), "This weed an ancient neighbour here" (198) and in a refrain that recalls the stanza quoted above, "– So where old marble citys stood/Poor persecuted weeds remain" (211–12). It is hard not to feel a self-identification in this sense of remaining even though one's place has been lost. And then, in the final affirming lines that draw together these strands, "& still the grass eternal springs/Where castles stood & grandeur died." This grass, the weeds, and the moss are further related to each other and the poetic lines through Clare's identification of moss with the paths of memory: "The mossy paths" (15), and "green lanes" (35) of Helpston are also lines of flight that share the same ground as the grass and weeds: "Below grass swells a velvet hill/and little footpaths sweet to see" (38–9). The moss in the stanza above is also described as "velvet."

It was not lost on Clare that the ability of substances like moss and weeds to remain, even after empires rise and fall, can also apply to poetry, as in "The Flitting." Yet moss in particular undergoes a specific transformation that sets it apart from weeds and grass. When the necessary conditions for life are not available, certain varieties of moss are known to undergo a process known as cryptobiosis, defined as a third state between life and death in which metabolic activity is slowed down to an undetectable rate. A recent study (Roads et al.) found that it was possible to revive moss that had been buried in a glacier in Antarctica for over 1,500 years. The perseverance and resilience of moss resembles the ability of poetry to reproduce itself more generally. As Clare states in "Song's Eternity" (1832), "Ballads of six thousand years/Thrive thrive" (17–18). Endurance was a quality Clare surely hoped for his own work, especially as he "had himself hung on through years of literary misjudgement and neglect, faithful both to his vision of the natural world and to his vocation to put that vision into words" (Mahood 141). Clare's work not only suffered neglect during his lifetime but would continue to do so long afterwards.[13] We might say his poetry undergoes its own form of cryptobiosis and the relatively recent revival of his work a sign of its unusual resilience. The ability of moss to undergo cryptobiosis and be brought back to life under the right conditions resembles the latent potential of text awaiting a reader, something exemplified by the history of the critical reception of Clare's work.

Clare's Fen Aesthetic

"The Flitting" describes an inherent relationship between social and ecological dwelling. Monique Allewaert's recent study of the "swamp sublime"[14] in the American plantation zone shows how boggy landscapes sheltered diasporic Africans who refused slave status. The way these Africans and others, such as Native Americans and poor whites, inhabited these spaces provides new ways of thinking about the construction of the subject during the period: "I argue that instead of simply producing subjects who gained power through an abstract and abstracting print culture, the plantation zone witnessed the emergence of agents who gained power by combining with ecological forces. This shift from subjectivity to agency testifies to an organization of political life that is not dependent on the separation of subjects from an object world" (341). Clare's own combination with ecological forces similarly testifies to a different way of conceiving the organization of political life. These allegiances allow him to reshape the ground of his political being, something also true of other subjected peoples in the world during the period.[15] And Clare's remaking takes place in the boggy fens around Helpston, similar ecologically to the swamps of the American South, both places that were shunned as unhealthy and unappealing by popular taste. Clare's celebration of the boggy landscape around Helpston not only resists a long tradition of the depiction of such spaces in English literature, it makes him part of a global resistance to the broader ideology of empire (including the notion of the inevitability of this ideology). What Alan Vardy writes about Clare's use of local language, "His defence of dialect, vernacular speech and orality in his poetry constituted a cultural intervention fully aware of its social and political implications" (1–2), can be productively applied, as in his "Song" (1821) to Clare's defence of his choice of subject:

> Swamps of wild rush beds & sloughs squashy traces
> Grounds of rough fallows wi thistle & weed
> Flats & low vallies of king cups & daiseys
> Sweetest of subjects are ye for my reed (1–4)

This is a landscape neither picturesque nor beautiful, in the sense in which these categories were generally defined and understood. Clare's poetry often asks us to think outside of received aesthetic categories and seek experience that defies the larger cultural and economic models these aesthetic expectations inhabit. The "rough," and "low," suggestive of an upper-class denigration of the labouring class, become here terms of praise and adulation. The unproductive land, or "fallows," similarly reverses the cliché of the lazy poor and reconfigures a lack of agricultural productivity as an opportunity for poetic propagation.

Though unproductive agriculturally, the plants that pack, and are barely held by these lines, are irresistibly fructifying and, significantly, all rhizomatous. Rushes, thistles, weeds, king cups (marsh marigolds), and daisies all make use of rhizomatic root systems and grow in colonies. This is what makes these plants so resilient and, for "improvers," difficult to eradicate; as long as one rhizome remains, they can reproduce themselves. Clare would also be aware that many of these plants were seen as invasive and unwanted, though they performed important ecological roles, especially as sources of nectar for pollinators (or poets). The thistle is emblematic, its sharp, bristly exterior, unattractive or even threatening to the casual observer, belies the invitation it offers to a host of butterflies, goldfinches, hummingbirds, and bumblebees. The plants culminate in the "reed," itself both a wetland plant and an instrument for poetic composition. The reed is also a rhizomatic plant, a significance that carries over into the types of horizontal open-ended connections Clare's poetics offer.

Clare's praise of wetland spaces take part in a swamping of the sublime that draws our attention to a different kind of landscape and a different sense of what landscapes can do. His panegyrics draw our attention to places disdained throughout the history of English verse and depart from a long tradition in British literature that treated such places as unhealthy, formless, monotonous, or worse. Bridget Keegan writes of the common associations of wetlands with "places of disease, of danger and of spiritual, physical and mental illness," and explains how "The notion that wetlands were threatening, even monstrous, is as old as the beginnings of … English literature. Grendel and his mother are creatures of the swamps, and their marshy monstrosity is linked with the dangerous material "in-betweenness" of wetlands, which are neither land nor water" (150). The association of swampy land with the monstrous parallels its association with sin. Mina Gorji has referenced Bunyan's "Slough of Despond" and similar treatments of wetlands in Milton and Cowper and pointed to Clare's close familiarity with these authors (111–13). Wetlands were viewed as locales of both physical and moral danger that bordered on the supernatural. Even into the twentieth century Seamus Heaney could remember "a warning that older people would give us about going into the bog. They were afraid we might fall into the pools in the old workings so they put it about (and we believed them) that *there was no bottom* in the bog-holes" ("Feeling into Words" 56; original emphasis). Clare writes, knowingly, in the context of this tradition.

In "Song," Clare develops his own way of, in Allewaert's words, "combining with ecological forces," testifying to a different way of conceiving the organization of political life. The close identification with the fenny landscape in "Song" demonstrates the basis for thinking about an ecological subject:

> Ye commons left free in the rude rags of nature
> Ye brown heaths be cloathed in furze as ye be
> My wild eye in rapture adores e'ery feature
> Yere as dear as this heart in my bosom to me   (5–8)

Clare puts his own identity and self-worth emphatically on the same ontological level as the environment he describes. The furze that clothes this landscape would have been seen by many as a sign of unproductive or "waste" land (much as the middle and upper classes often characterized the laziness of the poor), but Clare's alliance with it is precisely what is generative and a source of power. Incidentally, furze was an important source of fuel for the labouring classes (Rackham, qtd. in Ardon 7), something lost on those who did not engage themselves with the lives of the working poor.

Clare's treatment of these landscapes rescues them from a cultural history of infamy and records in detail the particular qualities that give these places value. In the process Clare creates a kind of fen aesthetic that uniquely expresses the relationship between place and poetry. This aesthetic bears close comparison to Allewaert's description of the swamp sublime: "[E]ighteenth-century Anglo-Europeans saw swamps as monstrosities that stalled the subject-making work of the sublime. But the swamping of the sublime gives way to an aesthetics that suffuses persons through places to remake the terrain of the political" (355). In his reiterative insistence on the landscape as suffused through him in "Song" ("Yere as dear as this heart in my bosom to me") and elsewhere, Clare takes part in the swamping of the sublime and the remaking of the political terrain that this effects. Along with others that insisted on the value of such landscapes, Clare was well ahead of his time. There are various wetland conservation and restoration projects underway in the United Kingdom today,[16] as the ecological importance of these environments for wildlife and of peat bogs as carbon sinks has become more widely recognized. Peat bogs are unique in their ability to store information about minute changes in climate and have been used by scientists as one of the primary archives for measuring human impact on the environment,[17] lately subsumed under the term "Anthropocene."

At the close of the "Song," Clare stirringly recognizes others' devaluation of this type of landscape within his own unabashed championing of it:

> Yer skies may be gloomy and misty yer mornings
> Yer flat swampy vallies unwholesome may be
> Still refuse of nature wi out her adorning[s]
> Yere as dear as this heart in my bosom to me

Swampy places, both in England and in the United States often harboured the threat of disease. In the southern United States this was in part what kept most whites away from the swamps and made them a habitable retreat for others. Clare's celebration of the fen indicates not only a deeply personal identification but understands this landscape as a receptacle of cultural memory, one increasingly subject to drainage and enclosure by the economic and political forces of the day. And just as similar places today provide a palaeoecological archive that is critical to understanding the global nature of climate change, so do they record a rich and varied social history that is critical to understanding cultural change.

Though much has been said about the importance of enclosure to Clare's poetics, not much attention has been given to the related draining of the fens, another widespread practice related to the industrialization of farming, and what Ian Rotherham has called "England's greatest ecological disaster."[18] The complete transformation of the landscape Clare describes in this poem parallels Clare's experience on his removal from Helpston, when all his surroundings appeared foreign. And the shrinkage of the peat that occurred as a result of the drainage of Whittlesey Mere, the setting of Clare's "To the Snipe" would create the lowest point on land in Britain, at approximately nine feet below sea level ("UK's Lowest Spot is Getting Lower").

This shrinkage is directly related to the social effects of enclosure as described by E.P. Thompson: "enclosure, as it came to each village, was experienced as catastrophic to the customary culture. Within the space of a year or two the labourers' world shrank suddenly, from 'our' parish to a cottage which might not be their own" (179). "The commons and wastes shrank, in the nineteenth century, to the village greens (if such survived) and communally-shared custom shrank to the "calendar customs" and survivals collected by the folklorists" (182). The erosion of common rights and customs thus parallels the shrinkage of peat as a result of fen drainage. Peat was itself often used as fuel for the drainage engines, just as local labourers were often employed in the processes of drainage and enclosure. What enclosure made visible in terms of social relations was something like what drainage removed from sight ecologically. If "Enclosure had a terrible but instructive visibility" (Neeson, qtd. in Thompson 180), then so too did the drainage of the fens.

This visibility becomes dramatically apparent in the subsidences that took place around many places where drainage was practiced. According to Oliver Rackham,

> In The Fens, more than half the original area of peat has disappeared altogether; houses, bridges, and railways subside and lean; and many rivers are now perched 14 feet or more above the surrounding farmland. A famous illustration of peat wastage is the Holme Fen Post, an iron column, 22 feet long, buried upright in the peat of Holme Fen (Huntingdonshire) when it was drained, apparently for the first time, in 1848. The peat shrank 6 feet in the first twelve years of drainage. By 1890, 10 feet of the Post was exposed. The drainage of Holme Fen was then abandoned, and shrinkage stopped for thirty-five years. Since 1925 the peat has continued to shrink slowly, being affected by the resumed drainage of other fens nearby. By 1978 the total shrinkage was 12 feet 8 1/2 inches. (379)

Holme Fen is on the southern edge of Whittlesey Mere. The subsidences here were not as disastrous as those caused by the salt industry in Cheshire, but they carry the same instructive visibility as to the soundness of the ideological structures upon which such "improvement" was justified. They also show how the effects of human interaction with the land can continue for hundreds of years after the event and make Clare's treatment, in "To the Snipe" of Whittlesey Mere as a refuge surrounded by danger, newly relevant.

"To the Snipe" is written almost twenty years before the drainage of Whittlesey Mere and describes the area as a refuge for the titular bird:

> Lover of swamps
> The quagmire overgrown
> With hassock tufts of sedge – where fear encamps
> Around thy home alone   (1–4)

Though peat is not mentioned by name, it is everywhere in the poem, from the "quagmire" of the opening stanza to the "gelid mass" of the fifth stanza or the "spungy lap" of the sixth. Peat digging here was a source of local employment and fuel for the community for centuries before it was drained. As one commentator, writing just before the drainage commenced, explains: "The turf or peat dug from the upper part of the soil constitutes the chief fuel throughout the fen districts. It is cut out in squares, put into sacks, carted away, and sold in shops or hawked about through the neighbouring towns and villages, at from ten to twelve shillings per 1,000" (Newcombe 278). The phrase "hassock tufts of sedge" is interesting in both its grammatical looseness and its apparent redundancy. The *OED* defines a hassock as "A firm tuft or clump of matted vegetation, esp. coarse grass or sedge" (1a). Thus "tufts of sedge" is already included in the meaning of "hassock," which appears to operate as an adjective here, though the *OED* gives no adjective for this word. Therefore, "hassock" may modify "tufts," which at the same time belongs to "sedge," which is a synonym for "hassock." These grassy plants also suggest lines, and the redundancy of the phrase suggests fecundity, as the lines sprout up everywhere and Clare finds them and writes them down.

Another way in which bogs offer a text to be read is through the history made available in the pollen grains which can be preserved in bogs for thousands of years. As P.V. Glob explains, "Since the pollen of every plant has its own special form, it is possible with the microscope to establish what plants were growing at different points in time. The distinct layers in peat-bogs thus become, as it were, the pages of a great picture-book illustrating the changing flora of the land through the ages" (42). The carving of peat from the earth over thousands of years, significantly shaping the landscape of many areas, also resembles a kind of writing. This cutting imprints itself upon the land, marking it irrevocably into a narration of human interface with the world. Paul Ardon gives an example of this shaping in describing the "extensive but discrete removals of peat" in the Upper Derwent Valley, amounting to "a minimum between 52,881,700 and 79,819,200 cubic metres" (i). In Scotland the changes were likely even more severe, given the predominance of peat deposits there: "over the centuries the use of turf ... has cleared and changed now unimaginable stretches of the countryside" (Fenton, qtd. in Ardon 7). If one considers the large number of peat deposits spread over the four nations, the drastic nature and importance of this landscape shaping comes more clearly into focus.

The rampant drainage of peaty land by "improvers" (also called "adventurers" and "undertakers" [Keegan 151])[19] in Clare's day was often met with resistance from those who dwelled in the fens.[20] Clare's poetry takes part in this resistance (E.P. Thompson refers to Clare as "a poet of ecological protest" [180]), decrying a mechanically regimented

142   In Common Things

appropriation of the natural world for both aesthetic and commercial purposes. Just as moss provides a palaeoecological archive, providing an invaluable source for determining changing weather and climate patterns over huge stretches of time, so Clare's poetry describes moss as an archive of cultural memory and makes possible a reading of a changing cultural climate through the history and use of this substance.

The history of drainage and peat digging in Britain and its importance to Clare's verse cannot be fully understood without reference to an unlikely source, the Dutch Golden Age. Not only did Holland's rise as a world power rely on its extensive use of peat, but Britain imported its methods and tools of drainage from Holland. According to Keegan: "Due to advances in engineering first imported from the Netherlands, the wetland ecosystem in England witnessed wholesale drainage and eradication from the mid-seventeenth century forward, thereby limiting the locations where leeches and other animals and plants dependent on such an environment might thrive" (148). The snipe is just such an animal effected by this widespread drainage.[21] The Dutch were one of the major commercial and colonial powers before Britain rose in dominance late in the eighteenth century and therefore played an integral role in shaping European empire and the growth of commerce with which it was associated. For most of the seventeenth century Holland was the envy of Europe, in its wealth, technical skill, global possessions, and social organization. England consciously imitated the Dutch,[22] as well as entered several wars with them, and though unsuccessful at first, it would in the eighteenth century inherit many former Dutch colonies.[23] The rise of Holland as a global power relied in part on its access to a large and ready supply of energy, specifically peat. Jan de Vries and An van der Woude, in *The First Modern Economy*, point to "the special position that the production of peat held at the intersection of three important physical phenomena: the Netherlands' unique access to low-cost energy, the reclamation of land, and the development of the transportation network" (37). And in "Peat and the Dutch Golden Age: The Historical Meaning of Energy-Attainability," J.W. de Zeeuw investigates how during the seventeenth century peat enabled the rise of a relatively small country with limited resources to a major world power. He poses the question "why were the Dutch able to make use of their peat, while the rest of Europe had to abstain from it?" and goes on to explain: "The Dutch had the good fortune to find their peat very near to, partly even just below the overall water table. This fortunate situation was caused by the rising of the sea level during the holocene. In this country the digging of navigable canals in the peat areas and, more important, the linkage of these canals to the already existing, extensive network of natural waterways was easily done. Since these natural waterways gave access to all important cities, the turf could be directly transported by ship from the peatery to the consumer" (5–6). As with many of the other substances treated in this book, accessibility, low overhead, and convenient means of transportation were essential qualities in contributing to their commercial success and place within broader everyday culture. Though relatively little has been written about the economic and geopolitical importance of peat, it appears worth further investigation, particularly in the role it, and the technologies associated with drainage, played in the rise of Holland as a world power and its role in the larger history of European empire. This would likely open up further unexpected connections between the economic and the literary applications of moss than those I have only been able to treat in a limited way here.

The absence of peat from a consideration of the energy sources that drove European colonialism is oddly related to the way it provides clues to other histories otherwise lost. In both Britain and Scandinavia, peat bogs were places in which relics and bog bodies were discovered, many of these finds likely the remnants of religious ceremonies involving human sacrifice, possibly with the purpose of ensuring a fertile ground and a plentiful harvest. These bodies and the items which attended sacrificial rites were deposited in bog holes where peat had been dug. Peat would then slowly regrow over the bodies in steady accretive layers over the millennia, usually amounting to several feet by the time the bodies were discovered. According to Clayton Tarr, it was during the nineteenth century that "[b]ogs began to be celebrated as portals to national, regional, and personal pasts. The bodies preserved in these bogs not only provided access to prehistoric civilizations predating Roman occupation, but also functioned as material evidence of ancient traditions that were unique to the British Isles" (84). And as Heaney explains, these places were unique storehouses of cultural memory: "So I began to get an idea of bog as the memory of the landscape, or as a landscape that remembered everything that happened in and to it. In fact, if you go round the National Museum in Dublin, you will realize that a great proportion of the most cherished material heritage of Ireland was 'found in a bog'" ("Feelings into Words" 54). The "squelch and slap" of Heaney's "Digging" are also the sounds of poetic production and share an acoustics and foot-feel with the "squashy traces" of Clare's "Song." An important, and often misunderstood aspect of Clare's verse, is that he did not simply value natural objects for their intrinsic wildness but understood a significant aspect of their value as arising from his, and his community's relationship with them over time. The memory of the landscape, and the objects of this memory, are ephemeral and plastic, especially subject to changes the landscape undergoes, and therefore always in danger of disappearance. Memory becomes, as Clare puts it, "both the shadow and the substance" of what no longer remains, and poetry therefore a method of its preservation.

As I began this section by proposing a connection between Clare and those who made wetlands their homes in the American south, I'll conclude it by considering the implications of Clare's work for current issues of global environmental justice. This connection is largely motivated by how the extractive methods taking root in the Romantic period are at the base of our current global environmental crises.[24] As Clare demonstrates so vividly, it is the poor who suffer the brunt of environmental degradation, which is as true today as it was in Clare's day. The forms of industrial agriculture which Clare everywhere decries in his poetry have grown and transformed into a global machinery, and it is now a global poor whose lives and cultures are increasingly threatened by a process that has been the historical source of wealth in the "developed" world. I do not mean here to turn Clare into a spokesperson or representative for those climate refugees that he could not have imagined but, rather, to point to the relevance Clare's work obtains when considered in terms of climate change and its associated injustices. In other words, Clare speaks to these developments now because he has been speaking about them all along.

Because so much of Clare's verse offers a commentary on our current global moment, I can only offer a few brief examples here. I will remain with the poetry discussed already in this chapter to demonstrate a line of continuity between the relation of substance and its historical use to current issues of environmental justice. The burgeoning number of those displaced by climate change is expected to increase as climate disasters become more frequent. Among the many places in Clare that are relevant to this development are the plaintive lines that open "The Flitting":

> Ive left mine own old home of homes
> Green fields & every pleasant place
> The summer like a stranger comes
> I pause & hardly know her face

The phrase "home of homes" creates a sense of internality and suggests something of the effect of loss of place on identity. The inability to recognize summer relates to the disruption of the seasons that is produced by climate change, wherein even the home places become less and less familiar. Clare's poetry, both before and after the move from Helpston, takes on new significance in the wake of what humanity is set to lose.

The precarious atmosphere Clare creates in "To the Snipe" is another example of the relevance of his poetry to our current moment. This poem is one of many that addresses the commons and their impending destruction, as the fens around Whittlesey Mere, where the poem is set, would be drained and enclosed about twenty years after the poem's composition. The poem offers a poignant commentary on the unstable ground that increasingly cannot bear "the weight of man" (7) many inhabit today, including the countless species that have faced extinction due to human activity. As a direct result of drainage, the peat found here in such abundance would dry up and decay, releasing the carbon stored there for millennia. Climate change now increasingly threatens the world's peat stocks, of which northern peatlands alone contain over 1,000 gigatons of carbon (Nichols and Peteet 920), double the estimates for all the carbon released into the atmosphere by humans. According to Ian Lawson, climate change "could destabilize the peatland carbon stores, adding very significantly to the total of human-caused greenhouse gas emissions" (qtd. in MacNamara). Periodic peat fires in current day Indonesia not only significantly contribute to carbon emissions, affecting air quality, and destroy the habitat of orangutans and other fragile species, they also cause serious health problems in humans, particularly in vulnerable segments of the population. These fires, set to clear plots of land for establishing palm oil plantations (not entirely unlike the drainage of land to plant crops), grow out of control due to dry weather conditions caused by El Niño and have caused major disasters in 1997, 2015, and 2019. Though "To the Snipe" is a poem that admires the bird's adaptation to its environment, it is also shot through with a precarity that becomes uncannily relevant to the eventual destruction of the ecosystem it describes and to the dwelling on which life and its expression depend. Clare shows us how the everyday substances around us contain worlds that are interwoven with our lives and our histories. How we value them will no doubt determine our fate.

"The Robin's Nest"

Clare closely considers the importance of moss in the formation of dwelling in his mid-period poem "The Robin's Nest," which opens with an imperative that is both invitation and invocation:

> Come luscious spring come with thy mossy roots
> Thy weed strown banks – young grass – & tender shoots
> Of woods new plashed sweet smells of opening blooms

The sign of spring is not a bud or flower, but moss. This is appropriate if we remember that mosses were thriving for millions of years before the arrival of flowers (Porley 5). Moss iterates a sense of origins, and what Clare expresses in "Emmonsails Heath" (1835) is equally appropriate here: "Things seem the same in such retreats/As when the world began."

The second line conveys a metonymic triad, as occurs, more diffusedly, in "The Flitting," rising vertically from the horizontal mossiness of the scene: "Thy weed strown banks – young grass – & tender shoots" which are also lines, joined by the lines of dashes, creating a structural metonym. "[S]trown" conveys a locality through its spelling and sounding, yet it is a place with no centre, it is a passive and scattered locality of weeds, plants which aggressively destabilize planned agricultural development. The triad of strong vowel sounds that begin the line: "I," "ee," and "o," are reinforced by the line-ending "oo," a euphonic rendering of the compositional harmony of the scene.

The next line further destabilizes a sense of hierarchical human-centred structure by breaking down grammatical hierarchies. Clare's rejection of grammatical and taxonomic structures operates similarly to Deleuze and Guattari's description of the rhizome as "not amenable to any structural or generative model" (12). The absence of a comma between "plashed" and "sweet" creates the possibility that "plashed" not only modifies "woods" but can also modify "smells" and even, adverbally, "sweet." The "Of" with which the line begins sends us back looking for a referent, which at first appears to be "tender shoots" but then spreads to the whole line, which itself refers back to the "mossy roots," the generic sign of spring. The line can be read normatively, with "sweet smells" modifying "new plashed," or it can be read rhizomatically, with the apparent collision between "plashed" and "sweet" breaking down the distinction between "woods" and "smells" and making all adjectives free to modify both/either "woods" and/or "smells." This doubling is also apparent with "blooms," which can normatively refer to flowers or as opening outwards into a verb, in which the "Sweet sunny mornings" of the next line are what blooms, or indeed it is the next line which blooms at the point of a clandestine enjambment. The dash after happiness appears to indicate a grammatical break, as the next words, "to seek & harbor in" appear to start a new sentence. This is not a restless seeking out of a latter-day Ulysses but a seeking to harbour in, to understand a poetics of dwelling as opposed to one of mastery. It is "far from the ruder worlds inglor[i]ous din" because that world now scorns "the splendid gift" that the mossy scene affords.

John Clare's Rhizomatic Poetics   147

The attachment of the speaker to the objects around him mimics the attachment of moss to the surroundings:

> Where nature's glory ever breaths and lives
> Seated in crimping ferns uncurling now
> In russet fringes ere in leaves they bow
> And moss as green as silk – there let me be
> By the great powdered trunk of an old oak tree
> Buried in green delights to which the heart
> Clings with delight and beats as loath to part   (10–16)

This dual clinging of the moss and the heart to its objects evokes the clinging of the poetry to the page, the "beats" which are "loath to part." The combined alliteration and assonance ("And moss as green as silk") blends the words into a textural uniformity. The poet wishes to be "Buried in green delights" and become like these mossy objects around him. The scene offers a protective layer, it "wraps me like a mantle from the storm." Moss establishes a certain interiority, much as it did historically in its widespread use as insulation. The solitude associated with both the observation of the natural world and poetic composition is here associated, not with a Coleridgean "Rime," but with a layering moss.

> The rest of peace the sacredness of mind
> In such deep solitudes we seek and find
> Where moss grows old and keeps an evergreen
> And footmarks seem like miracles when seen   (58–61)

"Footmarks," "leaves," "foot," "composed," and "lined" all have literary import that reinforce the relation between nest and poem. The metonymic relation between the lines of moss, grass and hair, brings to light the line they all create, a line with its own distinct poetic rhythm and pace. Acoustically, this line is echoed in the penultimate line, as "of moss & grass &" mirrors "& bye & bye a," the ampersands weaving the nest together as they link the moments of generation.

The poem comes to rest in dwelling:

> Where still the nest half filled with leaves remains
> With moss still green amid the twisting grains
> Here on the ground and sheltered at its foot
> The nest is hid close at its mossy root

> Composed of moss and grass and lined with hair
> And five brun-coloured eggs snug sheltered there
> And bye and bye a happy brood will be
> The tenants of this woodland privacy

The insistent "still" at the beginning of the line is echoed by "remains" at its end, as "half filled" also suggest a remainder, something left over, even final remains, still in another sense. The "leaves remains" at the end of the line presents a paradox that the physical presence of the nest somehow embodies. As the moss takes part in the nest, we take part in the poem; we are "amid the twisting grains" of the verse, "Here on the ground," sheltered at the metrical "foot" that is associated here, not with the tree as a whole, but with its "mossy root," an imbrication at the heart of the poem. We are led to a destination that is also, through the title, a point of departure. If, "any point of a rhizome can be connected to any other, and must be" (Deleuze and Guattari 7), then the "mossy root" is never an end or a beginning but always a mediation between.

The nest, like the poem, is suffused by moss, as it appears to spread invasively and metonymically through the scene. The mossy root returns here, and rather than a category gestured towards as an augury, appears as a concrete individual, suggesting the progress of the poem as one of individuation, leading to a point of projected genesis, the happy brood that "will be," or the generative effects of the poem on its "tenants" or readers. Clare generally resists enjambment and parodies its use in Wordsworth (Kovesi 80), so its appearance here in the final couplet, especially with the "will be" hanging over the final line, is suggestive. Though Clare could not have read it, the emphasis on a generative futurity in this enjambment recalls the "something evermore about to be" from Book Six of *The Prelude*. Moss not only provides the physical space which makes dwelling possible, it is also lined through this dwelling, it is both the fructifying "mossy root[s]" of spring, and the characteristic "mossy eaves"[25] of the Helpston cottage, enabling the very idea of home that everywhere lines Clare's poetics.

Conclusion: Plastic Rime

While the Romantics found a social value in the common thing, it can be difficult to see what this value might mean today; though we certainly have common things, they are no longer what they were, and we no longer hold them in common. Indeed, the centuries-old practices that revolved around holding things in common were disappearing in the Romantic period. E.P. Thompson writes that the eighteenth century was "the century in which the commoners finally lost their land, in which the number of offences carrying the capital penalty multiplied, in which thousands of felons were transported, and in which thousands of lives were lost in imperial wars; a century which ended … in severe rural immiseration" (18). These calamitous events were taking place at the same time Romantic authors were developing a new aesthetic, and they (as well as other global practices) provide a necessary context not only to this development but to the approach I have taken in this book, which has sought to demonstrate how common things inform cultural practice and production even as the very basis of that commonality began to undergo a dramatic shift.

This shift resonates throughout Romantic literature and culture, and its implications would be dramatic for the generations to follow, as rapid advancement in industrial methods of production followed by a technological revolution would place individuals at ever further removes from the everyday things that had, for thousands of years, made up such a large part of human daily experience. Not only has our relationship with things changed, the material objects of our daily life are no longer the same. We spend more time interacting with plastic today than we do with any of the telluric substances studied in this book. Matter, as we understand it, has thus gone through a kind of transmutation, as have we. The authors studied here remind us of an older system of material relations, less abstracted, less related to industrial production, less dependent on market forces, and more rooted in a flow between ecological relations and cultural production.

This conclusion argues that Samuel Taylor Coleridge's *The Rime of the Ancient Mariner* provides a way to think through the connection between the contemporary ubiquity of plastic in the environment and the Romantic depiction of the plastic relation between material qualities and cultural products. Plasticity, as Greg Ellerman points out, is an "unacknowledged but formative presence throughout romantic writing on nature and art" (212). I seek to demonstrate here that it is not only important to recognize the way the Romantics wrote about and experienced the natural world but that these forms of experience and of text are especially relevant to our own geohistorical moment. The Romantic regard for the plastic, mutually shaping relation between people and things has become fundamental to understanding what it now means to live on a plasticized earth.

The intimate relations between material things and cultural production that I have explored in this book attain another layer when considered in terms of our contemporary relation to plastic. Both miracle substance that has come to be part of every aspect of our lives, and waste product that in its spread into the ecosystem has become part of the food chain and part of our bodies, plastic is representative of the nature of capitalist economies and their effects on nature. This spread not only mimics the expansion of European empire over the face of the globe during the eighteenth and nineteenth centuries; it also engages in a microscopic form of colonization, known as "ecological invasion," in which pieces of plastic ferry organisms from one place to another, transforming the nature of local ecologies. In both a macro- and microscopic sense, modernity floats on these waters, its ideological investments long since detached from any landed locality or national identity, its essential and pervasive homelessness represented in Coleridge's figure of the Mariner floating on an unmanned vessel, which itself will become waste by the poem's end. This knowledge echoes in the first words the Mariner speaks in the poem: "There was a ship." The Mariner is interrupted, must begin again, and this line becomes redundant, disconnected from the tale, a floating constative in a sea of verse that can only repeat but can't get absorbed into a fuller narrative.[1]

Plastic is made possible by a trajectory of exploration and imaginative discovery that was foundational to the development of Romanticism. It's inventor, Leo Baekeland, claimed Benjamin Franklin as a seminal influence and left a promising academic career in Europe for an uncertain one as an inventor in America. The type of scientific endeavour of which he was part is all too often conceived of in

Figure 6.1 The original logo for the Bakelite Corporation, founded in 1910 by Leo Baekeland, the inventor of plastic.

terms of an altruistic pursuit of knowledge, belying its historical connection to European exploration and "discovery,"[2] that linked the pursuit of knowledge with that of personal enrichment and political gain, with little consideration of the rights of other human and non-human beings. Domination and appropriation is the "shared philosophy underlying industrial enterprise as well as so-called disinterested science, which are indistinguishable in this respect" (Serres 32). The way eighteenth-century explorers depicted the world as an endless resource there for the taking mirrors the way Baekeland saw the infinite potential uses of plastic.[3] Baekeland used this notion as a marketing tool, illustrated by the Bakelite corporate logo (see Figure 6.1 above), an ironic symbol in that it also represents the resistance of plastic to biodegradation, something with which Baekeland was unconcerned. The repetitive pattern in which plastic waste is released into the environment, to break down into ever more iterations, bears a resemblance to the poem's reiterative tendency, the "look with which they looked on me" that "never passed away" (255–6).

Since 2020, Coleridge's poem exists in a world in which human-made substances outweigh total biomass (Elhacham et al. 442). This unbearable, weary weight[4] is not only an environmental issue but interrogates the Romantic understanding of the relation between mind and world. The guilt and penance the Mariner undergoes, and the way that penance is often blocked, frame our own moment; we too are faced with our inability to escape, or even to meaningfully address, the unintended consequences of our actions. In this sense, the gothic imagery of the poem that appears, according to Raimonda Modiano, to overpower the Christian framing, mirrors the way environmental crisis today threatens to overwhelm our physical and mental frames. The billions of neurons in our brain now share a reciprocity with the billions of tons of plastic that litter the globe.

What follows provides a close reading of the poem that situates the romantic reciprocity between mind and world in the context of how "rime" is representative of plastic waste. I consider the dispersal of plastic into the environment in terms of the continual blockages to the flow of communication in *The Rime*, what Sean Barry calls a "poetics of interruption"[5] (379). The way rime (and plastic) encases its object indicates both the preservative capability of text and an imminent threat to the object's continued existence. Further, rime is composed of small ice particles with air pockets between them, thus its fragility, not unlike the way language in the poem is subject to interruption and fragmentation. The very grammatical unit of the particle behaves like the microplastic, in that it is a word "that does not change its form through inflection and does not fit easily into the established system of parts of speech" (McArthur and McArthur 454). The resistance of plastic particles to biodegradation leaves them to amass not only in the environment but in human and non-human bodies, with effects we are only beginning to understand. Just as rime is part of the Mariner (his "beard with age is hoar" [619]), so plastic is part of us. We appear at risk of increasingly becoming, like the Mariner, a composition of particulates, "as is the ribbed sea-sand" (227). Just as the Mariner's body is a site of guilt and recurring pain, so global sea sand today is infected with microplastics (Urban-Malinga et al.), producing what are now called "plastiglomerates," or organic materials encased in molten plastic. This journey of plastic from its consumption by the market to its consumption by bodies and by the earth is both example of and commentary on the romantic reciprocity between mind and world.

The preceding chapters appear in a new light when seen in the context of this commentary. Though John Clare's depiction of moss might appear diametrically opposed to the contemporary spread of plastic waste, the two substances share some important similarities. Both form a layer over things, both preserve, both are long-lasting, and both have aesthetic qualities that incorporate themselves into specific cultural fabrics. Yet moss is not made, but is self-generative, it does not threaten ecosystem survival, but contributes significantly to it, it does not harm human and animal bodies, but provides them with comfort and ease. Moss mirrors plastic in several ways, yet its fructification enriches life in its various forms rather than depriving it of its ability to thrive (see albatross). Unlike the alarming and seemingly unstoppable spread of microplastics into the ecosystem and food chain, the small, seemingly insignificant, and easily ignored become in Clare's work the basis for being, meaning, and living in the world.

The Rime's original publication is roughly equidistant from the publication of Ralph Cudworth's theory of plastic nature in 1678 and the invention of plastic by Leo Baekeland in 1907. The notion of a plastic principle, from which all things take their shape and character, was forwarded by the Cambridge Neoplatonists, Cudworth foremost among them, and was an important influence on Coleridge's earlier work.[6] This theory was meant to combat a rising tide of mechanistic and materialistic theories about the nature of the physical world that challenged orthodox Christian explanations of the place of God in the working of nature. Essentially, it posits a principle within nature that unconsciously unfolds divine will. Individual forms of life are embedded with a type of blueprint, that without the need of their self-awareness or will, expresses the divine plan for their specific life form.[7] Coleridge, in "The Eolian Harp," describes a "Plastic and vast ... intellectual breeze," giving consciousness to the natural world and putting it in direct dialogue with the mind. Yet, in *The Rime*, this reciprocity is experienced as a trauma that can today be read in terms of the relation between the plasticity of nature and the plastic that everywhere invades it. It is as if the divinely embedded directions for the operations of the natural world have been transformed, through Western industrial development, to a human direction of the operations of the material world, resulting in plastic embedded in bodies,[8] in the ocean, and in the earth. As Christina Flores describes Cudworth's plastic nature, it "penetrates and permeates nature down to its lowest plants and animals" (143). In its consumption by various species (including the human, the albatross, and the microorganism), the same can be said of plastic today. The plasticity of nature, its transformative capability, is penetrated and permeated by a plastic that resists transformation.

The strangeness of this relation between Romantic nature and contemporary ecological crisis is captured in the way the poem repeatedly unearths the reader's experience. Throughout the poem, we come upon things we think we know that on closer inspection turn out to be something stranger. Early in the poem the "ice, mast-high came floating by/ As green as emerald" (53–4). This striking image is transformed in the next lines:

And through the drifts of snowy clifts
Did send a dismal sheen:
Nor shapes of men nor beasts we ken –
The ice was all between.   (55–8)

The shapes of natural beings are missing, and the seascape takes on an artificiality (as it will do again and again in the poem). As the gloss explains, "no living thing was to be seen," and this is increasingly the case in the growing garbage patches in the world's oceans. This absence of living forms is compounded with a sense of siege: "The ice was here, the ice was there,/The ice was all around" (59–60). Like the ubiquity of plastic in the world today, the ice appears as ubiquitous, inescapable, and threatening.

The systems of production employed during the Romantic period laid the grounds for the contemporary spread of plastic waste. This threatening ubiquity and its relation to rime/plastic recalls the experience of Mary Prince in the salt ponds of Turks Island, where the salt invades the bodies of those producing it, "eating in some cases down to the very bone." The entering of salt into bodies has a historical relation to a host of physical ills, hypertension being prominent among them, setting the stage for the current entry of plastic into human bodies through exploitative methods of production and consumption. A substance that appears so uncommonly useful becomes, through a long process of accretion, suddenly ominous, infectious, and debilitating. This is true of both salt in Prince's narrative and plastic in our contemporary biosphere. The dulling of Prince's vision as a result of working in conditions of unbearable whiteness resembles the effects of the turn from natural substances to manmade ones in a host of applications and processes common to modern life. The homogeneity of plastic belies the unique variety of the objects of the natural world, creating experience of a sameness that is drastically different from our ancestors' experience of the natural variety of the world. Prince's narrative further brings to light the increasingly global nature of trade and the essential part the African diaspora played in the development of this global system. This contribution has all too often been considered separately from questions of Western economics and culture, and this study has attempted to recognize that these questions cannot be appropriately addressed without consideration of the diasporic experience.

When the albatross "ate the food it ne'er had eat" (67), we can see a phenomenon common to the consumption of commodities in Europe at the time Coleridge is writing, as exotic foreign consumables, often the product of slave labour, had become objects of desire for a growing middle class. It's now clear that a pattern of consumption rooted in the spread of global capitalism has brought about climate change, which in turn has unforeseen implications for cultural production, mediation, and preservation, concerns central to the circulation of the Ancient Mariner's tale. The context this pattern of consumption provides, considered alongside the poem's penitential economy, links the Romantic concern about the consequences of imperial expansion with contemporary attention to human effects on the biosphere.

The bond between empire and ecocrisis is found on the modern ocean, what Christopher Connery has termed "Western capital's primary myth element" (686). The new and rapidly spreading habits of consumption attending capitalism's global expansion parallel contemporary habits of consumption by the ocean's wildlife. Albatrosses are among a small group of tube-nosed seabirds that consume six times the amount of plastic as other seabirds, likely due to the resemblance of plastic to its prey. "It ate the food it ne'er had eat," taking part in the entry of plastic into the global food chain. Though we've known for some time that albatrosses eat plastic, only recently has evidence been offered as to why or how much. A study in the November 2016 issue of *Science Advances* demonstrates that albatrosses are attracted to plastic by the smell it gives off once it is in the ocean long enough to accumulate organic matter. According to the authors of the study, plastic debris provides a "substrate for biota that produce infochemicals" (Savoca et al. 1), one of which, Dimethyl Sulfide, or DMS, signals to the albatross that food is nearby, as this chemical is produced by the plankton which attract the albatross's prey.

The scientific term for the gradual accumulation of organic matter on human structures is "biofouling." This sense of being fouled by the bios is central to the action of *The Rime* (rime is also a type of biofouling). The first use of the term, according to the *OED*, is in the "Procedures of the 11th Mid-year Meeting of the American Petroleum Institute" in 1941 and refers to "deposits of slime … in refinery water circuits." The process whereby plastic is produced from petroleum is indicative of the "new spirit" of capitalism that relies on technological advances and fluid supply chains to produce seemingly endless growth. The biofouling of plastic in the oceans, and the resulting consumption by albatrosses and other biota, is a product of and commentary on this "new spirit," just as *The Rime* offers a commentary on the capitalist structures of its own day. In disguising plastic's appearance, biofouling makes it more likely to be mistaken for food. This misconception of plastic for food parallels the consumer's misconception of what it is they consume. Just as biofouling effaces the signs of plastic's manmade production, commodities efface the labour of those who produce them.

Much of the plastic in the ocean today can be found in large formations of garbage patches formed by circular patterns in ocean currents, known as gyres, that circle large areas of stationary, calm water, much like the calm of the setting of Parts II–IV of *The Rime*. This suggests an inevitable connection to Yeats's "Second Coming," where the farther the animal must turn in these gyres, the more things fall apart; the falcon cannot hear the falconer, nor can the albatross come to the Mariner's hollo. The lines which focus on the albatross's absence are indicative of what has been called a sixth mass extinction event, the first primarily caused by human activity. The consumption of plastic by microorganisms leads to chemicals being absorbed through each trophic level of the food chain through a process known as biomagnification; the resulting health effects for "higher" animals are still poorly understood. The consumption of plastic by the albatross is a sign of a larger ecological crisis, signalled by a second coming of the commodity, not slouching towards Bethlehem but rising from the ocean foam.

A recent study on the Great Pacific Garbage Patch (GPGP) found that the single biggest contributor to the total mass of its plastic comes from what are known as ghost nets. These are fishing nets, made of plastic for durability and longevity, that are discarded, lost, or forgotten, yet continue to function on their own. This product, designed to fulfil a specific task and that can do so without any human intervention, replicates the way the theory of plastic nature posits an unconscious expression of purpose within the natural world. It also pathologically mirrors the productive agency of substances described elsewhere in this book. One popular type of net, the gillnet, is suspended by buoys and forms a vertical wall hundreds of feet long. Once the net becomes over-full, it sinks to the sea floor, where the fish are eaten by crustaceans and other fish. The net then rises back to the surface to fill up again, and the cycle continues. This process is known as ghost fishing. This ghostly agency bears a resemblance to the ghostly actors that motivate the events of *The Rime*. And the recurring nature of this process parallels the cyclical, circulatory narrative of the poem, describing something not alien to human agency but an inevitable result of what it sets into motion.

Ghost nets and ghost fishing inevitably imply a ghost ship:

> At first it seemed a little speck,
> And then it seemed a mist:
> It moved and moved, and took at last
> A certain shape, I wist. (149–52)

All the seeming and moving here overwhelm the "certain shape" the object takes, which is anything but certain. The apparition, what we "wist" of it, changes radically between speck, mist, and shape, commenting on what it means to "wist" at all. This is intensified by the concentrated repetition in the following stanza: "A speck, a mist, a shape, I wist!/And still it neared and neared." The effect here is not only one of repetition but in its removal of time-order words it suggests a simultaneity of multiple incongruous qualities, creating a tension between dynamic change and consistent duration, the same tension elucidated by plastic as concept and as thing.

This transformation not only suggests a certain plasticity of knowing, it also resembles the way plastic breaks down in the marine environment into smaller and smaller pieces, moving in the opposite direction from a certain shape to a microscopic speck. The plasticity of knowledge over time resembles the resistance of plastic to final biodegradation and assimilation into the environment. The line "And still it neared and neared" is suggestive of both the increasing spread of plastic into all the earth's ecosystems (as witnessed by the recent discovery of a plastic bag at the bottom of the Mariana Trench), and the concomitant entry into the food chain and into our own bodies, pathologically blurring the subject/object division.

The way bodies become things in the poem is relevant to the way things become part of bodies in the animal, human, and ecosystem consumption of plastic waste. When the crew fall down dead, they do so as "a lifeless lump" (218), and the Mariner is described shortly afterwards in terms of "ribbed sea sand" (227). The seeming lack of agency of all the human actors in the poem is in one sense a sign of their becoming object-like. Marx's description of the worker's identification with the commodity is relevant here, but equally important is the way in which this replaces a former identification with the natural world. The Mariner is so "Alone, alone, all, all, alone" in this sense because he has lost the ability to identify his place in the broader ecosystem, the "all" which can now only serve to connote the Mariner's separation from the "all-one." As Robin Wall Kimmerer puts it, "As our human dominance of the world has grown, we have become more isolated, more lonely when we can no longer call out to our neighbors" (*Braiding Sweetgrass* 209). This inability to call out is figured in the Mariner's inability to pray (264) and his identification with the "thousand thousand slimy things" (258) that are highly suggestive of plastic waste. The fact that the dead crew do not "rot nor reek" (254) is another sign of the unnatural stasis that is repeated throughout the poem and parallels the ability of plastic (and verse) to preserve, which is so essential to its widespread production and use.

I cite the following stanza in its entirety for how it represents the poetics of waste in terms of an essential contradiction: that between the dynamic and the stagnant, the momentary and the lasting.

> Her beams bemocked the sultry main,
> Like April hoar-frost spread;
> But where the ship's huge shadow lay,
> The charmed water burnt alway
> A still and awful red. (267–71)

Moonlight is figuratively transformed into rime (synonymous with hoar-frost until late in the nineteenth century), and the fluid surface of the water appears to transform into a solid, similar to the way plastic is formed from liquid oil derivatives. A poetics of waste is furthered by the following lines in which an unnatural (or "charmed") water does what is antithetical ("burnt"), in a static, freezing way ("alway"). Plastic similarly captures the process of dynamic motion in the many forms it takes, and the quality of unmoving stillness in its persistence in the biosphere (the "hoary flakes" of the following stanza bear comparison to microplastics in this regard). The "red" of the water is suggestive; if the poem's first part had foreshadowed something infernal with its dropping out of sight from all recognizable systems of value, here that foreshadowing is brought to fruition (this is brought out even further in the 1798 edition, in which the Mariner's "own flesh/Was red as in a glare" [487–8]). The persistence of plastic in the marine environment resembles the persistence of the gaze of the dead mariners, "The look with which they looked on me/Had never passed away" (255–6). The Mariner must look "Beyond the shadow of the ship" (272), or of his received notions of human place and purpose, to see his essential ontological sameness with the other living things around him. It is in this recognition that the initial curse is expiated.

The redness of the waters (and the Mariner's flesh) allows us to grasp the ecological significance of Felicia Hemans's depiction of the palm and the origins of the modern palm oil industry in the trade between Britain and West Africa during the Romantic period. Raw palm oil is red in colour, and it was commonly used in early nineteenth-century Britain as both an industrial lubricant and as a primary ingredient in soap. The infernal atmosphere suggested by the red waters of the poem is literalized in the increasing intensity of forest fires in modern-day Indonesia (where much of the world's palm oil is produced) and their lasting effects on the health of children and other vulnerable groups. These forest fires are often the result of attempts to clear land for palm oil plantations, thus, like plastic production, equating the primacy of use value with the destruction of environmental and cultural ecologies. The subtle, yet persistently subversive, thread within Hemans's poetics shares a tendency in common with Coleridge's critique of empire in *The Rime*, both offering an important yet underappreciated way of reading contemporary environmental crises.

It would be tempting to argue that the vengeance required by the spirit of the deep (377) is carried out today in various ecological catastrophes, inflicting life-altering trauma on those in their wake,[9] were it not for the fact that the industrial West is largely responsible for these catastrophes. The sudden and superhuman acceleration of the ship in the following stanzas are suggestive of another "great acceleration" of carbon production, species extinction, and environmental degradation, beginning roughly at the end of the Second World War and continuing into our current moment.[10] Read in this light, the Mariner appears as a kind of climate refugee,[11] forced to wander and recount his tale of loss, driven by forces beyond his control. The excessive penance demanded of the Mariner is something like the excessive force unleashed by unabated human industrial activity. *The Rime* relates both what James McKusick calls "a parable of ecological transgression" (385) and one of human trauma, reflecting the plastic relationship between mind and world.

The affect of this relationship between mind and world in the context of ecological distress is aptly described by lines that oddly appear immediately after another layer of the curse "was snapt" (442). Regardless of our awareness, our situation is "Like one" who walks "in fear and dread,"

> And having once turned round walks on,
> And turns no more his head,
> Because he knows, a frightful fiend
> Doth close behind him tread.   (446–51)

Though these lines could be said to apply to ecological crises more broadly, they are particularly relevant in describing the threat of plastic waste, as its effects are only beginning to be understood, which adds to its impending menace. Desire and dread are conveniently wrapped for our precarious consumption. Like the reader of *The Rime*, we are both thoughtless wedding guest and cursed Mariner at once.

The way *The Rime* dramatizes the exchange between the Mariner and wedding guest provides a framework for reading the relationship between Armytage and the traveller in Wordsworth's "The Ruined Cottage." In both cases a long tale of woe is followed by a gesture of reconciliation, and in both cases this gesture fails to sufficiently account for the affective returns of the tale. In this sense, the Mariner's suffering reflects that of Robert, the unwilling mariner, who enlists out of desperation to fight in one of Britain's colonial conflicts. The way *The Rime* has something to tell us about contemporary plastic waste is mirrored in the way "The Ruined Cottage" narrates something about increasing conflict over the control of resources. The wood that serves mutely as participatory witness in the scenes of Robert's enlistment and Margaret's grief is emptied of its larger cultural significance through the vast deforestation of Britain and the broader instrumentalization of the natural world. It is just this instrumentalization that makes the invention and widespread use of a product like plastic possible. The comfortless and barren plain that sets the scene of "The Ruined Cottage" is something like the confining vastness of the Mariner's ocean; just as the Latin *vastus* describes vast spaces and provides the root for "waste," these poems both describe wastes and comment on waste.

The reciprocal relationship between mind and world is allegorized by the relationship between ships and wind in the poem, which itself can be read in terms of the relation between the plasticity of capitalism and the dependence of capitalism on plastic as an empowering force. Plastic mingles strangely with our own bodies, as the wind "mingled strangely" with the Mariner's fears. The Hermit's extended commentary on the sails early in part seven is relevant to the way plastic nature becomes plastic waste:

> "Strange, by my faith!" the Hermit said –
> "And they answered not our cheer!
> The planks look warped! and see those sails,
> How thin they are and sere!
> I never saw aught like to them,
> Unless perchance it were
>
> "Brown skeletons of leaves that lag
> My forest-brook along;
> When the ivy-tod is heavy with snow,
> And the owlet whoops to the wolf below,
> That eats the she-wolf's young." (527–37)

The strangeness of the ship's appearance, especially that of its sails, appears to fall outside the Hermit's understanding of the world. The lack of a customary response to the cheer of those witnessing the ship's arrival is indicative of the transformation that has occurred from life to life-in-death, from plastic nature to plastic-in-nature. The Hermit "never saw aught like" the sails that are the sign of this transformation, echoing the experience of the albatross that "ate the food it ne'er had eat," bookending the narrative in terms of the unprecedented. In struggling to find a likeness, it is no accident that the Hermit turns to "skeletons," or the detritus of what has been broken down that litters the local waterways. These skeletons "lag" as does the line itself through the stanza break, drawing attention once more to the dual sense of "rime." That the scene is set within the context of scarcity and predation recalls the Mariner's prey, while pointing to the important difference between the necessary and arbitrary taking of life.

The question of the Mariner's identity, which is soon to follow, is therefore impossible for the Mariner to answer, as he cannot claim an identity outside his relations with others, both human and non-human. He can only tell his story, the only anodyne available to the pain he suffers, an agony that, in the context of a poetics of waste, is related to the various ailments (suffered by humans and non-humans) brought about by environmental degradation. The Mariner's final words offer some sense of not only his penance but the actions that must be taken by those in the "developed" world, should we hope to prevent the most disastrous events from forever marking both the earth and the human culture that it sustains. It is not in consumption, nor in prayer, but in concerted action that there is any reason for hope. As the Mariner claims:

> Oh sweeter than the marriage-feast,
> 'Tis sweeter far to me,
> To walk together to the kirk
> With a goodly company! – (601–4)

The act of walking together is "sweeter" than the marriage-feast (and its heteronormative reproductive futurity), also calling into question the very quality of sweetness in an era where a great influx of sugar was transforming cultural norms. The Mariner points to an older notion of sweetness that is not dependent on this commodity imported from across the ocean or on the slave labour that produced it. Walking is here a habitual act of sociability that supplants the habitual consumption signified by the marriage-feast. Like the Mariner's opening gesture, it interrupts the act of consumption and in doing so not only replaces it but undermines a logic of economic relations based on a notion of continual growth and expansion. It is in a communal movement between the spaces of cultural institutions that the Mariner gestures towards another possible space for the creation of value. And by extending the notion of love towards "All things both great and small" (615), the Mariner goes beyond the command of "love thy neighbour," beyond the merely social obligation to invoke the necessity of love for all the earth's inhabitants, for the earth itself, even (or especially) one filled with plastic. As Michel Serres writes, the law of social obligation "remains silent about mountains and lakes, for it speaks to men about men as if there were no world" (49). It is now time to turn away from the bridegroom's door and face this world, no longer as shadow that follows close behind but in recognition of that other part of ourselves.

Love of the earth itself, or geophilia, stands in direct contrast to the history of Eurocentric exceptionalism that has abstracted the human from its communal reciprocity with the natural world. Mary Wollstonecraft's *Letters* dramatize how geophilia offers a salvific alternative to a hostile social world and an alienating view of materiality. Though, like the Mariner, she often experiences a paralyzing sense of loneliness, she is able to escape this through a communion with the natural objects surrounding her, especially the ever-present stone. We can learn from her, as from the Mariner, how to love when such an act appears both impossible and illogical.

The Mariner's exhortation to love "things both great and small" thus can achieve a meaning beyond its false purport to moralize the tale. The admonition corresponds with the lines with which I began the introduction to this book: "The admiration and the love, the life/In common things." In the introduction I focused heavily on the closing words of this phrase, and I would like now, by way of conclusion, to pay some attention to the opening ones.

"The admiration … the love" and "the life" ascend from the superficial, to the all-engrossing, to being itself. The Romantics ask us to gaze more intently upon what is common to us all, to realize what is ultimately the shared nature of our material and cultural existence. Admiration, love, life: each grows from the other, beginning from a relation with natural things. To hold something in common is not merely to establish a set of social relations, it is to develop a state of consciousness that is markedly different from that engendered by private ownership; it is to instill a sense of dignity through the recognition of an active reciprocity. There is an element of duty to this relationship, one that we so urgently need to rediscover today.

What Wordsworth describes as the inception of his poetic career through a relationship with things, like Coleridge's insistence on the primacy of things at the end of his arguably most influential poem, are not retreats from the political upheaval of their day but directly address the way social organization arises from particular forms of relationship with the natural world. What the great social contracts of the period forget is that the social world depends on the natural world, not the other way around. We are now faced with the difficult task of relearning the primacy of the natural world and resituating our social relations accordingly. But this task need not, indeed cannot, commence as an onerous one. It begins with admiration and leads to love, providing the path that will be necessary should we wish for life to flourish.

Notes

Introduction

1 *De Rerum Natura* 123–4; book 2.
2 For an insightful analysis of Lucretian *vestigia*, see Jacques Lezra, *On the Nature of Marx's Things: Translation as Necrophilology*, 49f.
3 The commentary on this history is too vast to summarize here. For an excellent study of the history of the commons in relation to Romantic literature (specifically the poetry of John Clare), see John Barrell, *The Idea of Landscape and the Sense of Place*. For a description of the commons as part of traditional common rights, see E.P. Thompson, *Customs in Common*.
4 Perhaps most famously is Hardt and Negri's influential *Commonwealth*, which develops a utopic theory around the concept of the common as beyond property rights but is still largely focused on human cultural production. Another important deployment of the concept is in Fred Moten and Stefano Harney's *The Undercommons*, which theorizes the Black radical tradition.
5 Katey Castellano finds that, for Thomas Bewick and John Clare, "it is not just the sensual life that we have in common with animals, but also a habitus in common" (89). It is this type of common I have in mind here, expanded to include what is shared with all natural things.
6 Alaimo's description of what the application of this idea means is similar to what this book aspires to: "[T]he movement across human corporeality and nonhuman nature necessitates rich, complex modes of analysis that travel through the entangled territories of material and discursive, natural and cultural, biological and textual" (3).
7 Like "the commons," the body of scholarship is too large to summarize here. The contemporary discussion usually begins with Heidegger's distinction between a thing and an object, the influence of this on the development of "thing theory" by Bill Brown and others, and more

recently the explosion of several new materialisms. Some representative examples include Jane Bennet's *Vibrant Matter*, Graham Harman's *Object Oriented Ontology*, Levi Bryant's *The Democracy of Objects*, Ian Bogost's *Alien Phenomenology*, Karan Barad's *Meeting the Universe Halfway*, and Daniel Miller's *Materiality*.

8 In the sense defined by the *OED*: "The action or fact of sharing or holding something in common with others; mutual participation; *the condition of things so held*, mutuality, community, union" (1a; my emphasis).

9 I use this term to indicate that this book comments on the history of the formation of disciplinary knowledge in the West. This is not meant as an attack on disciplinarity but, rather, a recognition of how it shapes ways of thinking and being in the world.

10 The conversation could be said to go back to the Romantics themselves.

11 Some notable exceptions include Vin Nardizzi's *Wooden Os: Shakespeare's Theatres and England's Trees* (2013), Jeffrey Jerome Cohen's *Stone: An Ecology of the Inhuman* (2015), and Jules David Law's *The Social Life of Fluids* (2010).

12 Donna Haraway makes the point that "We become-with each other or not at all" (4). Though Haraway is more concerned with the animal in this work than the vegetable or mineral, her statement is all the more relevant when applied to all these areas. Part of what this book seeks to accomplish is to provide a historical and cultural record of this becoming with.

13 Though the rhizome is theorized by Giles Deleuze and Felix Guattari, and I quote them later in this book, my treatment of the rhizome centres on its biological function rather than its theoretical significance.

14 *The Prelude* (401–5; book 2).

15 That is, if not wipe it out completely, as the science increasingly suggests.

16 An undated poem written at the Northampton General Lunatic Asylum at some time between 1842 and 1856 (*Major Works* 494).

17 "My Early Home was This" (17–24). In *The Later Poems of John Clare*, edited by Eric Robinson and David Powell, vol. 1, Oxford UP, 1984.

18 Nixon 241. This figure is for the flowers packed in Covent Garden. Nixon goes on to point out that "some of the leading firms of florists in London have factories on the Continent for the collection and preparation of moss" demonstrating the international scope of the industry in the nineteenth century.

19 The role of peat in the rise of Dutch empire and the importance of Dutch colonial expansion for the British empire is discussed in chapter 5.

20 The relation between enclosure and incarceration takes on a new relevance today, where in the United States the percentage of young Black men who can expect to be incarcerated (over 25 per cent, compared to around 4 per cent for their white peers [Bonzcar and Beck 1]) harkens back to the oppression of Jim Crow and occurs alongside a variety of new forms of

enclosure, including such phenomena as the nationalization of oceans, drilling in national nature reserves, and the many examples of the privatization of formerly public cultural products and activities.
21 Simon Gikandi describes the Atlantic slave trade as "one of the informing conditions of civilized culture" (i).
22 This movement and its implications are thoroughly detailed in Alan Bewell's *Natures in Translation*.
23 One way this interdependence was visible was through Romantic literature itself. In tracing the presence of Wordsworth abroad, Katherine Bergren observes that his poetry could serve to connect "Wordsworth's local sphere to other faraway local spheres and reveal their reciprocal implication and inextricable interdependence" (6).
24 Debates about disciplinarity and interdisciplinarity that both dwell on the nature of knowledge and the corporatization of the academy sometimes fail to acknowledge the extent to which disciplines have always borrowed from one another. It is difficult to imagine what English studies would be today, for example, were it not for the diverse disciplinary tools it routinely employs.
25 Siraj Ahmed demonstrates how the legacy of colonization continues to produce destruction through the practice of a colonial logic: "This colonial logic – wherein property and law metamorphose into environmental devastation and emergency – still defines conflicts throughout the peripheries" (13).
26 I refer here to an earlier phase of historicism, exemplified by the work of such critics as Jerome McGann, Marjorie Levinson, and the early work of Alan Liu, that was responding to purely aesthetic, text-isolating treatments of Romantic literature.

1 Mary Wollstonecraft's Social Geology

1 Stone as a subject of Romantic contemplation has been taken up to great effect elsewhere, perhaps most notably in Noah Heringman's *Romantic Rocks, Aesthetic Geology* and in chapter 8 of Mary Jacobus's *Romantic Things*. This chapter is indebted to these works, especially Heringman's interdisciplinary analysis of the relationship between geology, economics, and aesthetics during the Romantic period.
2 For the historical reception of this work, see Harriet Devine Jump, ed., *Mary Wollstonecraft and the Critics 1788–2001*, 2 vols., and Janet Todd's *Mary Wollstonecraft: An Annotated Bibliography*. The essays mentioned in this chapter provide some of the most innovative work on the *Letters* to date, from Nancy Yousef's "Wollstonecraft, Rousseau and the Revision of Romantic Subjectivity" (1999) to Mary Favret's "Wollstonecraft's Antigone" (2019).

3 Though there have been fingers pointed in this direction. Mary Heng, for example, notes how Wollstonecraft calls attention to material details of everyday life: "Wollstonecraft makes the condition of nursing women, heretofore hidden … concrete by bringing it to textual life" (374).
4 Of which Thomas Thomson, in his *Travels in Sweden* in 1812 notes: "The great rock of which it [i.e. Sweden] is almost wholly composed, is gneiss" (399). And as Robert Bremner writes of Norway in 1840, "The most abundant rock is gneiss" (107). The word most likely comes from a Middle High German verb meaning "to spark."
5 Besides William Godwin and Robert Southey's enthusiastic reception, the majority of reviews of the work were positive, many comparing the more personal tone in the *Letters* with the language of the two *Vindications*. The work was almost immediately translated into several European languages.
6 "[B]anding in some gneisses develops by an incompletely understood process called metamorphic differentiation. During differentiation chemical reactions segregate different minerals into different layers" (Marshak 195).
7 Mary Jacobus describes an excerpt from Wordsworth's *Guide to the Lakes*, in which he "notes that the initials W. (his own initial) and Y. are the characteristic shapes inscribed by the erosion of torrential water on the rocky slopes of Lake District mountains, as if written by the hand of nature" (152–3).
8 The rocks Wollstonecraft is contemplating form part of the Baltic shield, one of the oldest and most geologically stable parts of the earth's crust.
9 We might also consider the *Letters*, as Karen Hust does, as that which would help Wollstonecraft "rebuild the foundation of her moral and political philosophy" (1). Or, we might take the *Letters*' unique arrangement of various genres as providing a means to reconstruct reality (McConnell-Ginet 12).
10 In a similar vein, Christine Cheney writes that the *Letters* provide a "way of seeing selfhood as a communal, confessional project" (279). The "communal" is understood in this chapter as including the stone, and the non-human more generally.
11 The history of silver mining in New Spain and its connection to the rise of a newly global economy is complex. As Galeano writes, "The quantity of silver alone imported into Europe in a little more than a century and a half from the mines of colonial South America, exceeded by three times the total European reserves" (33). According to John Tutino, "New Spain's silver became pivotal to Europeans' profit in world trade. Britain and France fought to claim it, helping stimulate the wars and revolutions of 1789 to 1825 … China became a [British] source of silver, a new 'mine' for the first half of the nineteenth century" (174–5).

12 Gneiss was an attractive stone for various uses because of its aesthetic qualities. As Winckler explains, "some gneisses ... are marked with tight folds formed by plastic or semiplastic flow during metamorphism," and these folds "give a very desirable ornamental accent to the stone" (22). And as Schouenborg and his co-writers point out: "the Hallandia gneiss is a product of a complex poly-phase tectonic and metamorphic evolution that included repeated recrystallization and deformation at high-temperature conditions" (38). This bending, folding, stretching, and chemical reformation gives the stone particular aesthetic attributes: "the Hallandia gneiss excels with its characteristic strong deformational overprint and highly strained mineral fabrics, which define its unique aesthetic properties" (46). The strain these "fabrics" are under relates to the various strains that Wollstonecraft traveled under, that in part form the fabric of her text.

13 "Nowhere else other than Sweden was iron made in sufficient quantity or of suitable quality to meet British demand. Swedish iron was indispensable" (Evans and Ryden 228).

14 Swedish iron was used in the manufacture of scythes (Hildebrand 22) and carding combs (23) and is thus relevant to such Wordsworth poems as "The Solitary Reaper" and "The Brothers," where each of these items figures significantly.

15 For recent discussion of this connection, especially in terms of Novalis, see Kate Rigby: "'Mines aren't really like that': German Romantic Undergrounds Revisited," *German Ecocriticism in the Anthropocene*, edited by Caroline Schaumann and Heather L. Sullivan, Palgrave, 2014. Also, see Heather Sullivan's essay "Dirty Nature: Ecocriticism and Tales of Extraction – Mining and Solar Power – in Goethe, Hoffmann, Verne, and Eschbach," *Colloquia Germanica*, vol. 44, no. 2, 2014, pp. 133–48.

16 The invention of the seismograph by John Milne in 1880 enabled scientists to confirm that there were layers of different density within the structure of the earth. Andrija Mohorovičić is credited with discovering the boundary between the earth's crust and mantle in 1909.

17 See Freud, "The Aetiology of Hysteria," and Jung, *Psychology and Alchemy*.

18 The silver that is the substance of her business in Scandinavia thus takes on a new sense. Though we aren't told what directs her travels in the narrative, silver is brought up several times. In Letter VII she bemoans the lack of productivity of Norway's silver mines (45). In Letter X she comments on "some articles in silver, more ponderous, it is true, than elegant." Soon after, she suspects the owners of these objects "smuggle a little" (67), no doubt raising the suspicion that these silver objects might be part of the haul she was sent to retrieve, or at least get compensated for.

Mining and smuggling are both useful metaphors for thinking about the derivation of latent from manifest content in psychoanalysis.

19 Alum is a chemical compound that is crystalline in form and was primarily used in England in the textile industry as a fixative for dyes (see Balston, Appendix 1). It also was used in cosmetic, culinary, medical, and other applications. One use in England was as an additive to bread to make it appear whiter. Food additives were a major problem in England in the eighteenth and nineteenth centuries. What William Cobbett writes, in *Cottage Economy*, was generally the case for all sorts of consumables: "scarcely a week passes without witnessing the detection of some greedy wretch who has used, in making or in doctoring his beer, drugs forbidden by the law" (46). The poor (especially the urban poor) of course had little recourse or mechanism of complaint and regularly consumed various dangerous substances. Coincidentally, in the paragraph immediately following the one quoted above, Wollstonecraft describes a riot caused by the high price of grain.

20 A major influence on Wollstonecraft's letters was Laurence Sterne's *A Sentimental Journey through France and Italy*, which was published the same year Wollstonecraft's family moved to Yorkshire. Incidentally, one of Sterne's friends, and fellow member of the "Demoniacs" club, Zachary Moore, inherited, and subsequently dissipated, a substantial fortune that was earned through the alum industry.

21 A similar motif is present in Rousseau's Seventh Walk (in *The Reveries of the Solitary Walker*). Wandering through a wood, Rousseau imagines himself as lord of an undiscovered land before he hears a strange noise and, entering a clearing, finds, to his dismay, a stocking factory.

22 Cobbett also describes a landscape as deprived of sustenance that parallels in several ways Wollstonecraft's descriptions: "Their hilliness, bleakness, roughness of roads, render them unpleasant to the luxurious, effeminate, tax-eating crew, who never come near them, and who have pared them down to the very bone" (134).

23 Animal bones, ground into powder, were commonly used as fertilizer in Britain and were in great demand as population and the amount of land cultivated increased. The large importation of bones led the chemist Baron Justus von Liebig to comment: "Great Britain is like a ghoul, searching the continents for bones to feed its agriculture … robbing all other countries of the condition of their fertility" (qtd. in O'Connor, "Origins and Development of the Coprolite Industry"). By 1839 about 30,000 tons were being imported annually (46).

24 "Rag and bone" men sorted through household trash for items, such as rags, that could be sold. According to Henry Mayhew, writing in the

mid-nineteenth century: "The bone-picker and rag-gatherer may be known at once by the greasy bag which he carries on his back. Usually he has a stick in his hand, and this is armed with a spike or hook, for the purpose of more easily turning over the heaps of ashes or dirt that are thrown out of the houses, and discovering whether they contain anything that is saleable at the rag-and-bottle or marine-store shop" (139). As this description suggests, rag and bone men lived in extreme poverty and survived on what they found in the street. Human sweat, with the help of dirt and other environmental factors, was what broke down cloth into rags. Animal parts were boiled to make gelatin and glue, both products used in paper-making. Animal bones were sometimes also used in the making of ink.

25 According to Shorter, "in 1800 it was estimated that Great Britain's expenditure on foreign rags was nearly £200,000 per annum" (41). And as Koops records, Britain was by far the biggest consumer of rags, using "twenty-four million pounds weight of rags and other paper-stuff ... annually" before 1803 (74).

26 As Miranda Burgess details,

> When war curtailed rag imports, the remedies Britain grasped at intimated further encounters with violence and trauma. When naval uniforms provide furnish for the packaging of sugar, their blue dye highlighting the sugar's refined white, the symbols of maritime authority are metonymically yoked to the Atlantic slave economy naval authority enforces (Krill 56). The sails and hammocks that provide furnish for packaging and the newspaper trade not only memorialize the warships that return "in rags" from the maritime theatre but also convert the relics of violence into vehicles for violent narrative ("Principal Officers and Commissioners of His Majesty's Navy" 1; "Gallant Action"). Further sources of paper furnish include the "Condemned Barrack Linen" of executed criminals and the cast-off clothes of enslaved laborers on the plantations of the British Caribbean ("Condemned Barrack Stores" 1). (371)

2 Deforestation in "The Ruined Cottage"

1 From Wordsworth's note to his sonnet "On the Projected Kendal and Windermere Railway" composed in 1844 (*Poetical Works* 282). The preceding lines of the note provide the relevant context: "The degree and kind of attachment which many of the yeomanry feel to their small inheritances can scarcely be over-rated. Near the house of one of them stands a magnificent tree, which a neighbour of the owner advised him to fell for profit's sake."

2 In a September 1800 letter to William Godwin outlining a work on the evolution of language, Coleridge writes: "Are not words &c parts & germination of the Plant? And what is the Law of their Growth? – In something of this order I would endeavor to destroy the old antithesis of *Words & Things*, elevating, as it were, words into Things, & living Things too" (*Letters* 625–6; vol. 1).

3 James George Frazer, for example, writes that across ancient Europe Zeus's voice was heard "in the rustling of oak leaves" (184).

4 Today there are only two trees remaining of what was once Birnam wood. Besides deforestation, climate change has also caused forests to "move," as changing temperatures have altered tree habitats.

5 The following comparison by forest is given in *House of Commons Journal* (1792), 350:

	1608	1783
New Forest	123,927	32,611
Alice Holt	13,031	9,136
Whittlewood	51,046	5,211
Salcey	15,247	2,918
East Bere	5,363	256
Sherwood	23,370	(1789) 1,368

6 The term "deforestation" was not used until the late nineteenth century. Most of the words used to describe the process of cutting down trees did not carry a negative prefix. The legal term from the sixteenth century forwards was "to assart" and the land thus cleared was also known as an "assart." Various other terms, such as rid, stub, clot, grub, stock, extirpate, and shrub, all generally meant to clear a wooded area. Samuel Johnson provides the verb "averruncate" (*OED* 2), which he defines as "to root up; to tear up by the roots." The language suggests a local attitude rather than a consciousness of the practice as a national ecological phenomenon. The terms "disforest" or "disafforest" were also used, but these generally meant to disestablish a particular area as legally defined forest, not necessarily to cut down trees. A "forest" for most of modern English history did not imply thickly wooded landscape but a mixed-use area that included some wooded land. As E.P. Thompson memorably describes Windsor Forest during the eighteenth century: "Some part of this forest was made up of parkland and of widely spaced mature oaks, intersected by straight rides; other parts were enclosed arable and meadow land; on other parts were thick coppices, bushes and man-high bracken in which a deer could hide or shake off a dog; and yet other parts were moorland, on the edges of which squatters had settled" (28).

7 The complex, multilayered, and at times contentious history of the deforestation of the four nations can only be addressed here by a very general overview. In the modern period, the suppression of the monasteries by Henry VIII in the late 1530s marks the first major inroad into the nations' wood. As Robert Albion explains, "Most of the religious houses owned woodlands, and the oaks were one of the most readily negotiable parts of the confiscated property" (122). According to John Bellamy Foster, this phenomenon was in great part responsible for the origins of the Poor Laws: "With the seizure of church lands, innumerable peasants were driven out. So great was the increase in pauperization that Queen Elizabeth was forced to acknowledge it directly by the introduction of the poor rate – the beginning of the Poor Laws" (171). The rise in iron and copper forges under Elizabeth marks the next major stage (John Perlin [175–80] provides a historical overview of this development). Various depredations under James and Charles for the purpose of raising money further diminish the woods (Calendar of State Papers, Domestic Series, 1603–40; Victoria County History [various]: see Albion 124–7). Cromwell's reign did little to abate this process, as formerly royal forests, as well as woods on royalist property, became a ready source of revenue for the new state (Acts and Ordinances 2 785). War, the increase in British mercantile and colonial interests, and the growth of industry all accelerated the process of deforestation throughout the eighteenth century. Planting was sporadic and piecemeal and did little to abate the general and continuous destruction of woodlands from the late sixteenth century onwards, which was not only generally recognized but came to be viewed by certain factions with an air of triumphalism: "The Scarcity of Timber ought never to be regretted, for it is a certain proof of National Improvement; and for Royal Navies, Countries yet barbarous are the right and only proper nurseries" (Dr. Thomas Preston, *House of Commons Journal* (1792): 343, qtd. in Albion 119).

8 In "Lines Composed a Few Miles Above Tintern Abbey" Wordsworth famously "recognize[s]":

> In nature and the language of the sense
> The anchor of my purest thoughts, the nurse,
> The guide, the guardian of my heart, and soul
> Of all my moral being. (109–12)

This framing of "nature" is central to the very notion of Romanticism. Also, in Book One of *The Prelude*, Wordsworth uses Milton's description of Adam and Eve facing expulsion from paradise to evoke his own joyous entrance into a world filled with possibility: "The earth was all before me." In reversing the biblical plot, Wordsworth rejects the notion of a "fallen" nature and thus renews the association of nature with paradise.

9 Wordsworth most often uses this term to describe landforms, especially rocks. In *The Excursion*, of which "The Ruined Cottage" would become part, the epithet is associated with the bleak, miserable, deserted, and deprived.
10 Artaud's comment addresses the effects of capitalist modes of production on art and cultural practice. In the current context, the deforestation of Britain was often a gradual, piecemeal, and therefore under-noted phenomenon.
11 Spinoza 919. Another way this is described in reference to Spinoza's work is as a "mediate infinite mode" of extension, that is, "mediate" in the way it represents a system of dependence and logical necessity (as between Armytage and the tree, the ground and the clouds), and "infinite" in the sense that it represents a relationship between motion and rest that remains consistent throughout the universe. Another way of putting this, perhaps, is that the way particular finite objects come into being and pass away (Armytage, the landscape) demonstrates the relation between motion and rest that is an infinite mode of extension (the universe).
12 This inorganic body might also be thought of in terms of the "body without organs" first proposed by Artaud and later theorized by Deleuze, a body freed from mechanistic functioning to become a source, a point of origin.
13 In Book 11 of *The Prelude*, Wordsworth famously describes "spots of time" and narrates a particular incident as an example, where he is lost upon a "bare common" (302).
14 For a concise yet thorough scientific study, see Vitousek.
15 What Sir Walter Raleigh says of trade is also particularly apt: "Hee that commaunds the sea, commaunds the trade, and hee that is Lord of the Trade is Lord of the wealth of the worlde" (qtd. in Williams 134).
16 See Macpherson; Graham; Knight; Crimmin.
17 Several actions, including the Battle of Camperdown, were fought in the 1790s to protect British trade routes to the Baltic, which supplied wood and other resources necessary to a large and widely active British navy. Today, the control of dwindling natural resources is the single most prevalent cause of war.
18 Robert Nixon persuasively argues for the need to address slowly unfolding historical processes in opposition to spectacular and sensational events.
19 The relationship between industrialized agriculture and landscape aesthetics is compellingly discussed by Ann Bermingham.
20 "Brotherhood" might echo the *"fraternité"* of the French Revolution, though Wordsworth refers here to a relationship between humans and

natural things (specifically the members of the household and the spring). The broken bond could also suggest the action of the guillotine.
21. What E.P. Thompson writes of those accused under the Black Act also rings true here: "If this is a 'criminal subculture' then the whole of plebian England falls within the category" (194).
22. "Debates on the Law on Thefts of Wood." Cited as "Debates" hereafter.
23. Foster writes: "Five-sixths of all prosecutions in Prussia during this period had to do with wood, and in the Rhineland the proportion was even higher." Thompson notes that Marx's essay turns "upon many of the same issues disclosed also in the English forests of the eighteenth century" (241n1).
24. According to Thompson, "The rights and claims of the poor, if inquired into at all, received more perfunctory compensation, smeared over with condescension and poisoned with charity. Very often they were simply redefined as crimes: poaching, wood-theft, trespass" (241).
25. See King (12–13; 170) for the growth in imprisonment and transportation as punishments for petty crimes in the eighteenth century.
26. The rising poor rates and the increasing number of the dependent poor is taken up in David Davies's widely read 1795 account *The Case of Labourers in Husbandry*.
27. The costs of bringing a case before a magistrate in the eighteenth century fell upon the individual prosecuting the case.
28. Thus economy and ecology share the same Greek root, "oikos" or "home." When the term "ecology" was coined by Ernst Haeckl in 1866, it is unsurprising that he defines it as "the economy of nature" (qtd. in Bate 36).
29. Margaret Schabas, writing of "the denaturalization of the economic order" (2), details the ways in which economic considerations had, up until the late eighteenth century, remained rooted in natural history and how our modern notions of economics arise from the alienation of financial economy from material nature.

  An example of this development might be seen in the way the objects of nature were themselves abstracted into newly minted financial terms, a process the poem in many ways addresses. "Hedge" would become a term of financial speculation, so that today a "hedge fund" remains an abstraction of (etymologically pulled [tract] from [ab]) a hedge. "Hedge" is an Old English word, dating from before the composition of the Anglo-Saxon Chronicles, defined by the *Oxford English Dictionary* as "A row of bushes or low trees (e.g., hawthorn, or privet) planted closely to form a boundary between pieces of land or at the sides of a road: the usual form of fence in England" (1a). The word came to be used metaphorically to refer to any barrier or defense;

the *OED*'s first citation for this use is from the fourteenth century (4). The word is later found widely in the context of betting, as numerous examples from the late seventeenth through the late nineteenth centuries demonstrate (n.5, v.8). A relevant, and revealing, example from the Romantic period comes from the orator William Windham, speaking in Parliament in 1805: "What, in the sporting language was called 'a hedge', the effect of which was, that there was a chance the Right Honourable Gentleman would at all events win" (5). The earliest citation for the word as a term of market speculation is in the twentieth century, as in this representative example by Albert William Atwood in Exchanges and Speculation (1917): "Hedging … consists in making a purchase or sale for future delivery to offset and protect an actual merchandising transaction" (v.8c).

30 Something similar can be said of the tree stump in "Simon Lee." The speaker's grief at the end of the poem is involved in the act of grubbing up the stump and illustrates a broader growing inability in the culture to see the connection between humans and between humans and the objects of nature.

31 The sticks appearing to participate in Goody's curse reflects a historical tendency to ascribe magical qualities to wood. Samuel Pepys describes a drinking game which involved "kneeling on a faggot" to drink the King's health, a "strange frolique" in celebration of the Coronation of Charles II. Goody's kneeling is also interesting in that it mirrors that of the thief appealing for mercy: "The wretched thief begging on his knees for forgiveness is not a literary conceit, but a reality described in many legal dispositions" (Hay 41).

32 As Douglas Hay observes of the latter eighteenth century: "As the decades passed, the maturing trade, commerce and industry of England spawned more laws to protect particular kinds of property" (21). When it comes to trees, of course, "protect" is highly ironic, in that it is not the living object that is protected but its market value. This trend is further evidenced in twentieth-century U.S. law that sanctioned the patenting of living things (the Plant Patent Act of 1930 and the Plant Variety Protection Act of 1970 allowed particular plants to be patented, and the 1980 Supreme Court case, Diamond vs. Chakrabarty allowed patents on genetically modified organisms).

33 From its enactment in 1723, through the last case tried under it in 1814, the Black Act made the cutting down of trees a crime punishable by hanging (see Thompson 22–3; 255). Other attempts to legislate notions of common use include the enclosures of the commons under the Enclosure Acts, which deprived the poor, among other things, from access to the collection of fallen wood (Snell 179).

34 The situation of the poor, customary rights, and the imperial motivations of deforestation are similarly addressed in Keats's "Robin Hood" (1820). Marian and Margaret "weep" for their irreplaceable loss, and Robin's "craze" is not unlike Robert's:

> And if Robin should be cast
> Sudden from his turfed grave,
> And if Marian should have
> Once again her forest days,
> She would weep, and he would craze:
> He would swear, for all his oaks,
> Fall'n beneath the dockyard strokes,
> Have rotted on the briny seas;
> She would weep that her wild bees
> Sang not to her – strange! that honey
> Can't be got without hard money! (38–48)

35 I am grateful to Joshua Wilner for pointing out the relevance of this passage.
36 "The Ash Tree in St. John's Cottage." This essay gives an account of the trees at Cambridge mentioned by Wordsworth.
37 Wordsworth did what he could to save what was left: "This poem was composed in a grove at the north-eastern end of Grasmere Lake, which grove was in a great measure destroyed by turning the high-road along the side of the water. The few trees that are left were spared at my intercession" (*Fenwick Notes* 52).
38 John, on learning of the destruction of the grove, wrote Mary Hutchinson in 1801: "I wish I had the monster that cut them down in my ship, & I would give him a tight flogging" (qtd. in Rand 30).
39 "under Brehon Law … trees were divided into four categories with a scale of fines for their unlawful felling that diminished in severity according to the category" (Graves 202). The four categories, in order of importance, are given as Chieftan Trees, Peasant Trees, Shrub Trees, and Bramble Trees.
40 The history of May Day stretches back to early Celtic rites and forward to the working-class struggle for the eight-hour day. Anne Ross explains the origins of the practice: "The classics tell of a chief druid, while Caesar states that all the druids met together in assembly … in the tribal territory of the Carnutes, which was regarded as the centre of all Gaul. The Irish druids likewise had a chief druid … They used to assemble at Uisneach, in modern County Westmeath. The Assembly of Uisnech, which was regarded as the "navel" of Ireland, was held on Beltain, 1 May … The whole druidic system would seem to have been common to all the Celts" (428). Beltain was a spring festival that involved fertility

rites thought to be associated with a sun god and celebrated with ritual fires meant to purify and protect crops and livestock: "The calendar festivals and the great assemblies which accompanied them were fundamental to Celtic social life, when the people met not as tribes but as a nation" (Ross 437). During the middle ages, May Day festivals across Europe adopted some of the customs common to charivari, and this was when the phallic maypole was introduced. There were various attempts to suppress the practice of May Day in the modern period, which were never entirely successful. John Evelyn, the seventeenth-century author of a seminal work on trees, *Sylva*, demonstrates this resistance to May Day ritual: "And here we cannot but persistinge those Riouotous Assemblies of idle people, who under pretence of going a maying (as they term it) do oftentimes cut down, and carry away fine straight trees, to set up before some Ale-house, or traveling-place, where they keep their drunken Baccanalias" (qtd. in Bushaway 212).

41 The way the oak was a "contested symbol" (193) is examined in depth in two essays by Tim Fulford: "Britannia's Heart of Oak: Thomson, Garrick and the Language of Eighteenth-Century Patriotism," and "Cowper, Wordsworth, Clare: The Politics of Trees."

42 In Ireland, the oak also suggests an aristocratic absenteeism but with different implications. The word for oak in Irish can also mean "chief," and it is widely thought that the dispossession of the native land-owning gentry in Ireland was instrumental to the breakdown in the structure of Gaelic culture and the retreat of Irish Gaelic as the national tongue. Trees where rebels were hung in Ireland often served as commemorative sites, and as Guy Beiner relates, "Even when the trees were cut down, they continued to survive in the imaginary landscape of social memory" (216).

43 Thompson's biographer, Leonard George Johnson, gives this memorable portrait: "His ideal for Sierra Leone was a colony of free settlers owning and cultivating lands of their own, justly secured to them. For this ideal the headstrong Governor worked himself nearly to death. Time and again he was stuck down with fever. Once a report got about that he was dead and a procession of native women came to 'keen' him. He was dosed with calomel to such an extent that all his front teeth fell out" (54–5).

44 For an excellent overview of these theories and their relation to theories of cognition, see Alan Richardson, chapter 2.

45 Iain McCalman and Nicholas Roe both provide invaluable accounts of radical Romanticism that trace these developments in great detail.

46 Colonial mining also provided Europe the gold and silver that "not only stimulated Europe's economic development; one may say that they have made it possible" (Galeano 33).

47 McNeill further argues that deforestation contributed to loss of insectivorous birds and created new swampy areas, perfect conditions for the breeding of mosquitoes carrying malaria and yellow fever (48; 55).
48 Of Barbados, one of the first islands to be deforested by colonization, McNeill writes: "In 1631, Sir Henry Colt noted 'diuers sorts of birds' including blackbirds, turtle doves, pigeons, and pelicans. Ligon (1657: 60–1) recounted a dozen or more species, and allowed there were more he could not name. But a visitor in 1652, Heinrich von Utcheritz, claimed 'one hears no birds'" (28n32).
49 In the Second Maroon War of 1795, bloodhounds were brought from Cuba to terrorize the maroon population. Upon discovery, George III ordered that such methods be put to an end immediately. His order was received too late to matter (Campbell 229–33). A drawing of one of these dogs with his trainer amongst a picturesque landscape provides the frontispiece for Dallas's *The History of the Maroons*.
50 Examples of each author's response to Wordsworth's poem are given in Bergren, 1–2.
51 Wordsworth writes:

> We must then look for protection entirely amongst the dispassionate advocates of liberty and discussion. These, whether male or female, we must either amuse or instruct; nor will our end be fully obtained unless we do both. The clergy of the Church of England are a body from which periodical publications derive great patronage: they however will turn from us. At the Universities of Oxford and Cambridge, amongst the young men, we shall not look in vain for encouragement The dissenters, in general, are not rich; but in every town of any size there are some who would receive a work like ours with pleasure. I entirely approve of what you say on the subject of Ireland and think it very proper that an agent should be appointed in Dublin to disseminate the impression. It would be well if either of you have any friends there, to whom you could write soliciting their recommendation. Indeed it would be very desirable to endeavour to have, in each considerable town of Great Britain and Ireland, a person to introduce the publication into notice. To this purpose, when it is further advanced, I shall exert myself amongst all my friends. (qtd. in Knight 72–3)

Precisely what Matthews had to say on the subject of Ireland is unknown, as his letter is lost, but the content could hardly have been unsympathetic to the Irish cause of independence given the radical nature of Matthews's beliefs and the general and universal attitude towards liberty espoused by early supporters of the French Revolution.
52 "The Solitary Reaper" also mentions the cuckoo in negative and nostalgic terms: "No sweeter voice was ever heard / In spring-time from the

Cuckoo-bird, / Breaking the silence of the seas / Among the farthest Hebrides" (13–16).
53 This echoes an earlier situation described by a planter in the Caribbean: "at the Barbadoes all the trees are destroyed, so that wanting wood to boyle their sugar, they are forced to send for coales from England" (qtd. in McNeill, 27–8).

3 The Paradox of the Palm in the Poetry of Felicia Hemans

1 See, for example, Odysseus's comparison of Nausicaa to a palm in *The Odyssey*, or the praise of the bride in *Song of Solomon*: "thy stature is like to a palm tree" (7.7).
2 For a consideration of the historical reception of Hemans, including her fall from critical favour and more recent recovery, see Susan Wolfson's introduction to *Felicia Hemans: Selected Poems, Letters, Reception Materials*.
3 As Tricia Lootens writes, "Hemans's work suggests that national awarenesses are paradoxical and inescapably gendered and that gender is shaped by its own contradictory awarenesses, including conceptions of national identity" (243).
4 A number of books and articles followed Curran's essay, and a cursory overview is offered here. Marlon Ross's 1989 *The Contours of Masculine Desire* demonstrates the gender bias of earlier critical assessments. Anne Mellor's 1992 *Romanticism and Gender* offers an important reconsideration of the domestic in Hemans, stressing its precarious status. Jerome McGann's 1993 "Literary History, Romanticism, and Felicia Hemans" provides an important reassessment in the context of rethinking literary historicism, appearing in the same year as Isobel Armstrong's "A Music of Thine Own: Woman's Poetry – an expressive tradition?," which posits a subversive current in Hemans underneath the conservative exterior. The following year Tricia Lootens's "Hemans and Home" applies the Hegelian notion of an "internal enemy" to the workings of Hemans's verse. These currents were solidified in the dual publication in 2000 of Susan Wolfson's edited collection *Felicia Hemans: Selected Poems, Letters, Reception Materials* and Nanora Sweet and Julie Melnyk's collection *Felicia Hemans: Re-imagining Poetry in the Nineteenth-Century*, both of which firmly establish a broad critical consensus as to the renewed importance of Hemans's work. More recently, Kate Singer and Nanora Sweet's 2014 collection *Beyond Domesticity: Felicia Hemans in the Wider World* treats "the unfamiliar Hemans," stressing her philosophical tendencies and cosmopolitan investments, as well as offering a renewed consideration of her attention to and experimentation with poetic form.

5 In the way the identification with the tree creates a sense of shared power; for Wordsworth, in "The Excursion," (discussed above), "Like power abides / In man's celestial spirit." It is worth noting that the tree is gendered female in this passage.
6 It is worth mentioning here that the Romantic-period hope to find a point of origin bears an uncanny resemblance to our own moment's attempt to envision a future, itself increasingly something "more hoped for than believed in."
7 Jeffries, Martin O., Jacqueline Richter-Menge, and James E. Overland. "Executive Summary." *Arctic Report Card 2014*. National Oceanic and Atmospheric Association.
8 Global demand has grown "over the past few decades at a rate of 7.1 % per annum," and currently reaches well over 60 million tons per year (Lim et al. 13). According to Paul Tullis: "Between 1995 and 2015, annual production quadrupled, from 15.2m tonnes to 62.6m tonnes. By 2050, it is expected to quadruple again, reaching 240m tonnes. The footprint of palm oil production is astounding: plantations to produce it account for 10% of permanent global cropland. Today, 3 billion people in 150 countries use products containing palm oil. Globally, we each consume an average of 8kg of palm oil a year" ("How the World Got Hooked on Palm Oil"). This demand has created the destruction of sensitive ecosystems in Southeast Asia, contributing significantly to carbon emissions: "Draining and burning of peatland forest for palm oil production alone released about 2 billion tons of CO2 equivalent GHG emissions each year, contributing to 4% of global annual emissions" (Lim et al. 14). In addition, Indigenous people have been pushed from their traditional lands (15).
9 Though it is true, as Susan Wolfson and Elizabeth Fay point out in their edition of the poem, that in Hemans's experience it was the men who removed themselves (9), the poetry makes possible other formulations.
10 According to Gallegos, West Africans see palm oil like Italians see olive oil (24). Every part of the plant was made use of. Aghalino writes:

> the palm frond was used in burial ceremonies and in the propitiation of the gods ... The trunk of the palm was used in building houses, its fibre was woven into fish traps, while the fronds were used for construction of thatched fences ... Palm frond was also fed as fodder to goats, while the veins were used for making brooms. The palm kernel was chewed with maize, as snacks. Kernel was also fed to goats and chickens. The palm nut ... was used to cement marshy areas in compounds and footpaths (Usoro, 1974). The palm oil is ultimately used for cooking. The "banga" and "owo" soups [were] special delicacies ... made from the oil ... the

oil palm was tapped to yield palm wine. The pomade is therapeutic all-purpose oil which readily served as Sloan linament to the people (Okumagba, 1980; Ottic, 1972; Bradbury, 1957). (22)

11 According to the World Wildlife Fund, palm oil appears in over half of all packaged food products in the United States ("Palm Oil").
12 See, for example, K.S.V. Krishna Reddy et al., "Experimental Investigation on Usage of Palm Oil as a Lubricant to Substitute Mineral Oil in CI Engines." *Chinese Journal of Engineering*, vol. 2014.
13 The leisure associated with pastoral is a key association suggested by the palm, both in the past and today.
14 According to Manthorne, "the Tree of Life became historically identified with the date palm indigenous to the biblical lands" (376–7).
15 Hemans split with her husband when their children were young, and she raised and supported them on her own through her writing. This event had a significant impact on her writing and how she saw herself as an author.
16 Though other oils, such as olive oil, were used in the making of body soap, palm oil could be obtained significantly cheaper and thus made body soap more widely available to the British public.
17 The reasons for the growing popularity of washing with soap are many and complex. The changes to bathing habits readily apparent in the nineteenth century have their roots in developments of the eighteenth. One important contribution was William Buchan's immensely popular *Domestic Medicine* of 1769. This work was one of the first to talk about the skin as an organ that functioned to both protect the body as well as excrete waste. Without washing, Buchan argued, there was a danger that waste could be "reabsorbed" and cause illness (73). An increasing focus on hygiene was apparent in a number of ways (such as the letters of Lord Chesterfield or the obsessive cleanliness of Beau Brummell) and in some very successful attempts by the British navy to lower the death rate of sailors through a strict hygienic regimen. These successes would later be of great importance in the establishment of hygiene rituals in hospitals. And in the eighteenth century, "physiology took a turn towards the social sciences, towards seeing the human body en masse, observing the effects of personal hygiene from a distance. Secondly, a new phase of physiology opened up through the mid-century discovery of the nervous system, which ultimately led to the softening of the 'heroic' form of cold hygienic regimen" (Smith 247).But the washing of the body was not only a matter of health. The use of soap indicated an upward mobility that was in part about aspiring to gentility but also was tied to an important, potentially radical, political meaning: "After

1789, the French Revolution gave hygiene a new political status … Revolutionary hygiene [became] officially adopted as one of the rights of the healthy citizen, and one of the duties of the state, by the National Convention's Committee on Salubrity in 1793" (Smith 255). Bathing could be interpreted in a number of ways, but it appears to have tied the insistence by the middle class both for the potential to rise socially and in the notion of inherent rights forwarded by a variety of important eighteenth-century thinkers and defended for the first time, in certain ways, by the French Revolution. New notions of cleanliness were driven by a complex combination of economic change, scientific precedent, political upheaval, social aspiration, and the availability of colonial products.

18 I am grateful to Jennifer Wenzel for bringing this to my attention.
19 McClintock details a number of ads in the Victorian period in which Black boys bleach their skin white (220–3).
20 Just as Liverpool was the centre for the slave trade in Britain, it became the port of entry for palm oil as well, and it also, by the 1820s, had emerged as the major soap producer in Britain (Lynn 84f).
21 Katherine Ashenburg has detailed some of the ways bathing, especially in warm water, was deemed by many eighteenth-century writers to be enervating and sinful. Writing on the bidet, she notes "a persistent Anglo-Saxon suspicion that clean genitals might lead to lascivious behaviour (even oral sex) kept the chair of cleanliness mostly on the other side of the Channel" (153). She also comments that "Prudery in the name of religion or propriety may partly have been the socially acceptable face of an age-old disinclination to wash all over" (190).
22 In *A History of Classical Poetry: Sanskrit, Pali, Pankrit*, Siegfried Lienhard writes: "The commonest writing materials were palm leaves on which letters were scratched with the metal stylus" (14).
23 Classic Tamil poetry was written between c. 100 BC and 250 AD. These poems, known as "Cankam," vary in length from 3 to over 800 lines. There are 2,381 Cankam poems, of which 102 are anonymous (Ramanujan ix–x).
24 "In classical [Tamil] poetry … *akam* poems are love poems, *puram* are all other kinds of poems, usually about war, values, community: it is the 'public' poetry of the ancient Tamils" (Ramanujan 235).
25 This stands in contrast to the traditional importance of palms as providing food in a variety of cultures that utilized its oil, its nuts, and its fruits for a wide range of purposes.
26 In *The Natural History of Palms*, E.J.H. Corner describes the uniqueness of the palm in terms of its resistance to evolutionary change: "they maintain

their rigid character as if this great family had been pitched, as a block of special creation, into the Mesozoic world, and around, through, and over it the subsequent streams of life had flowed. The palm is an evolutionary challenge, primitive, standardized, and visible" (1).

27 The following pages provide a summary of some of the destructive aspects of palm oil production.

28 "[F]eathery cocoas" refers to the coconut palm and not the cocoa tree, though it is worth noting that the cocoa was introduced into India in the eighteenth century as part of the global and colonial movement of plants during this period.

4 Salt in *The History of Mary Prince*

1 Malleable because of the impossibility of finding any distinct line between the human and non-human. As Lewis Thomas puts it, "We are not made up, as we had always supposed, of successively enriched packets of our own parts. We are shared, rented, occupied" (2).

2 Though we have no record of Prince after 1833, we know that she left the Woods, her last owners, after their arrival in London. Though there is no record of her manumission, she was no longer under the command of the Woods from this point onwards.

3 Ernest Jones, in his essay "The Symbolic Significance of Salt", explains: "in all ages salt has been invested with a significance far exceeding that inherent in its natural properties, interesting and important as these are. Homer calls it a divine substance, Plato describes it as especially dear to the Gods ... Secondly, the idea of salt has in different languages lent itself to a remarkable profusion of metaphorical connotations, so that a study of these suggests itself as being likely to indicate what the idea has essentially stood for in the human mind, and hence perhaps the source of its exaggerated significance" (113). If one considers the seemingly endless uses of salt in a wide variety of processes over the course of human history to the current day (over 14,000 uses are cited by the modern salt industry [Kurlansky 5]), the significance Jones refers to appears far less exaggerated. And because of its ubiquity and its necessity to human life, salt has provided a basis for taxation throughout history and thus has been fundamental to the economic makeup and survival of government.

4 Largely, though not entirely, untold, as Michele Speitz's recent essay in *Romantic Circles*, "Blood Sugar and Salt Licks," attests. This essay has been an important impetus and departure point for this chapter. Also, Cynthia Kennedy's "The Other White Gold" has been an important historical resource.

5 For a detailed discussion of the importance of slavery to the development of capitalism, see Solow and Engerman.
6 The salt-producing island where Prince lived is known today as "Grand Turk," part of a chain collectively known as the Turks Islands. I will be following Prince's usage here and refer to Grand Turk Island as Turks Island.
7 See Hoffer, "Reflections on *Cathexis*."
8 This metaphor is reversed in a letter from Keats to Fanny Brawne, where he imagines he would "uncrystallize and dissolve" (84) as a result of continued dwelling on her.
9 Kerry Sinanan has recently shown that there continue to be problems with the reception of Prince's *History*. The desire to access a "real" speaker "occludes the forces at work to fulfill the mode of consumption within antislavery commemoration to the neglect of what we really do or can know about Prince" (70).
10 Though some salts contain colouring taken from materials involved in their production, the salt produced on Grand Turk was white enough that "partial or total blindness was common" ("Salt Industry") among salt workers from the prolonged exposure to the reflection of the sun off the salt. In a postscript to his introduction, Pringle mentions that Prince is effected by a "disease in the eyes" which "may terminate in total blindness" (ii).
11 Among the vast number of conditions which salt was used to treat, Eberhard Wormer indicates that "pharmacists of the 19th century recommended internal use of salt against digestive upsets, goitre, glandular diseases, intestinal worms, dysentery, dropsy, epilepsy, and syphilis. Externally applied salt (e.g. cold or warm hip-baths) was said to be locally stimulating but acerbic to skin and mucous membranes at high doses. External application was advised in cases of rash and swelling and, in ophthalmology, to drive off stains and stain-obscurations of the cornea. A clyster (enema) of salt was even supposed to work for patients who were '*seemingly dead and apoplectical*'" (author's emphasis). Salt was also used as a medicine in cases where the ailment was uncertain or undefined. Charles Rogers, in *Scotland, Social and Domestic* (1869), writes:

> When a child met with an accident, a table-spoonful of water mixed with salt was applied to its brow and poured into its mouth; when an adult complained, and the cause of his ailment was unknown, an old sixpence was borrowed from a neighbour, its intended use being kept secret. As much salt as could be raised on the coin was then placed in a table-spoonful of water and melted. The sixpence was next put into the

solution, and the soles of the patient's feet and the palms of his hands were moistened three times with the liquid. The patient was made to taste the mixture thrice. His brow was stroked with the solution. The liquid which remained in the spoon was thrown over the fire, with these words, "Lord, preserve us frae a' skaith." The cure was then held to be complete. (215)

12 For an overview of this debate, see George J. Armelagos's essay "The Slavery Hypertension Hypothesis: Natural Selection and Scientific Investigation: A Commentary" in *Transforming Anthropology*, vol. 13, no. 2, 2005. Here Armelagos details the contemporary argument for a genetic cause of African American hypertension and the counterargument which followed. That the scientific community lacks consensus on this issue is likely due in part to the persistence of ahistorical notions of race within all types of discourses and institutions.

13 The structure of the salt trade, as it became increasingly centralized and monopolized in Liverpool, appears to be subject to the same shifting ground as commodity production in the West Indies. This is doubly so, as those responsible for the exploitation of both products and people generally escaped sanction for their behaviour. Because subsidence often occurred far from the spot from where the brine was drawn, salt manufacturers vehemently denied responsibility. By enabling this distance, sponsoring pseudoscientific studies that forwarded alternative causes, and wielding their significant political clout, salt manufacturers were successful for many decades in squashing legislation aimed to provide aid to those affected by subsidence. The violent effects of subsidence upon the English landscape mirror the environmental destruction carried out in the colonies under similarly exploitative methods. The ground shifts under the feet of those in Cheshire and Bermuda, both places where salt was central to the economy.

14 Andrew Symmer, the king's agent for the Turks Islands in 1779, writes to the Colonial Office, "most of the inhabitants of Bermuda are inclined to the American cause" (CO 23/10).

15 John Murray had previously been governor of Virginia and New York.

16 Though it is impossible to be entirely certain, a father and son with the names Robert and Richard Darrell ("Master Dickey" in Prince's text) resided on Turks Island during Prince's time there, and this father and son seem to be the only candidates with these first names with a last name ending in "D."

17 As Hartman writes, "Through stealing away, counterclaims about justice and freedom were advanced that denied the sanctity or legitimacy of property rights in a double gesture that played on the meaning of

theft" (69). This double gesture is also woven into the fabric of Prince's narrative.

18 According to the excise office as given in BT 6/183: "In 1780 the Duty was increased, and again in 1782, making the whole 5 shillings per Bushel. This Duty was doubled in 1798 ... and in 1805 an additional Duty of 5 shillings per Bushel was imposed ... constituting the present [1817] Duty of 15 shillings per bushel." The salt tax, or *gabelle*, was so high in some provinces in France that it is considered a major factor leading to the outbreak of the French Revolution (see following note).

19 The tax in France was even more injurious and was an important factor in fomenting the French Revolution. As Kurlansky summarizes, "The salt tax in France ... was not the singular cause of revolution, but it became a symbol for all the injustices of government" (233).

20 Cochrane was the 9th Earl of Dundonald, "an important pioneer of the chemical industry" (Sugden 8). He inherited the title but not much else and experimented with various industrial processes in an attempt to recoup the family fortune. His production of soda from salt was his most commercially successful endeavour. He was, incidentally, a distant relation of Alexander Murray. His ancestor, Colonel John Campbell Cochrane (4th Earl of Dundonald) married Lady Anne Murray (daughter of 1st Earl of Dunmore) on 4 April 1706.

21 Salt was produced by boiling brine from naturally occurring springs in Kanawha, as opposed to the solar method used on Grand Turk, or the mining of rock salt in England and elsewhere.

22 Ilendo is the name of a village in current-day Gabon. I have not been able to determine the exact significance of the use of the word here, though it appears that Jeki is calling to an ancestral spirit for inspiration.

23 It is important to note that the National Archives house the Colonial Office records dealing with the governance of the Turks Islands during the period Prince was resident there.

24 The nuclear energy venture Terraform, recently founded by Bill Gates, hopes to use molten salt as a way to store reactor power.

25 For the importance of Lagos to the Transatlantic slave trade, see Kristin Mann, *Slavery and the Birth of an African City: Lagos, 1760–1900*.

5 John Clare's Rhizomatic Poetics

1 Some of these many uses of the many species of moss include: fuel to heat homes, insulation (in clothing as well as homes), building material, cushioning (in pillows and matresses), cattle bedding, smelting, smithing, pottery making, salt production, alum production, dam construction,

embarkment work, burial mound construction, fertilizer, bandages, diapers, sanitary napkins, packaging (for flowers, leeches, and brittle wares), as a fire-retardant, for scouring worms, for growing orchids, and for brooms. This list is by no means exhaustive. See Dixon; Brunskill; Kimmerer.

2 According to Paul Ardon, "Peat cutting has directly or indirectly changed the appearance of a great proportion of upland Britain by effecting widespread, visually obvious, vegetation change and breaking up the uniformity of the land surface" (165). Alexander Fenton, describing the impact of cutting in Scotland, writes "over the centuries, the use of turf ... has cleared and changed now unimaginable stretches of the countryside (qtd. in Ardon 7).

3 For an assessment of the importance of peat to climate, see "Towards Climate-Responsible Peatlands Management" by the United Nations Food and Agriculture Organization.

> The major ecological functions of peatlands are crucial for providing ecosystem services. These services include storing freshwater, providing wildlife refuges and sequestering carbon over long periods of time. This carbon is often essentially "locked up" and removed from the near-term global carbon cycle due to the slow (or negligible) decomposition processes within peatlands ... Because of their biodiversity, peatlands can deliver ecosystem services that contribute to the provision of important products, such as crops, berries, timber and fibre, livestock and purified water (Kimmel and Mander, 2010). Harvesting these resources and draining peatlands for other uses can change the landscape in ways that reduce peat at rates much faster than it can be created. The slow rate of peatland growth and development, associated with waterlogged and anaerobic subsurface conditions, requires active management over much longer time horizons to restore these landscapes when they are destroyed or degraded. This final point reflects the fragility of peatlands and indicates that short-term interventions like draining, harvesting, or construction can cause significant damage to landscape functioning. (9)

The current destruction of peatland in Southeast Asia to meet the global demand for palm oil contributes to 4 per cent of total annual global carbon emissions (Lim et al. 14).

4 A close second would be Seamus Heaney, who in "Digging" and elsewhere explicitly relates the labour of peat production with that of poetic labour.

5 See, for example, Theresa M. Kelley's chapter, "Clare's Commonable Plants" in *Clandestine Marriage: Botany & Romantic Culture*.

6 According to his editor John Taylor, "written before Clare was seventeen" (*Poems Descriptive* xxii).

7 Clare derived themes, inspiration, and content from both the traditional ballads sung in Helpston and in the broadsheet ballads he grew up reading. An eighteenth-century ballad tradition protesting enclosure also has relevance to Clare's anti-enclosure poetry. For a discussion, see *Songs of Protest, Songs of Love: Popular Ballads in Eighteenth-Century Britain* by Robin Ganev, pp. 77–99.
8 Given the closeness of moss and flowers here, it is worth noting their commercial interrelation: "An immense quality of moss, amounting in the year to millions of bundles, is required for the packing of flowers dispatched from Covent Garden … some of the leading florists in London have factories on the Continent for the collection and preparation of the moss" (Nixon 241).
9 Unlike vascular plants, which have conductive tissue to distribute resources and incubate in temperate zones in the warmer months, mosses reproduce at varying times of the year depending on the species. This is in part because mosses are able to reproduce asexually as well as sexually, and they tend to require only moisture to reproduce.
10 I am grateful to Beth Gargano for bringing this sense to my attention.
11 According to Mahood, Clare had detailed knowledge of the way flowers relied on wind to spread pollen, so it seems very likely he would be aware of the reproductive habits of mosses.
12 According to Alan Bewell: "In northern English and Scottish dialect, the word flitting refers not just to a kind of flickering movement, but to moving from one place of habitation to another. It also can refer to the removable goods and furniture, the 'flitting,' that one carries on such a move" (568).
13 Though Clare's first volume of poetry, *Poems Descriptive of Rural Life and Scenery* (1820), was highly successful, in part due to the way Clare was fetishized as a "peasant poet" or "natural genius," interest in his later work waned, which was to remain the case not only during the remainder of his lifetime, but for over a hundred years after his death. An interpretive line, apparent as recently as in the criticism of Harold Bloom, dismisses Clare as a minor poet, both misreading his poetry and misidentifying his strengths.
14 I am grateful to Katie Hogan for bringing my attention to this essay.
15 Alan Bewell and Gary Harrison have also independently made this point. In Bewell's words, "English rural laborers were not the only people who lost their traditional nature during this period. Read in light of what was happening elsewhere, Clare's poetry can also give us some idea of what it might have meant to other people in other parts of the world who were also grappling with the catastrophic loss of their own local natures" (552).

16 See, for example, the Great Fen project of Bedfordshire, Cambridgeshire, and Northamptonshire, which seeks to restore the area that includes the setting of Clare's "To the Snipe" (discussed below).

17 See "Holocene Environmental Change: Contributions from the Peatland Archive" by Frank M. Chambers and Dan J. Charman.

18 From the title, *The Lost Fens: England's Greatest Ecological Disaster*.

19 Keegan relates how drainage often occurred as a prelude to land enclosure: "The Enclosure Act movement was very hostile to wetlands. Although we did not, as the French Revolution did, 'abolish' all marshes by statute, agricultural writers treated the existence of even small fens as a scandal; the greedier landowners, not deterred by the poor results from draining the bigger peatlands, repeated the same mistakes on the smaller ones" (149).

20 "From the seventeenth century forward, fen dwellers retaliated through legal action and through direct destruction of drainage works" (Keegan 151).

21 The effect this produced on leech gatherers seems worthy of further investigation in terms of the eponymous Wordsworth poem.

22 As indicated by William Cunningham in *The Growth of English Industry and Commerce* and by Thorold Rogers, in *History of Agriculture and Prices*, qtd. in Clark 15.

23 Including the Dutch Gold Coast of Africa, Malabar, Suratte, Ceylon, Bengal, Coromandel, Mallaca, and its colonies in North America.

24 As I have tried to show throughout this book, from the brutal methods employed in New Spain mines to the clear cutting of plantations for sugar in Haiti, to the deforestation of Britain and its colonies, these processes and many others have provided the basis of an extractive methodology that has only accelerated since its initial significant expansion in the eighteenth century.

25 From "My Bonny Jane" (c. 1845–50). There are other descriptions of mossy thatch or mossy eaves in both Clare's prose and poetry, and a visitor to Helpston can still find moss resiliently growing on rooftops today.

Conclusion

1 The isolation of this phrase both foreshadows the Mariner's isolation and indicates the centrality of the sea voyage to the development of Western culture – in this sense, there is always a ship.

2 The language of both science and exploration often used a sexualized imagery during this period, in which a "virgin" territory is "discovered" or a female nature is "penetrated" by a male explorer/scientist. The lines "We were the first to ever burst / Into that silent sea" (105–6) reflect this pattern. The Pacific was navigated for centuries before European arrival.

Vincente Diaz has detailed how Austronesian seafarers used outrigger technology to "fan out and settle roughly four fifths of the globe's southern oceanic hemisphere," a process that "has been underway for at least four thousand years" (93). Tim Fulford, Peter J. Kitson, and Debbie Lee, in their study *Literature, Science and Exploration in the Romantic Era*, point to the way exploration of the globe influenced Romantic imaginative literary exploration. In "Unspeakable Discovery: Romanticism and the 'Rime of the Ancient Mariner,'" Matthias Rudolf argues that maritime discovery provides an allegory for literary criticism.

3   As Barthes also recognized: "more than a substance, plastic is the very idea of its infinite transformation" (97). It is interesting to note that Barthes, like Baekeland, is uninterested in the non-biodegradable aspect of plastic, the paradoxical form of "its infinite transformation."

4   What Wordsworth describes as "the heavy and the weary weight / Of all this unintelligible world" takes on another layer of meaning in this context.

5   Though Barry is interested in the way Coleridge creates new spaces for meaning through an attention to the way different communities interpret specific terms, the notion of a "poetics of interruption" might also usefully be applied to the way Wollstonecraft employs tropes of the picturesque landscape only to repeatedly interrupt them at the moment when they rise to a height of expected aesthetic recompense.

6   For an excellent reading of this influence and its ties to that of Berkeley and Hartley, see Michael Raiger's "The Intellectual Breeze, the Corporeality of Thought, and the Eolian Harp." For a summary of Coleridge's reading on the theory of plastic nature, see Halmi, in *Coleridge's Poetry and Prose*, 19n7.

7   Cudworth describes plastic nature as "an inferior and subordinate instrument" that "doth drudgingly execute that part of his providence, which consists in the regular and orderly motion of matter" (150; book 1).

8   This recalls the experience described by Mary Prince, in which salt becomes pathologically embedded within the body, discussed further below.

9   See E. Ann Kaplan's *Climate Trauma* for the most comprehensive account of this type of trauma as it relates to literature and film, and Michael Richardson's "Climate Trauma, or the Affects of the Catastrophe to Come" for a response to Kaplan. See Morganstein and Ursano, "Ecological Disasters and Mental Health" for a community psychology–based approach to the subject.

10 One piece of data that illustrates this acceleration is the ten-fold increase in the amount of plastic produced from 1970 to 2015, from around 30 million tons to 322 million tons (Kosuth al. 2).

11 A recurring claim of individuals directly affected by climate change is how the natural world, once viewed as friendly support, becomes feared adversary (see the documentary *The Human Face of Climate Change* for several first-hand accounts).

Works Cited

Acts and Ordinances of the Interregnum, 1642–1660. Eds. C.H. Firth and R.S. Rait. London: His Majesty's Stationery Office, 1911. *British History Online*, https://www.british-history.ac.uk/no-series/acts-ordinances-interregnum. 29 July 2021.

Aghalino, Sam Ovuete. "British Colonial Policies and the Oil Palm Industry in the Niger Delta Region of Nigeria." *African Study Monographs*, vol. 21, no. 1, 2000, pp. 19–33.

Ahmed, Siraj. *Archaeology of Babel: The Colonial Foundation of the Humanities*. Stanford UP, 2018.

Alaimo, Stacey. *Bodily Natures: Science, Environment, and the Material Self*. Indiana UP, 2010.

Albion, Robert. *Forest and Sea Power: The Timber Problem of the Royal Navy, 1652–1862*. Harvard UP, 1926.

Allewaert, Monique. "Swamp Sublime: Ecologies of Resistance in the American Plantation Zone." *PMLA*, vol. 123, no. 2, March 2008, pp. 340–57.

Anglicus, Barthalomaeus. *De proprietatibus rerum*. Translated by John of Trevisa, Thomas East, 1582.

Appadurai, Arjun. "Introduction: Commodities and the Politics of Value." *The Social Life of Things*, edited by Arjun Appadurai. Cambridge UP, 1986.

Ardon, Paul. *Peat Cutting in Upland Britain with Special Reference to the Peak District*. 1999. University of Sheffield, PhD dissertation.

Armelagos, George J. "The Slavery Hypertension Hypothesis: Natural Selection and Scientific Investigation: A Commentary." *Transforming Anthropology*, vol. 13, no. 2, 2005, pp. 119–24.

Armstrong, Isobel. "A Music of Thine Own: Woman's Poetry – An Expressive Tradition?" *Victorian Poetry: Poetry, Poetics and Politics*. Routledge, 1993.

Aronsohn, Marie DeNoia. "Palm Trees Are Spreading Northward. How Far Will They Go?" *Climate Response News*. Columbia University Faculty of Arts and Sciences, 19 March 2018.

Artaud, Antonin. "Theater and the Plague." *The Theater and its Double*, translated by Mary Caroline Richards. Grove, 1958.

"The Ash Tree in St. John's Cottage." *Wordsworth at Cambridge: A Record of the Commemoration Held at St John's College, Cambridge in April 1950*. Cambridge UP, 2009.

Ashenburg, Katherine. *The Dirt on Clean: An Unsanitized History*. Farrar, Straus, and Giroux, 2007.

Balston, John Noel. *The Whatmans and Wove Paper*. J.N. Balston, 1992.

Barad, Karen. *Meeting the Universe Halfway: Quantum Physics and the Entanglement of Matter and Meaning*. Duke UP, 2007.

Barker, Juliet. *Wordsworth, A Life*. Harper, 2000.

Barker, T.C. "Lancashire Coal, Cheshire Salt and the Rise of Liverpool." *Transactions of the Historical Society of Lancashire and Cheshire*, vol. 103, 1951, pp. 83–101.

Barrell, John. *The Idea of Landscape and the Sense of Place, 1730–1840*. Cambridge UP, 1972.

Barry, Sean. "Old Words, New Words, Wrong Words: Coleridge's Poetics of Interruption in 'The Rime of the Ancyent Marinere.'" *European Romantic Review*, vol. 28, no. 3, 2017, pp. 379–85.

Barthes, Roland. "Plastic." *Mythologies*, translated by Annette Lavers, Hill and Wang, 1957.

– "Soap-Powders and Detergents." *Mythologies*, translated by Annette Lavers, Hill and Wang, 1957.

Batchelor, Thomas. *General View of the Agriculture of the County of Bedford*. Sherwood, Neely and Jones, 1813. *HathiTrust*, https://catalog.hathitrust.org/Record/008600240.

Bate, Jonathan. *Romantic Ecology: Wordsworth and the Environmental Tradition*. Routledge, 1991.

Behrendt, Stephen C. "'Certainly Not a Female Pen': Felicia Hemans's Early Public Reception." *Felicia Hemans: Reimagining Poetry in the Nineteenth Century*, edited by Julie Melnyk and Nanora Sweet, Macmillan, 2000.

– "Placing Irish Romanticism in the Same Frame: Prospects." *Ireland and Romanticism*, edited by Jim Kelly, Palgrave Macmillan, 2011.

Beiner, Guy. *Remembering the Year of the French: Irish Folk History and Social Memory*. U of Wisconsin P, 2007.

Benjamin, Walter. "Theses on the Philosophy of History." *Illuminations*, translated by Harry Zohn, Schocken Books, 1969.

Bennett, Jane. *Vibrant Matter: A Political Ecology of Things*. Duke UP, 2009.

Benso, Silvia. *The Face of Things: A Different Side of Ethics*. SUNY Press, 2000.

Bergquist, Lars. *Swedenborg's Secret: The Meaning and Significance of the Word of God, the Life of the Angels, and Service to God*. The Swedenborg Society, 2005.

Bergren, Katherine. *The Global Wordsworth: Romanticism out of Place*. Bucknell UP, 2019.

Berlant, Lauren. "Intimacy: A Special Issue." *Critical Inquiry*, vol. 24, no. 2, Winter 1988, pp. 281–8.
Bermingham, Ann. *Landscape and Ideology: The English Rustic Tradition, 1740–1860*. U of California P, 1986.
Bewell, Alan. *Romanticism and Colonial Disease*. John Hopkins UP, 1999.
– "John Clare and the Ghosts of Natures Past." *Nineteenth Century Literature*, vol. 65, no. 4, March 2011, pp. 548–78.
– *Natures in Translation*. Johns Hopkins UP, 2017.
Biancalani, Ricardo, and Armine Avagyan, editors. "Towards Climate-Responsible Peatlands Management." Food and Agriculture Organization of the United Nations, 2014.
Billingsley, John. *A General View of the Agriculture in the County of Somerset, 1795*. 2nd ed., R. Cruttwell, 1798. *HathiTrust*, https://babel.hathitrust.org/cgi/pt?id=nyp.33433006512390&view=1up&seq=11.
Bogost, Ian. *Alien Phenomenology, or What It's Like to Be a Thing*. Minnesota UP, 2012.
Bohls, Elizabeth. *Women Travel Writers and the Language of Aesthetics, 1716–1818*. Cambridge UP, 1995.
Boland, Eavan. "Discovering the Sonnet." *The Making of the Sonnet: A Norton Anthology*, edited by Eavan Boland and Edward Hirsch, Norton, 2008.
Bonzcar, Thomas P., and Allen J. Beck. "Lifetime Likelihood of Going to State or Federal Prison." *Bureau of Justice Statistics Special Report*. U.S. Department of Justice, 1997.
Bremner, Robert. *Excursions in Denmark, Norway and Sweden*, vol. 2, Henry Colburn, 1840.
Brown, Bill. "Thing Theory." *Things*, edited by Bill Brown, U of Chicago P, 2004.
Brunskill. R.W. *Traditional Buildings of Britain: An Introduction to Vernacular Architecture*. Yale UP, 2006.
Buchan, William. *Domestic Medicine*. Kruskshank, Bell, and Muir, 1784.
Buell, Laurence. *The Future of Environmental Criticism*. Blackwell, 2005.
Burgess, Miranda. "Jane Austen on Paper." *European Romantic Review*, vol. 29, no. 3, 2018. pp. 365–75.
Burke, Edmund. *The Correspondance of Edmund Burke*. Edited by Lucy S. Sutherland, vol. II, Cambridge UP, 1960.
– *A Philosophical Enquiry into the Origin of our Ideas of the Sublime and Beautiful*. Edited by Adam Phillips, Oxford UP, 1990.
Burkett, Andrew. "Wordsworthian Chance." *Romanticism and Victorianism on the Net*, vol. 54, 2009.
Bushaway, Bob. *By Rite: Custom, Ceremony and Community in England, 1700–1880*. Junction Books, 1982.
Calvert, Albert F. *Salt and the Salt Industry*. Pitman & Sons, 1919.
Cameron, Dorothy. "Goethe – Discoverer of the Ice Age." *Journal of Glaciology*, vol. 5, no. 4, 1964, pp. 751–4.

Campbell, Mavis C. *The Maroons of Jamaica, 1655–1796: A History of Resistance, Collaboration & Betrayal*. Bergin & Garvey, 1988.
Canuel, Mark. "Wollstonecraft and World Improvement." *Wordsworth Circle*, vol. 41, no. 3, 2010, pp. 139f.
Castellano, Katey. *The Ecology of British Romantic Conservatism, 1790–1837*. Palgrave, 2013.
Celan, Paul. "Conversation in the Mountains." *Paul Celan: Selections*. U of California P, 2005.
Certeau, Michel de. *The Practice of Everyday Life*. Translated by Steven Rendall, U of California P, 1984.
Chambers, Frank M., and Dan J. Charman. "Holocene Environmental Change: Contributions from the Peatland Archive." *The Holocene*, vol. 14, no. 1, December 2003, pp. 1–6.
Cheney, Christine. "The Rhetorical Strategies of 'Tumultuous Emotions': Wollstonecraft's Letters Written in Sweden." *Journal of Narrative Theory*, vol. 34, no. 3, Fall 2004, pp. 277–303.
Chisolm, JJ. "Lead Poisoning." *Oski's Essential Pediatrics*, edited by M. Crocetti, M.A. Barone, and F.A. Oski, Lippincott Williams & Wilkins, 2004.
Choi, Hojin, and Seung Hyun Kim. "Air Pollution and Dementia." *Dementia and Neurocognitive Disorders*, vol. 18, no. 4, December 2019, pp. 109–12.
Clare, John. *Poems Descriptive of Rural Life and Scenery*. Taylor and Hessey, 1820.
– *The Later Poems of John Clare*. Edited by Eric Robinson and David Powell, vol. 2, Oxford UP, 1984.
– *Poems of the Middle Period, 1822–1837*. Edited by Eric Robinson, David Powell, and P.M.S. Dawson, Oxford UP, 1996.
– *"I AM": The Selected Poetry of John Clare*. Edited by Jonathan Bate, Farrar, Straus and Giroux, 2003.
– *Major Works*. Edited by Eric Robinson and David Powell. Oxford UP, 2008.
Claridge, John. *A General View of the Agriculture in the County of Dorset, 1793*. W. Smith, 1793. *Google Books*, https://books.google.com/books?id=PKwQAAAAIAAJ&printsec=frontcover&source=gbs_ge_summary_r&cad=0#v=onepage&q&f=false.
Clark, G.N. *The Seventeenth Century*, 2nd ed., Oxford UP, 1957.
Cobbett, William. *Rural Rides*. A. Cobbett, 1853.
– *Cottage Economy*. Oxford UP, 1979.
Cochrane, Archibald. *The Present State of the Manufacture of Salt Explained*. W. & A. Strahan for T. Cadell, 1785.
Cohen, Jeffrey Jerome. *Stone: An Ecology of the Inhuman*. Minnesota UP, 2015.
Coleridge, Samuel Taylor. *Coleridge's Poetry and Prose*. Edited by Nicholas Halmi, Paul Magnuson, and Raimonda Modiano, Norton, 2004.
Collings, David. *Monstrous Society: Reciprocity, Discipline, and the Political Uncanny at the End of Early Modern England*. Bucknell UP, 2009.

Connery, Christopher. "Sea Power." *PMLA*, vol. 125, no. 3, May 2010, pp. 685–92.

Cooke, Majid Fadzilah, and Dayang Suria Mulia. "Migration and Moral Panic: The Case of Palm Oil in Sabah, East Malaysia." *The Palm Oil Controversy in Southeast Asia: A Transnational Perspective*, edited by Oliver Pye and Jayati Bhattacharya, Institute of Southeast Asian Studies, 2013.

Corner, E.J.H. *The Natural History of Palms*. U of California P, 1966.

Cox, Keiran, et al. "Human Consumption of Microplastics." *Environ. Sci. Technol.*, vol. 53, no. 12, 2019 pp. 7068–74.

Crimmin, P.K. "Searching for British Naval Stores: Sources and Strategy c.1802–1860." *The Great Circle*, vol. 18 no. 2, 1996, pp. 113–24.

Critser, Greg. *Fat Land: How Americans Became the Fattest People in the World*. Houghton Mifflin, 2003.

Crowder, Michael. *West Africa under Colonial Rule*. Northwestern UP, 1968.

Cudworth, Ralph. *The True Intellectual System of the Universe*. Printed for Richard Royston, 1678.

Curran, Stuart. "The I Altered." *Romanticism and Feminism*, edited by Anne Mellor, Indiana UP, 1988.

Dallas, Robert Charles. *The History of the Maroons*. T.N. Longman and O. Rees, 1803.

Daniels, Stephen. "The Political Iconography of Woodland in Later Georgian England." *The Iconography of Landscape*, Cambridge UP, 1988.

Davies, David. *The Case of Labourers in Husbandry*. R.Crutwell, 1795.

Deleuze, Giles, and Felix Guattari. *A Thousand Plateaus: Capitalism and Schizophrenia*. Translated by Brian Massumi, U of Minnesota P, 1987.

Diaz, Vincente. "Voyaging for Anti-colonial Recovery: Austronesian Seafaring, Archipelagic Rethinking, and the Re-mapping of Indigeneity." *Pacific Asia Enquiry*, vol. 2, no. 1, Fall 2011, pp. 21–32.

Dickson, Joshua. *The Highland Bagpipe: Music, History, Tradition*. Ashgate, 2009.

Dixon, H.N. "The Economic Value of Mosses." *Journal of the Northamptonshire Natural History Society & Field Club*, vol. 8, Jos. Tebbutt, 1894–5.

Doubleday, Arthur H., editor. *Victoria County History. Hampshire ii*. Constable and Company, 1903.

Douglas, Mary. *Purity and Danger: An Analysis of Concepts of Pollution and Taboo*. Routledge, 1966.

Eisenstein, Paul, and Todd McGowan. *Rupture: On the Emergence of the Political*. Northwestern UP, 2012.

Elhacham, Emily, et al. "Global Human-Made Mass Exceeds All Living Biomass." *Nature*, vol. 588, December 2020, 442–4.

Eliasson, Per, and Sven G. Nilsson. "'You Should Hate Young Oaks and Young Noblemen': The Environmental History of Oaks in Eighteenth- and Nineteenth-Century Sweden." *Environmental History*, vol. 7, no. 4, October 2002, pp. 659–77.

Ellerman, Greg. "Plasticity, Poetry, and the End of Art: Malabou, Hegel, Keats." *Romanticism and Speculative Realism*, edited by Anne C. McCarthy and Chris Washington, Bloomsbury 2019.

Equiano, Olaudah. *The Interesting Narrative of the Life of Olaudah Equiano, or Gustavus Vassa, The African. Written by Himself*, 9th ed., printed for and sold by the author, 1794.

Evans, Chris, and Goran Ryden. *Baltic Iron in the Atlantic World in the Eighteenth Century*. Brill, 2007.

Everitt, Alan. "Farm Labourers." *The Agrarian History of England and Wales v.4: 1500–1640*, edited by Joan Thirsk, Cambridge UP, 1967.

Falconbridge, Alexander. *An Account of the Slave Trade on the Coast of Africa*. J. Phillips, 1788.

Favret, Mary. *War at a Distance: Romanticism and the Making of Modern Wartime*. Princeton UP, 2010.

– "Wollstonecraft's Antigone." *Mary Wollstonecraft Even Now*, edited by Sonia Hofkosh, Romantic Circle PRAXIS, 2019.

Flood, John, and Phil Flood. *Kilcash 1190–1801*. Geography Publications, 1999.

Flores, Christina. *Plastic Intellectual Breeze: The Contribution of Ralph Cudworth to S. T. Coleridge's Early Poetics of the Symbol*. Peter Lang, 2008.

Forman, Cyrus. "A Briny Crossroads Salt, Slavery, and Sectionalism in The Kanawha Salines." Thesis, *CUNY Academic Works*, 2014.

Fosso, Kurt. "Community and Mourning in William Wordsworth's 'The Ruined Cottage 1797–1798.'" *Studies in Philology*, vol. 92, no.3, Summer 1995, pp. 329–45.

Foster, John Bellamy. *Marx's Ecology: Materialism and Nature*. Monthly Review Press, 2000.

Frank, Andre Gunder. *ReOrient: Global Economy in the Asian Age*. U of California P, 1998.

Freud, Sigmund. *The Interpretation of Dreams*. Translated by James Strachey, *The Standard Edition of the Complete Works of Sigmund Freud*, vol 4, Hogarth, 1953.

– "The Aetiology of Hysteria." *The Standard Edition of the Complete Psychological Works of Sigmund Freud*, translated by James Strachey, vol. 3, Hogarth Press, 1962.

– *New Introductory Lectures in Psychoanalysis*. Translated by James Strachey, Norton, 1965.

Fulford, Tim. "Cowper, Wordsworth, Clare: The Politics of Trees." *The John Clare Society Journal*, vol. 14, 1995, pp. 47–59.

– "Britannia's Heart of Oak: Thomson, Garrick and the Language of Eighteenth-Century Patriotism." *James Thomson: Essays for the Tercentenary*, edited by Richard Terry, Liverpool UP, 2000.

Fulford, Tim, et al. *Literature, Science, and Exploration in the Romantic Era: Bodies of Knowledge*. Cambridge UP, 2004.

Gadd, Carl-Johan. "The Agricultural Revolution in Sweden." *The Agrarian History of Sweden: 4000 BC to AD 2000*, edited by Janken Myrdal and Mats Morell, Nordic Academic Press, 2011.

Gadsby, Meredith. *Sucking Salt: Caribbean Women Writers, Migration, and Survival*. U of Missouri P, 2006.

Galeano, Eduardo. *Open Veins of Latin America: Five Centuries of the Pillage of a Continent*. Translated by Cedric Belfrage. Monthly Review Press, 1973.

Gallegos, Danielle. "Palm Oil Tensions." *New Formations*, vol. 74, 2011, 18–32.

Galloway, Stephen. "Which Hollywood Studio Hid Its Priceless Papers in an Underground Salt Mine?" *The Hollywood Reporter*, 21 Oct. 2019, https://www.hollywoodreporter.com/movies/movie-news/hollywood-studio-hid-priceless-papers-an-underground-salt-mine-1247668/#:~:text=There%2C%20in%20a%20still%2Dfunctioning,the%20dryness%20and%20the%20cold.

Ganev, Robin. *Songs of Protest, Songs of Love: Popular Ballads in Eighteenth-Century Britain*. Manchester UP, 2009.

George, Sam. "The Cultivation of the Female Mind: Enlightened Growth, Luxuriant Decay and Botanical Analogy in Eighteenth-Century Texts." *History of European Ideas*, vol. 31, 2005, pp. 209–23.

Gikandi, Simon. *Slavery and the Culture of Taste*. Princeton UP, 2011.

Gilroy, Paul. *The Black Atlantic: Modernity and Double Consciousness*. Verso, 1993.

Glob, P.V. *The Bog People: Iron-Age Man Preserved*. New York Review Books, 1965.

Gorji, Mina. *John Clare and the Place of Poetry*. Liverpool UP, 2008.

Gottleib, Evan. Introduction. *Global Romanticisms: Origins, Orientations, and Engagements, 1760–1820*, edited by Evan Gottleib, Bucknell UP, 2015.

Graham, G.S. *Sea Power and British North America, 1783–1820: A Study in British Colonial Policy*. Harvard UP, 1941.

Graves, Robert. *The White Goddess*. Noonday Press, 1948.

Gray, Richard. "Inside Cheshire's Salt Mine: Britain's Only Underground Hazardous Waste Facility." *Telegraph*, 22 Sept. 2013.

Green, T.A. *Folklore: An Encyclopedia of Beliefs, Customs, Tales, Music and Art*. ABC-CLIO, 1998.

Haraway, Donna. *Staying with the Trouble: Making Kin in the Chthulucene*. Duke UP, 2016.

Hardiman, David. Introduction. *Healing Bodies, Saving Souls: Medical Missions in Asia and Africa*, edited by David Hardiman, Brill, 2016.

Hardt, Michael, and Antonio Negri. *Commonwealth*. Harvard UP, 2010.

Harman, Graham. *Object Oriented Ontology: A New Theory of Everything*. Pelican, 2018.

Harrison, Gary. "Hybridity, Mimicry, and John Clare's Child Harold." *The Wordsworth Circle*, vol. 34, no. 3, Summer 2003, pp. 149–55.

Hartman, Geoffrey. *The Unremarkable Wordsworth*. U of Minnesota P, 1987.
Hartman, Saidiya V. *Scenes of Subjection: Terror, Slavery, and Self-Making in Nineteenth-Century America*. Oxford UP, 1997.
Hassett, Maurice. "Palm in Christian Symbolism." *The Catholic Encyclopedia*, vol. 11, Robert Appleton Company, 1911.
Hay, Douglas. "Property, Authority and the Criminal Law." *Albion's Fatal Tree*, Pantheon Books, 1975.
Heaney, Seamus. "Feeling into Words." *Preoccupations: Selected Prose, 1968–78*, Faber & Faber, 1980.
– "John Clare: A Bi-centenary Lecture." *John Clare in Context*, edited by Geoffrey Summerfield, Hugh Haughton, and Adam Phillips, Cambridge UP, 1994.
Heidegger, Martin. *Poetry, Language, Thought*. Translated by Alfred Hofstadter, Harper & Row, 1971.
Hemans, Felicia Dorothea. *The Poetical Works of Mrs. Felicia Hemans; Complete in One Volume*. Grigg & Elliot, 1836.
– *The Complete Works of Mrs. Hemans*. Vol. 2, D. Appleton & Co., 1847.
– *Felicia Hemans: Selected Poems, Letters, Reception Materials*. Edited by Susan Wolfson, Princeton UP, 2000.
– *The Siege of Valencia*. Edited by Susan Wolfson and Elizabeth Fay, Broadview, 2002.
Heng, Mary. "Tell Them No Lies: Reconstructed Truth in Wollstonecraft's *A Short Residence in Sweden*." *The Journal of Narrative Technique*, vol. 28, no. 3, Fall 1998, pp. 366–87.
Herder, Johann Gottfried von. "Essay on the Origin of Language." *On the Origin of Language*, translated by Alexander Gode and edited by John H. Moran and Alexander Gode, U of Chicago P, 1966.
Heringman, Noah. *Romantic Rocks, Aesthetic Geology*. Cornell UP, 2010.
Herodotus. *The Histories*. Vol II. Translated by A.D. Godley, The Loeb Classical Library. Heinemann, 1921.
"Herring and the Herring Fishery." *The Westminster Review*, vol. 26, Trubner & Co., 1864.
Hess, Scott. *William Wordsworth and the Ecology of Authorship: The Roots of Environmentalism in Nineteenth-Century Culture*. U of Virginia P, 2012.
Hildebrand, K.G. "Foreign Markets for Swedish Iron in the 18th Century." *Scandinavian Economic History Review*, vol. 6, no. 1, 1958, pp. 3–52.
Hoffer, Peter. "Reflections on Cathexis." *The Psychoanalytic Quarterly*, vol. 74, no. 4, October 2005, pp. 1127–35.
Horner, E.J.H. *The Natural History of Palms*. U of California P, 1966.
Houben, Jan E.M., and Saraju Rath. "Manuscript Culture and its Impact in 'India': Contours and Parameters." *Aspects of Manuscript Culture in South India*, edited by Saraju Rath, Brill, 2012.

Hunter, J.P. Introduction. *Frankenstein*, by Mary Shelley, edited by J.P. Hunter, Norton, 2012.
Hust, Karen. "In Suspect Terrain: Mary Wollstonecraft confronts mother nature in *letters written during a short residence in Sweden, Norway, and Denmark*." *Women's Studies*, vol. 25, no. 5, 1996, 483–505.
Hutton, James. *Theory of the Earth*. Outlook, 2020.
Huxley, Aldous. *Collected Essays*. Harper & Brothers, 1959.
Inglis, Brian. *Poverty and the Industrial Revolution*. Hodder & Stoughton, 1971.
Inikori, Joseph. "Slave Trade and Capitalism." *British Capitalism and Caribbean Slavery: The Legacy of Eric Williams*, edited by Barbara Lewis Solow and Stanley L. Engerman, Cambridge UP, 1987.
Irigaray, Luce. *This Sex Which Is Not One*. Translated by Catherine Porter, Cornell UP, 1985.
Jacobus, Mary. *Romantic Things: A Rock, a Cloud, a Tree*. U of Chicago P, 2012.
Jeffrey, Francis. "Felicia Hemans." *Edinburgh Review*, vol. 50, October 1829, pp. 32–47.
Johnson, Leonard George. *General T. Perronet Thompson*. George Allen & Unwin, 1957.
Jones, Ernest. "The Symbolic Significance of Salt." *Essays in Applied Psychoanalysis*, edited by Ernest Jones, The International Psycho-analytical Press, 1923.
Jump, Harriet, editor. *Mary Wollstonecraft and the Critics 1788–2001*. Vols. 1–2, Taylor & Francis, 2003.
Jung, C.G. *Psychology and Alchemy*. Translated by Gerhard Adler and R.F.C. Hull, Princeton UP, 1980.
Kaplan, E. Ann. *Climate Trauma: Foreseeing the Future in Dystopian Film and Fiction*. Rutgers UP, 2015.
Karera, Axelle. "Blackness and the Pitfalls of Anthropocene Ethics." *Critical Philosophy of Race*, vol. 7, no. 1, 2019, pp. 32–56.
Keats, John. *The Complete Works of John Keats*. Edited by H. Buxton Forman, Gowers and Gray, 1901.
– *The Major Works*. Edited by Elizabeth Cook, Oxford UP, 1990.
Keegan, Bridget. *British Labouring-Class Nature Poetry 1730–1837*. Palgrave, 2008.
Kelly, Theresa M. *Clandestine Marriage: Botany & Romantic Culture*. Johns Hopkins UP, 2012.
Kennedy, Cynthia. "The Other White Gold: Salt, Slaves, the Turk's and Caicos Islands, and British Colonialism." *The Historian*, vol. 69, no. 2, Summer 2007, pp. 215–30.
Kimmerer, Robin Wall. *Gathering Moss: A Natural and Cultural History of Mosses*. Oregon State UP, 2003.
– *Braiding Sweetgrass*. Milkweed Editions, 2015.
King, Peter. *Crime and Law in England, 1750–1840*. Cambridge UP, 2006.

Klein, Herbert S., and Ben Vinson. *African Slavery in Latin America and the Caribbean*. Oxford UP, 2007.

Knight, R.J.B. "New England Forests and British Seapower: Albion Revised." *American Neptune*, vol. 46, 1986, pp. 221–9.

Knight, William, ed. *The Letters of the Wordsworth Family, 1787–1855*. Haskell House Publishers, 1907.

Koops, Mathias. *Historical Account of the Substances Which Have Been Used to Describe Events and Convey Ideas from the Earliest Date to the Invention of Paper*. T. Burton, 1800.

Kosuth, Mary, et al. "Anthropogenic Contamination of Tap Water, Beer, and Sea Salt." *PLOS One*, vol. 13, no. 4, April 2018.

Kovesi, Simon. "John Clare &…&…&…Deluze and Guattari's Rhizome." *Ecology and the Literature of the British Left: The Red and the Green*, edited by John Rignall and H. Gustav Klaus, with Valentine Cunningham, Routledge, 2016.

Krishna Reddy, K.S.V., et al. "Experimental Investigation on Usage of Palm Oil as a Lubricant to Substitute Mineral Oil in CI Engines." *Chinese Journal of Engineering*, vol. 2014.

Kurlansky, Mark. *Salt: A World History*. Walker and Company, 2002.

Lacan, Jacques. *The Ethics of Psychoanalysis 1959–1960: The Seminar of Jacques Lacan*, Book VII. Edited by Jacques-Alain Miller and translated by Dennis Porter, Routledge, 1992.

Lamb, Jonathan. "Persons and Things." *The Material Cultures of Enlightenment Arts and Sciences*, edited by Adriana Craciun and Simon Schaffer, Palgrave, 2016.

Langan. Celeste. *Romantic Vagrancy: Wordsworth and the Simulation of Freedom*. Cambridge UP, 1995.

Latour, Bruno. *Politics of Nature: How to Bring the Sciences into Democracy*. Translated by Catherine Porter, Harvard UP, 1999.

– "The Berlin Key." *Matter, Materiality and Modern Culture*, edited by P.M. Graves-Brown, Routledge, 2000.

Law, Jules David. *The Social Life of Fluids: Blood, Milk, and Water in the Victorian Novel*. Cornell UP, 2010.

Lee, Debbie. *Slavery and the Romantic Imagination*. U of Pennsylvania P, 2002.

Lefebvre, Henri. *The Critique of Everyday Life*. Translated by John Moore, Verso, 1991.

Levin, Phillis. Introduction. *The Penguin Book of the Sonnet: 500 Years of a Classic Tradition in English*, by Levin, Penguin, 2001.

Levinson, Marjorie. *The Romantic Fragment Poem: A Critique of Form*. UNC Press, 2011.

Lezra, Jacques. *On the Nature of Marx's Things: Translation as Necrophilology*. Fordham UP, 2018.

Lienhard, Siegfried. *A History of Classical Poetry: Sanskrit, Pali, Prakrit*. Otto Harrassowitz, 1984.

Lim, Chye Ing, et al. "Review of Existing Sustainability Assessment Methods for Malaysian Palm Oil Production." *Procedia CIRP*, vol. 26, 2015, pp. 13–18.

Linebaugh, Peter. *Stop Thief!: The Commons, Enclosure and Resistance*. Spectre, 2014.

Liu, Alan. *Wordsworth: The Sense of History*. Stanford UP, 1989.

Ljungman, Axel Vilhelm. "The Great Bohuslan Herring-Fisheries." *The Miscellaneous Documents of the Senate of the United States for the Third Session of the Forty-Fifth Congress, 1878-'79*, translated by Herman Jacobson, Government Printing Office, 1879.

Lo Bue, Maria C. "Indonesia's Huge Fires and Toxic Haze will Cause Health Problems for Years to Come." *Phys.org*, 7 Oct. 2019, https://phys.org/news/2019-10-indonesia-huge-toxic-haze-health.html.

Lootens, Tricia. "Hemans and Home: Victorianism, Feminine 'Internal Enemies,' and the Domestication of National Identity." *PMLA*, vol. 109, 1994, pp. 238–53.

Lowe, Lisa. *The Intimacies of Four Continents*. Duke UP, 2015.

Lucretius. *De Rerum Natura*. Translated by W.H.D. Rouse and edited by Martin Ferguson Smith, Harvard UP, 1992.

Lukács, György. "Reification and the Consciousness of the Proletariat." *History and Class Consciousness*, Merlin Press, 1967.

Lynn, Martin. "Trade and Politics in Nineteenth Century Liverpool: the Tobin and Horsfall Families and Liverpool's African Trade." *Transactions of the Historic Society of Lancashire and Cheshire*, vol. 142, 1993, pp. 99–120.

– *Commerce and Economic Change in West Africa: The Palm Oil Trade in the Nineteenth Century*. Cambridge UP, 1997.

– "Liverpool and Africa in the Nineteenth Century: The Continuing Connection." *Transactions of the Historic Society of Lancashire and Cheshire*, vol. 147, 1998, pp. 27–54.

MacNamara, Mark. "We Need to Talk About Peat." *Nautilus*, no. 78, 7 November 2019.

Macpherson, D. *Annals of Commerce, Manufactures, Fisheries, and Navigation with Brief Notices of the Arts and Sciences Connected with Them: Containing the Commercial Transactions of the British Empire and Other Countries: With a Large Appendix; in Four Volumes*. Nichols and Son, 1805.

Maddison-MacFadyen, Margo. "Toiling in the Salt Ponds." *Times of the Islands*, vol. 84, Fall 2008, https://www.timespub.tc/2008/09/toiling-in-the-salt-ponds/.

Mahood, M.M. *The Poet as Botanist*. Cambridge UP, 2008.

Mann, Kristin. *Slavery and the Birth of an African City: Lagos, 1760–1900*. Indiana UP, 2007.

Manthorne, Katherine. "The Quest for a Tropical Paradise: Palm Tree as Fact and Symbol in Latin American Landscape Imagery, 1850–1875." *Art Journal*, vol. 44, no. 4, 1984, pp. 374–82.

Marshak, Stephen. *Essentials of Geology*. 4th ed., U of Illinois P, 2013.
Marx, Karl. "Debates on the Law on Thefts of Wood," translated by Clemens Dutt, *Rheinische Zeitung*, no. 298, Supplement, 25 October 1842.
– "The Fetishism of the Commodity and the Secret Thereof." *Capital: A Critique of Political Economy*, translated by Ben Fowkes, vol. 1, Penguin Classics, 1990.
– *Capital: A Critique of Political Economy*. Translated by Ben Fowkes, vol. 1, Penguin, 2004.
Mayhew, Henry. *London Labour and the London Poor*. Vol. 2, Cass, 1851.
McArthur, Tom, and Roshan McArthur. *The Concise Oxford Companion to the English Language*. Oxford UP, 2005.
McCalman, Iain. *Radical Underworld: Prophets, Revolutionaries, and Pornographers, 1795–1840*. Clarendon Press, 1988.
McClintock, Anne. *Imperial Leather: Race, Gender, and Sexuality in the Colonial Contest*. Routledge, 1995.
McConnell-Ginet, Sally. "Linguistics and the Feminist Challenge." *Women and Language in Literature and Society*, Praeger, 1980.
McGann, Jerome. *The Romantic Ideology: A Critical Investigation*. Chicago UP, 1983.
– "Literary History, Romanticism and Felicia Hemans." *MLQ*, vol. 54, no. 2, 1993, pp. 215–35.
McKusick, James. "Coleridge and the Economy of Nature." *Studies in Romanticism*, vol. 35, no. 3, Fall 1996, pp. 375–92.
McNeill, J.R. *Mosquito Empire: Ecology and War in the Greater Caribbean, 1620–1914*. Cambridge UP, 2010.
Mellor, Anne. *Romanticism and Gender*. Routledge, 1992.
Melville, Herman. *Moby-Dick*. Penguin, 1986.
Miller, Daniel, editor. *Materiality*. Duke UP, 2005.
Mintz, Sidney. "Color, Taste and Purity: Some Speculations on the Meanings of Marzipan." *Etnofoor Jaarg*, vol. 4, no. 1, 1991, pp. 103–8.
Modiano, Raimonda. "Words and 'Languageless' Meanings: Limits of Expression in The Rime of the Ancient Mariner." *Modern Language Quarterly*, vol. 38, no. 1, 1977, pp. 40–61.
Moore, Jason. *Anthropocene or Capitalocene? Nature, History, and the Crisis of Capitalism*. PM Press, 2016.
Morganstein, Joshua, and Robert Ursano. "Ecological Disasters and Mental Health: Causes, Consequences, and Interventions." *Frontiers in Psychiatry*, vol. 11, no. 1, February 2020.
Morrison, Toni. *Playing in the Dark: Whiteness and the Literary Imagination*. Harvard UP, 1992.
Morton, Timothy. *The Poetics of Spice: Romantic Consumerism and the Exotic*. Cambridge UP, 2000.
– *Ecology without Nature: Rethinking Environmental Aesthetics*. Harvard UP, 2007.

Moten, Fred, and Stefano Harney. *The Undercommons: Fugitive Planning & Black Study*. Minor Compositions, 2013.

Nardizzi, Vin. *Wooden Os: Shakespeare's Theatres and England's Trees*. U of Toronto P, 2013.

Nassau, Robert Hamill. *Fetichism in West Africa: Forty Years' Observation of Native Customs and Superstitions*. Duckworth & Co, 1904.

National Archives, United Kingdom. Colonial Office (CO) Papers. Various. Manuscript.

Nau, Ignace. "Dessalines." *Poetry of the Haitian Independence*, edited by Doris Kadish and Deborah Jenson and translated by Norman R. Shapiro, Yale UP, 2015.

Negele, Rainer. *Reading after Freud: Essays on Goethe, Holderin, Habermas, Nietzsche, Brecht, Celan, and Freud*. Columbia University Press, 1987.

Newcombe, S.P. *Pleasant Pages*. Vol. 6, Houlston & Stoneman, 1853.

Nichols, Jonathan E., and Dorothy M. Peteet. "Rapid Expansion of Northern Peatlands and Doubled Estimate of Carbon Storage." *Nature Geoscience*, vol. 12, November 2019, pp. 917–21.

Nixon, H.N. "The Economic Value of Mosses." *Journal of the Northamptonshire Natural History Society & Field Club*, vol. 8, Jos. Tebbutt, 1894–6.

Nixon, Rob. *Slow Violence and the Environmentalism of the Poor*. Harvard UP, 2011.

Nussbaum, Felicity. *Torrid Zones: Maternity, Sexuality, and Empire in Eighteenth-Century English Narratives*. Johns Hopkins UP, 1995.

Nyström, Per. *Mary Wollstonecraft's Scandinavian Journey*. Kungl Vetenskaps- och Vitterhets-Samhället, 1980.

O'Connor, Bernard. "The Origins and Development of the British Coprolite Industry." *Mining History*, vol. 14, no. 5, Summer 2001.

Orwell, George. *1984*. Signet Classics, 1977.

"Palm Oil." *World Wildlife Fund*, https://www.worldwildlife.org/industries/palm-oil.

Perlin, John. *A Forest Journey: The Story of Wood and Civilization*. Countryman Press, 1989.

Piersen, William D. "White Cannibals, Black Martyrs: Fear, Depression, and Religious Faith as Causes of Suicide Among New Slaves." *The Journal of Negro History*, vol. 62, no. 2, April 1977, pp. 147–59.

Place, Francis. *The Autobiography of Francis Place*. Edited by Mary Thale, Cambridge UP, 1972.

Plant, Marjorie. *The English Book Trade*. Allen & Unwin, 1974.

Porley, Ron D. *England's Rare Mosses and Liverworts: Their History, Ecology, and Conservation*. Princeton UP, 2013.

Potkay, Adam. "Wordsworth and the Ethics of Things." *PMLA*, vol. 123, no. 2, March 2008, pp. 390–404.

Prince, Mary. *The History of Mary Prince, A West Indian Slave, Related by Herself*. Edited by Moira Ferguson, U of Michigan P, 1997.

Pross, Jorg, et al. "Persistent Near-Tropical Warmth on the Antarctic Continent during the Early Eocene Epoch." *Nature*, vol. 488, August 2012, pp. 73–7.

Prynne, J.H. *Field Notes*: *'The Solitary Reaper' and Others*. Cambridge Printers Ltd., 2007.
Rackham, Oliver. *Ancient Woodland: Its History, Vegetation, and Uses in England*. Edward Arnold, 1980.
– *The History of the Countryside*. Dent, 1986.
Raiger, Michael. "The Intellectual Breeze, the Corporeality of Thought, and the Eolian Harp." *Coleridge Bulletin*, vol. 20, Winter 2002, pp. 76–84.
Ramanujan, A.K., editor and translator. *Poems of Love and War*. Columbia UP, 1985.
Rand, Frank Prentice. *Wordsworth's Mariner Brother*. The Newell Press, 1966.
Rauwerda, A.M. "Naming, Agency, and 'A Tissue of Falsehoods' in *The History of Mary Prince*." *Victorian Literature and Culture*, vol. 29, no. 2, September 2001, pp. 397–411.
Raven, Peter H., et al. *Biology of Plants*, 7th ed., W.H. Freeman and Company, 2005.
Reichgelt, Tammo, et al. "The Relation between Global Palm Distribution and Climate." *Scientific Reports*, vol. 8, no. 4721, March 2018.
Rhodes, Barbara J., and William W. Streeter. *Beyond Photocopying: The Art and History of Mechanical Copying, 1780–1938*. Oak Knoll Press, 1998.
Richardson, Alan. *British Romanticism and the Science of the Mind*. Cambridge UP, 2001.
Richardson, Michael. "Climate Trauma, or the Affects of the Catastrophe to Come." *Environmental Humanities*, vol. 10, no. 1, 2018, pp. 1–19.
Richens, R.H. *Elm*. Cambridge UP, 2012.
Rigby, Kate. *Topographies of the Sacred: The Poetics of Place in European Romanticism*. U of Virginia P, 2004.
Rituale Romanum. Edited by Philip T. Weller. The Bruce Publishing Company, 1964.
Roads, Esme, et al. "Millennial Timescale Regeneration in a Moss from Antarctica." *Current Biology*, vol. 24, no. 6, March 2014, R222–3.
Roe, Nicholas. *Wordsworth and Coleridge: The Radical Years*. Clarendon Press, 1988.
Rogers, Charles. *Scotland, Social and Domestic: Memorials of Life and Manners in North Britain*. Printed for the Grampian Club, 1869.
Ross, Anne. "Ritual and the Druids." *The Celtic World*, edited by Miranda J. Green, Routledge, 1995.
Ross, Marlon. *The Contours of Masculine Desire: Romanticism and the Rise of Women's Poetry*. Oxford UP, 1989.
Rotherham, Ian. *The Lost Fens: England's Greatest Ecological Disaster*. Stroud, 2013.
Rousseau, Jean Jacques. *The Reveries of the Solitary Walker*. Translated by Charles E. Butterworth, Hackett Publishing, 1992.

Rudolf, Matthias. "Unspeakable Discovery: Romanticism and the 'Rime of the Ancient Mariner.'" *European Romantic Review*, vol. 24, no. 2, 2013, 185–210.

Said, Edward H. *Culture and Imperialism*. Vintage, 1993.

"Salt Raking in the TCI." *Turk's and Caicos Islands National Museum*, https://www.tcmuseum.org/culture-history/salt-industry/.

Samuel, Arthur Michael. *The Herring: Its Effect on the History of Britain*. John Murray, 1918.

Samuel, John G. "Preservation of Palm-Leaf Manuscripts in Tamil." *IFLA Journal*, vol. 20, no. 3, October 1994, pp. 294–305.

Sassen, Saskia. *Expulsions: Brutality and Complexity in the Global Economy*. Harvard UP, 2014.

Savoca, Matthew, et al. "Marine Plastic Debris Emits a Keystone Infochemical for Olfactory Foraging Seabirds." *Science Advances*, vol. 2, no. 11, November 2016.

Scarry, Elaine. *On Beauty and Being Just*. Princeton UP, 1999.

Schabas, Margaret. *The Natural Origins of Economics*. U of Chicago P, 2007.

Schon, James Frederick, and Samuel Crowther. *Journals of the Rev. James Frederick Schon and Mr. Samuel Crowther*. Hatchard and Son, 1842.

Schouenborg, B., et al. "The Hallandia Gneiss, a Swedish Heritage Stone Resource." *Geological Society*, vol. 407, November 2014, pp. 35–48.

Serres, Michel. *The Natural Contract*. Translated by Elizabeth MacArthur and William Paulson, U of Michigan P, 1995.

Seshardi-Crooks, Kalpana. *Desiring Whiteness: A Lacanian Analysis of Race*. Routledge, 2002.

Sharpe, Jenny. "'Something Akin to Freedom': The Case of Mary Prince." *differences: A Journal of Feminist Cultural Studies*, vol. 8, no. 1, Spring 1996.

Shelley, Mary. *Frankenstein*. Edited by J. Paul Hunter, Norton, 2012.

Shi, Xilin, et al. "Geological Feasibility of Underground Oil Storage in Jintan Salt Mine of China." *Advances in Materials Science and Engineering*, vol. 2017.

Shorter, Alfred H. *Paper Making in the British Isles: An Historical and Geographical Study*. David & Charles, 1971.

Sinanan, Kerry. "The 'Slave' as Cultural Artifact: The Case of Mary Prince." *Studies in Eighteenth-Century Culture*, vol. 49, 2020, pp. 69–87.

Singer, Kate, and Nanora Sweet, editors. "Beyond Domesticity: Felicia Hemans in the Wider World." *Women's Writing*, vol. 21, no. 1, 2014, pp. 1–8.

Smith, Honor Ford. "A Message from Nian." *My Mother's Last Dance*, Black Women and Women of Colour Press, 1997.

Smith, Virginia Sarah. *Clean: A History of Personal Hygiene and Purity*. Oxford UP, 2008.

Snell, K.D.M. *Annals of the Labouring Poor: Social Change and Agrarian England, 1660–1900*. Cambridge UP, 1985.

Snyder, Terri L. *The Power to Die: Slavery and Suicide in British North America*. U of Chicago P, 2015.
Solow, Barbara L., and Stanley L. Engerman, editors. *British Capitalism and Caribbean Slavery: The Legacy of Eric Williams*. Cambridge UP, 1987.
Southey, Robert. *Collected Letters, Part Two: 1798–1803*. Edited by Ian Packer and Lynda Pratt, A Romantic Circles Electronic Edition, 2011.
Speitz, Michelle. "Blood Sugar and Salt Licks: Corroding Bodies and Preserving Nations in *The History of Mary Prince, a West Indian Slave, Related by Herself*." *Circulations: Romanticism and the Black Atlantic*, edited by Paul Youngquist and Frances Botkin, Romantic Circles, 2011.
Spinoza, Baruch. *Complete Works*. Edited by Michael L. Morgan and translated by Samuel Shirley, Hackett Publishing, 2002.
– A Letter to Jarig Jelles, 1674, *Improvement of the Understanding of Ethics and Correspondence*, translated by R.H.M. Elwes, Cosimo, 2006.
Spivak, Gayatri Chakravorty. "Can the Subaltern Speak?" *Marxism and the Interpretation of Culture*, edited by Cary Nelson and Lawrence Grossberg, U of Illinois P, 1988.
Stealey, John E. *The Antebellum Kanawha Salt Business and Western Markets*. West Virginia UP, 2016.
Steever, Sanford. "Tamil Writing." *The World's Writing Systems*, edited by William Bright and Peter T. Daniels, Oxford UP, 1996.
"Strataca: Underground Salt Museum." Roadsideamerica.com.
Studnicki-Gizbert, Daviken, and David Schecter. "The Environmental Dynamics of a Colonial Fuel-Rush: Silver Mining and Deforestation in New Spain, 1522 to 1810." *Environmental History*, vol. 15, no. 1, January 2010, pp. 94–119.
Sugden, J. "Archibald, 9th Earl of Dundonald: An Eighteenth-Century Entrepreneur." *Scottish Economic & Social History*, vol. 8, no. 1, September 2010, pp. 8–27.
Sunstein, Emily. *A Different Face: The Life of Mary Wollstonecraft*. Harper & Row, 1975.
Sweet, Nanora, and Julie Melnyk. *Felicia Hemans: Reimagining Poetry in the Nineteenth Century*. Palgrave, 2001.
Tacitus. *The Complete Works of Tacitus*. Translated by Alfred John Church, William Jackson Brodribb. Edited by Moses Hadis, Random House, 1942.
Tarr, Clayton Carlyle. "Absolute Heathenism: Bog Bodies and the Archaeology of Nineteenth-Century Literature." *Nineteenth Century Studies*, vol. 27, 2013, pp. 81f.
Theocritus. "Idyll 1," translated by C.S. Calverley, *The Classics in Sarasota*, 16 September 2009.
Thomas, Lewis. *The Lives of a Cell*. Penguin, 1974.
Thompson, E.P. *Whigs and Hunters: The Origin of the Black Act*. Random House, 1975.
– *Customs in Common: Studies in Traditional Popular Culture*. The New Press, 1993.

Thomson, Thomas. *Travels in Sweden, During the Autumn of 1812*. Robert Baldwin, 1813.
Todd, Janet. *Mary Wollstonecraft: An Annotated Bibilography*. Routledge, 2012.
Tomlinson, P.B. *The Structural Biology of Palms*. Clarendon Press, 1990.
The Treasuries of the Deep: Or, a Descriptive Account of the Great Fisheries and Their Products. T. Nelson and Sons, 1876.
Trevino, Javier A. *The Sociology of Law: Classical and Contemporary Perspectives*. Transaction Publishers, 2008.
Tullis, Paul. "How the World Got Hooked on Palm Oil." *The Guardian*, 19 Feb. 2019, https://www.theguardian.com/news/2019/feb/19/palm-oil-ingredient-biscuits-shampoo-environmental.
Tutino, John. *The Mexican Heartland: How Communities Shaped Capitalism, a Nation, and World History, 1500–2000*. Princeton UP, 2018.
"UK's Lowest Spot is Getting Lower." *BBC News*, 29 Nov. 2002, http://news.bbc.co.uk/2/hi/uk_news/england/2529365.stm.
Urban-Malinga, Barbara, et al. "Microplastics on Sandy Beaches of the Southern Baltic Sea." *Marine Pollution Bulletin*, vol. 155, June 2020, pp. 111–70.
Vardy, Alan. *John Clare, Politics and Poetry*. Palgrave, 2003.
Vitousek, P.M. "The Effects of Deforestation on Air, Soil, and Water." *The Biogeochemical Cycles and Their Interactions*, edited by B. Bolin and R.B. Cook, John Wiley and Sons, 1983.
Vries, Jan de, and Ad van der Woude. *The First Modern Economy: Success, Failure, and Perseverance of the Dutch Ecomony, 1500–1815*. Cambridge UP, 1997.
Washington, Booker T. *An Autobiography by Booker T. Washington: The Story of My Life and Work*. J.L. Nichols & Co, 1901.
Williams, Isabel M., and Leora H. McEachern. *Salt – That Necessary Article*. Wilmington, 1973.
Williams, Michael. *Deforesting the Earth: From Prehistory to Global Crisis*. U of Chicago P, 2006.
Winckler, E.M. *Stone: Properties, Durability in Man's Environment*. Springer-Verlag, 1975.
"What Are Metamorphic Rocks?" U.S. Geological Survey, https://www.usgs.gov/faqs/what-are-metamorphic-rocks-0?qt-news_science_products=0#qt-news_science_products.
White, William M. *Geochemistry*. Wiley-Blackwell, 2013.
Whitehurst, John. *An Inquiry into the Original State and Formulation of the Earth: Deduced from Facts and the Laws of Nature*. W. Brent, 1778.
Wilson Shiner, Carol, and Joel Haefner, J., editors. "Literary History, Romanticism, and Felicia Hermans." *Re-visioning Romanticism: British Women Writers, 1776–1837*. U of Pennsylvania Press, 1994.
Wollstonecraft, Mary. *Mary: A Fiction*. Garland Publishing, 1974.
– *Collected Letters*. Edited by Ralph M. Wardle, Cornell UP, 1979.

– *The Vindication of the Rights of Women*. Penguin Random House, 2001.
– *Letters Written During a Short Residence in Sweden, Norway, and Denmark*. Edited by Tone Brekke and Jon Mee, Oxford UP, 2009.
Woodmansee, Martha, and Mark Osteen. Introduction. *The New Economic Criticism: Studies at the Intersection of Literature and Economics*, edited by Martha Woodmansee and Mark Osteen, Routledge, 1999.
Wordsworth, Dorothy. *The Grasmere and Alfoxden Journals*. Edited by Pamela Woof, Oxford UP, 2002.
Wordsworth, William. *The Major Works*. Edited by Stephen Gill. Oxford UP, 2018.
– *The Poetical Works of William Wordsworth*. Edited by Thomas Hutchinson, Oxford UP, 1910.
– *The Prelude 1799, 1805, 1850*. Edited by Jonathan Wordsworth, M.H. Abrams, and Stephen Gill, Norton, 1979.
– *The Major Works*. Edited by Stephen Gill, Oxford UP, 1984.
– *The Fenwick Notes of William Wordsworth*. Edited by Jared R. Curtis, Humanities Ebook, 2008.
Wormer, Eberhard J. "A Taste for Salt in the History of Medicine." *Science Tribune*, March 1999, http://www.tribunes.com/tribune/sel/worm.htm.
The Young Tradesman; Or, Book of English Trades: Being a Library of the Useful Arts for Commercial Education. Whittaker & Co., 1839.
Youngquist, Paul. "Black Romanticism: A Manifesto." *Studies in Romanticism*, vol. 56, no. 1, Spring 2017, pp. 3–14.
Yousef, Nancy. "Wollstonecraft, Rousseau and the Revision of Romantic Subjectivity." *Studies in Romanticism*, vol. 38, no. 4, Winter 1999, pp. 537f.
Yusoff, Kathryn. *A Billion Black Anthropocenes or None*. U of Minnesota P, 2018.
Wolfson, Susan, and Elizabeth Fay. Introduction. *The Seige of Valencia*, edited by Susan Wolfson and Elizabeth Fay, Broadview, 2002.
Zeeuw, J.W. de. "Peat and the Dutch Golden Age: The Historical Meaning of Energy-Attainability." *AAG Bijdragen*, vol. 21, 1978, pp. 3–31.

Index

Abolition Act, 108
abolitionism, 105, 108, 109, 113, 120
Africa, 87, 90, 96, 102, 106, 107, 113, 115, 118, 136; diaspora, 19, 102, 109–10, 113, 117, 136, 154; "Flying Africans," 118–20; Niger river, 91, 95, 118; Sierra Leone, 64, 178n43; West Africa, 16, 18, 76–8, 84, 89, 91, 95, 98, 102, 103, 117–18, 120–1, 158, 182n12, 187n25, 190n23. *See also* Black Atlantic
African American, 115, 186n12
Aghalino, Sam Ovuete, 85, 181–2n12
Ahmed, Siraj, 109, 167n25
Alaimo, Stacey, 4, 165n6
albatross. *See* birds
Albion, Robert, 62, 173n7
Allewaert, Monique, 136, 138
alum, 30–1, 39, 170n19, 187n1
ampersand, 128–30, 132, 135, 147
anagnorisis, 49
Anglicus, Barthalomaeus, 37
animals, 38, 40, 42, 66, 87, 97, 114, 127, 142, 152, 153, 156, 157, 165n5, 166n12, 170n23, 171n24. *See also* birds; fish
anthimeria, 128
Anthropocene, 139, 169n15
Appadurai, Arjun, 7

archive, 19, 93, 94, 103, 109, 110, 111, 116, 120–1, 123, 126, 139, 142, 187n23, 190n17
Arctic, 78, 135, 181n9; Antarctica, 78, 135
Ardon, Paul, 127, 138, 141, 188n2
aristocracy, 24, 60, 62, 112, 178n42
Armstrong, Isobel, 76–7, 81, 180n6
Aronsohn, Marie DeNoia, 99
Artaud, Antonin, 48, 174n10, 174n12

Baekeland, Leo, 150–1, 153, 191n3
ballad, 53, 124, 126, 128, 133, 135, 189n7
Balston, John Noel, 30, 39, 170n19
Barker, Juliet, 70
Barker, T.C., 121
Barry, Sean, 152
Barthes, Roland, 87, 191n3
Batchelor, Thomas, 53–4
Beckett, Samuel, 121
Behrendt, Stephen, 70, 84, 88
Benjamin, Walter, 35
Benso, Silvia, 49
Bergquist, Lars, 27
Bergren, Katherine, 65, 167n23, 179n50
Berlant, Lauren, 10
Besetzung, 104–5

Bewell, Alan, 15, 65, 95, 167n22, 189n12, 189n15
Billingsley, John, 50
biofouling, 155
biomagnification, 156
biosphere, 6, 58, 75, 102, 124, 154, 155, 158
birds, 61, 67, 68, 70, 72, 125, 127, 137, 155, 179n47, 179n48; albatross, 90, 152–6, 161; birds' nests, 125, 127, 145, 147–8; cuckoo, 67, 70, 179–80n52; goldfinch, 137; hummingbird, 137; linnet, 71–2; nightingale, 67; robin, 125, 145; snipe, 125, 139, 140, 142, 145, 190n16; thrush, 71–2; wren, 61, 72
Black Atlantic, 77, 103, 108, 109, 114
bog, 124, 125, 127, 136, 138, 139, 141, 143
Bohls, Elizabeth, 21, 32, 39–40
Boland, Eavan, 128
bone, 16, 17, 21, 24, 32–4, 37, 38, 40, 43, 55, 104, 105, 154, 170n22, 170n23, 170–1n24
Brazil, 65
British Navy, 33, 107, 171n26, 174n17, 182n19
Brown, Bill, 7, 165n7
Browne, Montfort, 113–14
Brunskill, R.W., 127, 187–8n1
bryosphere, 133
Buell, Laurence, 47, 59
Bunyan, John, 137
Burgess, Miranda, 38, 171n26
Burke, Edmund, 32, 62, 107
Burkett, Andrew, 5

Calvert, Albert F., 110
Cambridge Neoplatonists, 153
Cameron, Charles, 112, 113, 114
Cameron, Dorothy, 41
cannibalism, 91, 105

Canuel, Mark, 31
capitalism, 4, 17, 25, 29, 54, 90, 105, 155, 160; capital, 9, 14–15, 32; environmental effects, 20, 32, 47, 72, 99, 150, 154–5, 174n10; and slavery, 14, 91, 104, 121, 185n5; spread of, 6, 9, 17, 24, 46, 155; and subjectivity, 26, 33
Capitalocene, 47
Caribbean, 66, 68, 69, 102, 104, 117, 171n26, 180n53; Bahamas, 111–14; Bermuda, 103, 111–14, 186n13, 186n14; Caicos, 114; Haiti, 67, 69, 108, 114, 190n24; Jamaica, 68; Turks Island, 19, 33, 102, 103, 104, 108, 110, 111–12, 114, 115, 116, 121, 154, 185n6, 186n14, 186n16, 187n23
Celan, Paul, 21, 25
Certeau, Michel de, 37
Cheshire, 110, 114, 118, 121, 140, 186n13
Clare, John, 8, 11–13, 19, 32, 62, 123–48, 152, 165n3, 165n5, 166n17, 178n41, 187–90; fen aesthetic, 19, 125, 136–45; "The Flitting," 125, 133–6, 144; "The Lament of Swordy Well," 32; "My Early Home was This," 11–12; "On Seeing Some Moss in Flower in Early Spring," 124–5, 125–33; rhizomatic poetics, vii, 19, 123, 129–30, 133, 134, 137, 146; "The Robin's Nest," 125, 145–8; "Song" ("Swamps of wild rush beds & sloughs squashy traces"), 125, 136–9; "To the Snipe," 125, 139–41, 145
Claridge, John, 50–1, 52
Cliff, Michelle, 69
climate change, 6, 12, 14, 35, 139, 144–5, 154, 159, 172n4, 192n11
Cobbett, William, 32, 170n19, 170n22
coccolith, 43

Cochrane, Archibald, 114, 187n20
Cohen, Jeffrey Jerome, 11, 22, 25, 166n11
Coleridge, Samuel Taylor, 37, 147, 150–63, 172n2, 191n5, 191n6; "The Eolian Harp," 153; "The Rime of the Ancient Mariner," 37, 90, 147, 150–63, 191n2
Collings, David, 60
Colonial Office papers, 103, 111–14, 186n14, 187n18
colonization, 12, 13–17, 18, 33, 45, 47, 50, 64–71, 76, 77, 79, 81, 83, 87, 88, 90, 92, 102–20, 124, 142, 143, 150, 160, 166n19, 167n25, 168n11, 173n7, 178n43, 178n46, 179n48, 183n19, 184n30, 186n13, 190n23, 190n24
commerce, 1, 6, 11, 14, 16, 18, 24, 26, 33, 42, 51, 63, 66, 77, 78, 82, 83, 84, 87, 99, 102, 118, 120, 124, 142, 143, 176n32, 187n20, 189n8, 190n22
commodity, 6, 9, 10, 15–16, 19, 26, 33, 39, 55, 56, 60, 65, 71, 78, 83–4, 87, 90, 92, 93, 101, 103, 104, 112, 114, 119, 120, 130, 154–6, 157, 161, 186n13; commodity fetishism, 15, 79, 90, 96
common rights, 3, 13, 52–5, 140, 165n3, 177n34, 183n19
Commons, 4, 13, 45, 47–8, 61, 66, 138–40, 145, 165n3, 165n4, 165n6, 174n13, 176n33
common things, 1–20, 42, 45–6, 54, 72, 124, 125–8, 130–1, 149–50, 162, 166n8
communis, 5
community, 48, 60, 68, 98, 102, 119, 141, 143, 166n8, 183n26
Connery, Christopher, 155
Cooke, Majid Fadzilah and Dayang Suria Mulia, 85

Cowper, William, 62, 137, 178n41
Crister, Greg, 85–6
Crowder, Michael, 79, 91
cryptobiosis, 125, 135–6
Cudworth, Ralph, 153, 191n7
Curran, Stuart, 76, 180n6
custom, 3, 13, 26, 52–4, 60, 99, 117, 139–40, 165n3, 177n34, 177–78n40
Cuvier, Georges, 33

Dallas, Robert Charles, 68, 179n49
Daniels, Stephen, 60, 62
Davidson, William, 107
deforestation, 13, 15, 17–18, 45–73, 84, 160, 171–80, 190n24
Deleuze, Gilles and Felix Guattari, 129, 134, 146, 148, 166n13, 174n12
dendrochronology, 45
Derbyshire, 29, 36
desertification, 67
Dessalines, Jean-Jacques, 67
diaspora. *See* Africa
Dickson, Joshua, 96
dimethyl sulfide, 155
Dixon, H.N., 127, 187–8n1
domesticity, 9, 39, 54, 76, 77, 81, 84, 85–8, 89, 92, 93, 95, 97, 180n6
Dorset, 47, 50, 52
Douglas, Mary, 89
drainage, 13, 99, 125, 139–43, 145, 190n19, 190n20. *See also* peat
Dutch Golden Age, 12, 124–5, 142
dwelling, 12, 22, 24, 45, 58–9, 61, 85, 124, 126, 131, 134, 136, 145–8

Ebos Landing, 120
ecocriticism, 16, 47, 169n15
ecology, 1, 4, 6, 7–8, 12, 26, 31, 34, 42, 47, 48, 54, 62, 64, 65, 66, 69, 75, 77–9, 82, 123–4, 126, 131, 134, 136–40, 141, 150, 166n11, 172n6, 175n28, 188n3; ecocrisis, 11, 16, 20,

24, 34–5, 50, 76, 85, 99, 124, 153, 156, 159, 190n18, 191n9; ecological invasion, 150; palaeo-ecology, 19, 123, 139, 142, 158
Eden, 78, 81–2, 83, 85
Eisenstein, Paul and Todd McGowan, 108
ekphrasis, 86–8
Elaeis guineensis, 75
El Greco, 86
Elhacham, Emily, et al., 151
Eliasson, Per and Sven Nilsson, 34
empire, 8, 9, 14, 18, 19, 20, 33–4, 50, 65–71, 75–6, 79, 83–4, 92, 98, 102, 110–14, 134–5, 136, 142–3, 150, 155, 159, 166n19
enclosure, 3, 12, 13, 48, 133, 139–40, 166–7n20, 176n33, 189n7, 190n19
Enlightenment, 7, 17, 27, 35, 40
environmental justice, 8, 144
Equiano, Olaudah, 91, 107
erosion, 50, 66, 68, 140, 168n7
Everitt, Alan, 54
evolution, 4, 7–8, 101, 123, 184n28
exoticism, 18, 77–85, 92–3, 118, 154
extinction, 14, 66, 68, 76, 145, 156, 159

Falconbridge, Alexander, 91
Favret, Mary, 25, 96, 167n2
Fay, Elizabeth, 79, 181n11
Fenton, Alexander, 141
fish, 156, 181n12; commercial fishing, 33–4, 156; ghost fishing, 156; herring, 33–4
flax, 52
Flood, John and Phil Flood, 70
Flores, Christina, 153
Flying Africans. *See* Africa
Forman, Cyrus, 116
Fosso, Kurt, 46
Foster, John Bellamy, 53, 173n7, 175n23
Frank, Andre Gunder, 24
Franklin, Benjamin, 150
Frazer, James George, 61, 172n3
Freud, Sigmund, 27, 104, 129–30, 169n17
fuel, 9, 11, 17, 18, 34, 51–2, 85, 99, 123–5, 138, 140–1, 187n1
Fulford, Tim, 50, 61, 62, 178n41, 191n2
furze, 138

Gadd, Carl-Johan, 26, 34
Gadsby, Meredith, 117–18
Galeano, Eduardo, 65, 168n11, 178n46
gall, 39–40
Gallegos, Danielle, 84–5, 87, 181n12
Galloway, Stephen, 121
garbage patch, 154–6
gelatin, 39, 171n24
gender, 76, 82, 84, 86, 92, 97, 180n5, 180n6, 181n7
geology, 17, 18, 21, 23, 27–8, 41, 42, 167n1, 168n8
geophilia, 162
George, Sam, 31
Germain, George, 113
ghost nets. *See* fish
Gilroy, Paul, 106, 107, 108
glacial erratic. *See* stone
Glob, P.V., 141
global, 6, 12, 13–17, 18, 19, 24, 35, 41, 46, 47, 65, 76, 78, 84, 87, 94, 96, 98–9, 103, 108, 113, 116–20, 136, 139, 142, 144, 149, 152, 154–5, 168n11, 181n10, 184n30, 188n3
glue, 30, 38, 39–40, 171n24
Godwin, William, 39, 168n5, 172n2
Goethe, Johann Wolfgang von, 27, 40, 169n15
Goodison, Laura, 69
Gorji, Mina, 137
gorse, 61, 63, 72
Gottleib, Evan, 15

Gray, Richard, 121
"great acceleration," 159
Green, T.A., 126

habitat, 25, 67, 84, 125, 127, 145, 172n4
Hall, Stuart, 69
Hamblyn, Richard, 28
Hardiman, David, 89–90
Hardt, Michael and Antonio Negri, 10, 165n4
Harrison, Gary, 133, 189n15
Hartman, Geoffrey, 56
Hartman, Sadiya, 113, 186n17
Hassett, Maurice, 90
Heaney, Seamus, 133, 138, 143, 188n4
Hegel, Georg Wilhelm Friedrich, 10, 63, 180n6
Heidegger, Martin, 58, 165n7
Hemans, Felicia, 8, 16–17, 18, 75–99, 158–9, 180–4; "The Abencerrage," 98; "The Crusader's Return," 88–92; "Death and the Warrior," 98; "England's Dead," 98; "Forest Sanctuary," 98; "The Image in the Heart," 81–3; "The Indian City" 98; "The Palm Tree," 78, 80–1, 92–8; "Repose of a Holy Family," 86–7; *The Siege of Valencia*, 85, 98
Herder, Johann Gottfried von, 64
Heringman, Noah, 28, 167n1
Herodotus, 56
herring. *See* fish
Hess, Scott, 47
Highland Clearances, 66
Hildebrand, K.G., 26, 169n14
Holland, 12, 124–5, 142–3, 166n19, 190n23. *See also* Dutch Golden Age
Holt, John, 121
Homer, 86, 184n3
Houben, Jan E.M. and Saraju Rath, 94
Hunter, J.P., 78
Hutton, James, 23

Huxley, Aldous, 68
hypertension, 19, 109, 154, 186n12

Imlay, Gilbert, 22–3, 24–5, 30, 169n12
India, 93, 94, 97, 98, 184n30
Indonesia, 17, 98, 145, 158
industrialization, 3–4, 6, 9, 14, 18, 24, 25, 26, 28, 30, 32, 39, 48, 49, 51, 76, 77, 79, 104, 115, 139, 144, 149, 151, 153, 174n19
Ingles, Mary, 116
Inglis, Brian, 51–2
Inikori, Joseph, 104
ink, 38–40, 171n24
Ionesco, Eugene, 121
Ireland, 28, 60, 69–71, 113, 127, 143, 177–8n40, 178n42, 179–80n52
Irigaray, Luce, 81–3, 93
iron, 24, 26–8, 34, 140, 169n13, 169n14, 173n7

Jacobus, Mary, 41, 167n1, 168n7
Jeffrey, Francis, 80
Jěki and his Ozâzi, 117–20, 187n22
Jung, Carl, 27, 169n17

Kant, Immanuel, 32
Karera, Axelle, 109
Keegan, Bridget, 137, 141, 142, 190n19, 190n20
Kennedy, Cynthia, 104, 184–5n4
Kimmerer, Robin Wall, 71, 123, 127, 133, 134, 157, 188n1
Kincaid, Jamaica, 69
Klein, Herbert S. and Ben Vinson, 24–5
Kovesi, Simon, 129, 148
Kubrick, Stanley, 121
Kurlansky, Mark, 114, 184n3, 187n19

labouring classes, 3, 12, 13, 33, 51–2, 54, 59, 137, 138, 139–40, 175n26
Lacépède, Bernard Germain de, 33, 34

216 Index

Lamb, Jonathan, 9
Langan, Celeste, 37, 41
Latour, Bruno, 7, 12
law, 9–10, 16, 53–6, 105, 110, 111, 167n25, 170n19, 173n7, 175n22, 176n32, 177n39. *See also* enclosure
Lawson, Ian, 145
Lee, Debbie, 90–1, 109, 191n2
Lefebvre, Henri, 20
L'Estrange, Roger, 33
Levin, Phillis, 127
Levinson, Marjorie, 51, 167n26
Lienhard, Siegfried, 94, 183n24
Lim, Chye Ing et al., 99, 181n10, 188n3
Lim, Shirley, 69
Liverpool, 104, 110, 118, 121, 183n22, 186n13
Ljungman, Axel Vilhelm, 34
Locke, John, 10
L'Overture, Toussaint, 67
Lowe, Lisa, 14, 65, 82, 111
Lukács, György, 56
luxury, 80–1, 87, 96, 170n22
Lynn, Martin, 79, 84, 91, 95, 102, 118, 183n22

MacNamara, Mark, 145
Maddison-McaFadyen, Margo, 104
Mahood, M.M., 130, 135, 185n11
Malaysia, 17, 85, 98
Manthorne, Katherine, 82, 182n16
Maroons, 68–9, 179n49
Marx, Karl, 15, 49, 53–6, 157, 165n2, 175n23
materialism, 3, 7–12, 15–16, 21–2, 38–41, 101, 129, 149–50, 153, 166n7
Matthews, William, 70
May, John, 37
McArthur, Tom and Roshan McArthur, 152
McClintock, Anne, 88, 89, 90, 183n21

McDaniel, Lorna, 118
McGann, Jerome, 75, 77, 167n26, 180n6
McKusick, James, 159
McNeill, J.R., 65–6, 67–8, 179n47, 179n48, 180n53
memory, 48–9, 58, 63, 66–8, 116, 121, 131, 135, 139, 142, 143–4, 178n42
metonym, 5, 42, 51, 86, 89, 103, 106, 134, 146–8, 171n26
Milton, John, 137, 173n8
mining, 9, 24, 25, 26–8, 51, 65, 103, 115–16, 120–1, 168n11, 169n15, 170n18, 178n46, 187n21, 190n24
Mintz, Sidney, 105
Modiano, Raimonda, 151
Morrison, Toni, 106
Morton, Timothy, 47, 105
moss, 4, 8, 9, 10, 11–12, 13, 19, 31, 61, 95–6, 123–48, 152, 166n18, 187n1, 189n8, 189n9, 189n11, 190n25. *See also* peat

Naipaul, V.S., 69
Nassau, Robert Hamill, 117
nationalism, 47, 81, 89, 98
Nau, Ignace, 67–8
Navigation Act, 33
Neeson, Jeanette, 140
neurons, 151
New Spain, 24, 66, 168n11, 190n24
Nichols, Jonathan E. and Dorothy M. Peteet, 145
Novalis, 27, 169n15
Nussbaum, Felicity, 82, 92
Nyström, Per, 24

Ogham, 70
oracle, 46, 48
orientalism, 78
Origen, 90
Orwell, George, 72
Ovid, 29

Index   217

palm oil. *See* palm tree
palm tree, 10, 16–17, 18, 75–99, 158, 180–4; palm oil, 4, 8, 9, 16–17, 18, 75–99, 101–2, 118, 121, 145, 158, 180–4, 188n3; palm oil plantation, 85, 89, 145, 159, 181n10
paper, 38–9, 171n24, 171n25, 171n26
parataxis, 126, 129
pastoral, 18, 28, 48, 60, 65, 80, 83, 86, 96, 110, 182n15
peat, 9, 11, 19, 99, 123–4, 125, 127, 132, 139–43, 145, 166n19, 181n10, 188n2, 188n3, 188n4, 190n17, 190n19. *See also* moss
Perlin, John, 71, 173n7
petroleum, 120, 155
picturesque, 17, 28–33, 36, 137, 179n49, 191n5
Piersen, William D., 91
Pinter, Harold, 121
Place, Francis, 89
Plant, Marjorie, 40
plantation. *See* palm oil; sugar
plastic, 144, 149–63, 169n12, 191n3, 194, 207; microplastic, 152, 158; plasticity, 8, 150, 153, 157, 160; plastic nature, 153, 156, 191n6, 191n7; plastiglomerates, 152
poetic meter, 16, 52, 75, 81, 147, 148
pollen, 141, 189n11
pollution, 14, 99
postcolonial, 16, 117, 119
Potkay, Adam, 49
Poussin, Nicolas, 86
Priestley, Joseph, 39, 64
Prince, Mary, 8, 16, 18–19, 33, 154, 185n6, 185n9, 185n10, 186n16, 187n17, 191n8; *The History of Mary Prince*, 101–21, 184–7
Pross, Jorg, et al., 78

Quran, 86

race, 6, 89, 107, 110, 113, 186n12; racism, 14, 19, 105, 113, 186n12
Rackham, Oliver, 138, 140
Rauwerda, A.M., 105
Raven, Peter H., 133
Rayner D.H. and J.E. Hemingway, 30
reciprocity, 23, 60, 151–2, 162
Reichgelt, Tammo et al., 78
Rembrandt, 86
revolution, 61, 108, 109, 168n11; American, 104; French, 22, 175n20, 179n51, 183n19, 187n18, 187n19, 190n19; Haitian, 67, 108
rhizome, 10, 126, 129–30, 137, 146, 148, 166n13
Rhodes, Barbara J. and William W. Streeter, 39
Richens, R.H., 60
Rigby, Kate, 47, 169n15
rime, 149, 152, 154, 155, 158, 161
Roads, Esme, et al., 135
Ross, Marlon, 76, 77, 180n6
Rossetti, W.M., 80
Rotherham, Ian, 139

Said, Edward, 64–5
salt, 4, 8, 9, 10, 13, 16, 18–19, 33, 34, 101–21, 140, 154, 184–7, 191n8; brine, 110, 186n13, 187n21; rock salt, 121, 187n21; salt duty, 112, 114, 187n18, 187n19; salt furnace, 115–16; salt tectonics, 102; solar salt, 16, 19, 33, 154
Samuel, Arthur Michael, 33
Samuel, John G., 94
Sassen, Saskia, 85
Savoca, Matthew et al., 155
Scandinavia, 16, 17, 21–3, 25, 26, 27, 31, 34, 36, 40, 143, 169n18; Denmark, 16, 25; Norway, 21, 22, 27, 28, 38, 42, 168n4, 169n18;

Sweden, 21, 22, 25–6, 34, 38, 42, 168n4, 169n13
Scarry, Elaine, 93–4, 132
Schon, James Frederick and Samuel Crowther, 91
Scotland, 66–7
seasonality, 50, 126, 127, 128, 130–1, 144
Serres, Michel, 12, 23, 151, 162
Shakespeare, William, 166n11, 204; *Macbeth*, 46, 64; *Othello*, 64
Sharpe, Jenny, 105
Shelley, Mary, 36; *Frankenstein*, 78, 82
Shi, Xilin et al., 120
Shorter, Alfred, 39, 171n25
silver, 17, 24, 27, 28, 42, 63, 72, 96, 168n11, 169n18, 178n46
slave trade, 14, 39, 64, 77, 79, 90–1, 95, 99, 101–2, 103–5, 108, 109–10, 112–13, 114–15, 116, 118–20, 121, 136, 154, 167n21, 171n26, 183n22, 185n5, 187n25
Smith, Honor Ford, 69
smuggling, 104, 112–14, 116, 169n18, 170n18
Snyder, Terry, 120–1
soap, 9, 17, 18, 30, 77, 78, 79, 87–90, 99, 118, 158, 182n18, 182n19, 183n22
Somerset, 47, 50
sonnet, 67, 127–31, 171n1
Southey, Robert, 37, 168n5
spinning, 51–2
Spinoza, Baruch, 49, 75, 174n11
Spivak, Gayatri Chakravorty, 101
Standish, Arthur, 50
Steever, Sanford, 94
stone, 4, 8, 9, 10, 13, 16, 17, 21–43, 45, 75, 96, 162, 166n11, 167–71; compositional layering, 17, 23; foliation, 22–3; glacial erratic, 40–2; gneiss, 10, 17, 22–3, 25, 36, 38, 168n4, 168n6, 169n12; granite, 23; metamorphic differentiation, 23, 168n6; metamorphic rock, 21, 22, 209; strata, 10, 75; Valley of Stones, 37
Studnicki-Gizbert, Daviken and David Schecter, 65, 66
subjectivity, 4, 7–8, 10, 19, 21–4, 26, 33, 41, 48, 78, 79, 82–3, 99, 124, 129, 136, 138, 157, 167n2
sublime, 23, 24, 38, 107, 138; "swamp sublime," 136, 138
subsidence, 110, 140, 186n13
sugar, 39, 66, 68, 85, 104, 161, 171n26, 180n53, 184n4, 190n24; sugar plantation, 13–14, 33, 69, 114, 118, 136, 171n26, 190n24
Sunstein, Emily, 30
surfactant, 87
Swedenborg, Emanuel, 27

Tacitus, 56
Tamar, 86–7
Tamil poetry, 94, 183n25, 183n26
Tarr, Clayton, 143
Theocritus, 60
Thompson, E.P., 54, 139–40, 141–2, 149, 165n3, 172n6, 175n21, 175n23, 175n24, 176n33
Thompson, T.P., 64, 178n43
Titian, 86
Tobin, John, 118
Tomlinson, P.B., 78
trans-corporeality, 4, 14, 165n6
trauma, 21, 29–36, 41, 107–8, 153, 159, 171n26, 191n9
trees, 5, 11, 17, 18, 40, 45–73, 75, 131, 134, 147, 148, 166n11, 171–80, 182n16; African blackwood, 96; ash, 58–9, 177n36; ebony, 96; elm, 18, 45, 47, 48, 49, 58–61, 63, 70, 72; fir, 31, 58; laburnum, 95, 96; oak,

18, 45, 50, 58, 59, 61–3, 70, 147, 172n3, 173n7, 177n34, 178n41, 178n42; pine, 29, 59. *See also* palm tree; wood
Tullis, Paul, 87, 181n10
Tutino, John, 24, 168n11

Urban-Malinga, Barbara et al., 152

Vardy, Alan, 133, 136
Vries, Jan de and An van der Woude, 142

war, 48, 50, 63, 64, 90, 95, 104, 121, 142, 149, 159, 168n11, 171n26, 173n7, 174n17, 179n49. *See also* revolution
Warwickshire, 56
Washington, Booker T., 103, 115
Watt, James, 39
Wedgwood, Thomas, 39
West Indies. *See* Caribbean
White, William M., 27
Whitehurst, John, 29, 36, 37
whiteness, 19, 38, 103–8, 154
Williams, Isabel M. and Leora H. McEachern, 114
Williams, Jane, 80
Williams, Raymond, 65
Wolfson, Susan, 77, 79, 180n4, 180n6, 181n11
Wollstonecraft, Mary, 8, 16, 17, 21–43, 45, 167–71, 168n3, 168n8, 168n9, 169n12, 170n20, 191n5; *Collected Letters*, 30; *Letters Written During a Short Residence in Sweden, Norway, and Denmark*, 16, 17, 21–43, 167–71, 170n20; *Vindication of the Rights of Women*, 31, 168n5
wood, 4, 8, 9, 10, 13, 15, 17–18, 34, 38, 46, 50–6, 58, 65, 68, 70–1, 96, 160, 166n11, 173n7, 174n17, 175n22, 175n23, 175n24, 176n31, 180n53. *See also* trees
Woodmansee, Martha and Mark Osteen, 26
Wordsworth, Dorothy, 58
Wordsworth, William, 4–5, 8, 11, 14, 15, 17, 18, 32, 37, 41, 45–73, 82, 96, 127, 148, 159, 162, 167n23, 168n7, 169n14, 171–80, 181n7, 190n21, 191n4; "The Brothers," 58, 169n14; *The Excursion*, 57, 60, 174n9, 181n7; "Expostulation and Reply," 45; "Goody Blake and Harry Gill," 52–6; Intimations Ode," 58; *Lyrical Ballads*, 37, 45, 58; "Michael," 58; *The Prelude*, 4–5, 37, 49, 57–8, 59, 62–3, 127, 148, 166n14, 173n8, 174n13; "The Ruined Cottage," 15, 17–18, 45–53, 59–66, 71–3; "The Solitary Reaper," 66–7, 70, 169n14, 179–80n52

Yeats, William Butler, 156
Yorkshire, 30, 170n20
Youngquist, Paul, 101
Yousef, Nancy, 23–4, 31, 167n2
Yusoff, Kathryn, 101, 102

Zeeuw, J.W. de, 142–3